GUIDE TO
PROFESSIONAL SERVICES

The *Entrepreneur Magazine* Small Business Series

ENTREPRENEUR MAGAZINE
Guide to Professional Services

Leonard Bisk

John Wiley & Sons, Inc.

New York • Chichester • Weinheim • Brisbane • Singapore • Toronto

This text is printed an acid-free paper.

Copyright © 1997 by Leonard Bisk.
Published by John Wiley & Sons, Inc.

All rights reserved. Published simultaneously in Canada.

Library of Congress Cataloging-in-Publication Data:

Bisk, Leonard.
    Entrepreneur magazine : guide to professional services / Leonard
Bisk.
        p.   cm. — (The Entrepreneur magazine small business series)
    Includes bibliographical references and index.
    ISBN 0-471-15517-9 (pbk. : alk. paper)
        1. Small business—Management—Handbooks, manuals, etc.
    2. Business consultants.   3. Industrial procurement.
    I. Entrepreneur (Santa Monica, Calif.)   II. Title.   III. Title:
    Working with consultants, professionals, and freelancers.
    IV. Series.
    HD62.7.B4146   1997
    658.02'2—DC21   96-46319

Printed in the United States of America

10 9 8 7 6 5 4 3 2 1

In memory of my father, Max, who epitomized, more than anyone else I have ever met, the word "entrepreneur." Dad gave me my first lesson in dealing with professionals. He showed his patent attorneys how to satisfy the requirement for a patent to be new and inventive by pointing out that his design made assembly easier than the prior art. That one experience illustrated to me that often entrepreneurs understand their businesses better than any service provider and entrepreneurs must control their professional advisors.

This book is also dedicated to all the entrepreneurs with whom I have worked throughout my career: To the inventors who approached me when I ran Independent Products Company; to the inventors I met during my involvement with the incubator movement in Israel; and to each reader who picks up this book and takes one positive benefit from it in developing a business.

ACKNOWLEDGMENTS

Writing a book can be an entrepreneurial exercise. And like most entrepreneurial ventures, it does not occur in a vacuum. Because I took on a different role as author, my banker, lawyer, accountant, and mentors took on different roles as well. My banker, for example, instead of critically analyzing my financial projections had to critically analyze my chapter on banks.

I added some advisers to the group I would normally have in a business venture. My thanks first and foremost to Deborah Streeter for planting the seed. My gratitude to Michael Steinberg, my agent, who recognized the value of the project from the outset and who gave me encouragement and sound advice. At John Wiley & Sons, Ruth Mills, my most important adviser and newest friend, is an editor who knows how to assuage the anxieties of a newly minted author. It was truly my good fortune to have such an experienced and upbeat editor for my first book.

A special thanks to all those old friends and new friends who offered insights about their professions and acted as editors of related chapters: Marvin Gevurtz of Basman, Smith; Jerry Marks of Marks, Kent and O'Neill; Bob Bifolco with Progress Bank; Howard Stredler of Stredler and Stredler; Al Soffa, my mentor and friend; Lottie Gatewood of Vanguard Communications; Ray Rauth from the Independent Computer Consultants Association (ICCA); Mike Shoop from Professional Finance; Jack Shapiro of the Penn Management Group; Ed Bobrow; and many more.

Finally, most authors, like most entrepreneurs, have families. It takes the support and encouragement of spouses and other family members to help through the dry spells and the moments of self-doubt. I am blessed with a wife who thinks I can do no wrong—Miri, thanks!

CONTENTS

LIST OF EXHIBITS

HOW TO USE THIS BOOK

Nothing will ever be attempted if all possible objections must be first overcome.

There are some important caveats to consider before you begin using the information in this book.

My observations and guidelines are not intended to be substitutes for your common sense and intuitive management skills. I have tremendous respect and admiration for entrepreneurs. Often, I express more confidence in an entrepreneur's ability than does the entrepreneur in question. Follow your instincts if the advice you receive from someone or from this book is contrary to your own experience and inner wisdom. I make this observation for two reasons. First, your personal situation may not apply to a generalization. For example, if you have a good personal friend who is an accountant in whom you have absolute confidence, then you don't need to go through a process of evaluating candidates and you may not have to bother "managing" the relationship. Second, you must be certain you have a problem, realize you don't have the internal resources to solve the problem, and be willing to make the effort to resolve the problem. If you are happy with the status quo, don't turn your business upside down simply for the sake of change.

No matter what advice you receive from other sources or from this book, unless you are prepared to invest sufficient time and energy on both the selection process and the ongoing management of your outside service providers, you will ultimately be dissatisfied with the results. As described in greater detail in Chapter 6, a close friend admitted to me that he had not spent enough time qualifying the architect he hired and he had not invested sufficient time on monitoring the construction project as it went forward. He was too busy running his business. This failure to prioritize his time resulted in costly mistakes. While making the investment of time and energy in the selection process can reduce your "aggravation ratio," you also must continue managing most adviser relationships after the selection process, to control costs and maximize effort and benefits. Construction projects, litigation, and many other aspects of management fall outside the realm of day-to-day demands on your time. As a result, it may seem to be more expedient to focus on the routine management functions rather than devote sufficient energy to the special projects. You may then be unhappy with the outcome. The recommendations in this book are only tools to be used by you as a manager; they are not substitutes for your conviction that you have to spend time managing these diverse professionals.

It is a human weakness to avoid doing what we don't enjoy doing and don't know, and to focus our attention on what we do like and know. Most entrepreneurial managers do not have the luxury of delegating unpleasant management responsibilities to someone else, especially in critical situations. At one point in my business career, I delegated the planning and implementation of a major factory relocation to my staff, who carried it off with incredible precision and success. Yet that same staff could not select and implement a computerization effort. The question I had to ask myself was, Could I have done a better job? The answer in both cases was, probably not. Might my team have done a better job with the computerization effort had this book been available to them? I believe the answer would have been yes. The team had good basic management skills but lacked adviser management skills.

I have structured the chapters in Part I so that you do not have to read the entire book to extract meaningful information on a given profession. Each discussion of a profession opens with a listing of the functions of that profession from the perspective of the manager or entrepreneur. Too often, managers and entrepreneurs misunderstand the role of their lawyers, accountants, and other consultants in the day-to-day operation of a business. I hope to assist you in focusing on what these professionals can contribute to your business, by stating at the outset the functions you can expect to be fulfilled. This will aid in the search for a new firm or individual and also provide a method for periodically reviewing your relationship with the service provider.

The information in Chapter 1, "Beginning the Search," is fundamental in hiring any professional and should be read and reviewed before reading the specific professions discussed in the book.

Almost every chapter and section within a chapter, relating to selection and hiring concludes with information that I call *"the three Rs."*

- *Recap.* This is a summary of the key points. The discussions of specific professions and law specialties are short enough, however, that I urge you to read them through and not to rely solely on the recap for your information. Since I have not duplicated information from profession to profession, you can read the entire book without being bored by a lot of repetition and will find that ideas from one section can be applied to other professions.

- *Resources.* These are sources for additional information (current at the time of publication; for more up-to-date information on national associations, several directories are available in public libraries, including *National Trade and Professional Associations of the United States,* which has a companion directory of state and regional associations, and Gales *Encyclopedia of Associations*). Depending on the population of your area, there may be local chapters and even hot lines or referral services of the local or regional Bar Association, the American Institute of Architects and some consulting associations. It makes sense to check your chamber of commerce and both the Yellow Pages and the white pages of telephone directories. Many Yellow Pages directories include a "Lawyer's Guide" with listings by specialty and by geographic area. Some of the resources I have encountered have been gold mines of information; I have noted ones that have been especially helpful. Often these resources publish directories and other useful information, and have extremely customer-oriented and knowledgeable staffs.

- *References.* This section lists books, magazines, and articles relating to the topic. Some of these books are out of print and you may need to request them from your public library or possibly a local college or university library. Out-of-print books are indicated with an asterisk (*). The Bibliography at the end of the book lists titles alphabetically for easier cross-referencing and in each case includes the author's name, publisher, copyright date, and a telephone number and price, if available. Many books have been written about operating a specific business (e.g., how to start a restaurant), others have chapters on dealing with specific professions, and new books are coming out all the time. I have only listed those books that I have personally examined or have been recommended to me. A valuable "how-to" booklet or book, may appear in both the *References* and *Resources* sections. Occasionally, I will list or refer to books that I haven't examined and will so note. Books that I recommend highly are identified with four asterisks (****). If you are interested in building a reference library for your business, the four-star books are excellent candidates for your collection.

The book also features many anecdotes that are indented and prefaced with the title "War Story." They are valuable and pertinent, but are not essential for understanding the issues. Many of these stories reflect my personal experiences. Others are stories I have recorded from people I interviewed for the book, and there are a few stories I have extracted from material I have read. To the best of my knowledge, all the stories are true accounts.

Chapter 2, "Attorneys," is the longest chapter in the book. The law profession has become such an integral part of business today, it is only natural that a book dedicated to managing outside service providers would be weighted heavily toward dealing with attorneys. Also, there are many specialties in law, each with its own idiosyncrasies. This chapter opens with a general discussion of legal services and then describes various specialties.

Part II of the book focuses on the compensation and management elements of your ongoing relationships with outside service providers. These later chapters are not profession specific although they include profession-specific issues.

I have not relied solely on my own experiences, or research in compiling this book. I have interviewed many entrepreneurs and managers, and many practitioners of the professions discussed. I am neither arrogant enough nor naive enough to believe that this book will be a sufficient reference for you in dealing with professionals. At the same time, I am confident that I have given you an excellent base on which to build your management skills, if you are new to the effort. And if you are a seasoned manager, you will find a lot of useful material here.

I would like to receive feedback from you, good or bad! If you send me your comments care of the publisher, I promise I will respond. And if the subject matter is applicable to many entrepreneurs, your comments and/or experiences may find their way into a second edition.

INTRODUCTION

Operating a business, especially one's own business, requires a wide range of skills. Although we learn many of these skills through formal education, work experience, and trial and error, we may not develop one of the capabilities we need most—effective management of the professionals who provide us and our business with services.

You may be asking yourself, "Why do I need these professionals, and why should I buy this book?" The answer is you cannot survive in the modern business world without at least an attorney and an accountant. The accountant will keep you from making errors that would allow the Internal Revenue Service or your state or local taxing authorities to destroy your business. You may need an accountant to set up your bookkeeping system, so you will know how much you are spending and how much you are making. An accountant can assist you in preparing a budget and can review your financial calculations for accuracy and logic.

A lawyer keeps the "wolves from your business door." You will use a lawyer to incorporate your business; if you are applying for a patent, you will work with a patent attorney; and if you are being sued or wish to sue someone, you will retain a litigator.

As your business grows, you will require the services of many of the other professions discussed in this book:

- You will need a bank and a banker from which to borrow money to grow your business.
- You will need an insurance agent. Even if you just want to lease some office space, you will want to protect the furnishings and equipment from loss and protect yourself from liability in case someone suffers an injury on the premises.
- Whether you have been in business before or are a first-time owner, you will seek out consultants for all sorts of advice and help—from market research to operation of a production line.
- You will most likely use creative services, for example, to design a logo and stationery. Many businesses require a much

broader range of such services including sales material, package design, and even product design.

Part I of this book provides guidelines for the selection and hiring of many of the professions typically utilized by entrepreneurs and managers both in the start-up phase and in the ongoing management of a business.

Part II of the book offers guidance and methods for the successful management of professional advisers including:

- *Compensation.* Negotiating fees and monitoring costs.
- *Administration.* Measuring performance and keeping records.

I love being in business. Some of my best friends are and have been suppliers, customers, employees, lawyers, and other professionals. That said, not every supplier, customer, employee, or outside service provider has your best interest at heart. This book is like the cold medicine you put in your medicine cabinet as a precaution at the beginning of each winter. You may not need my information every day, but the investment will be worthwhile when you have to retain a practitioner of one of the professions discussed in the following chapters.

The academic literature and the general business literature are sadly lacking in resource material on this area of management. It is also safe to say that I haven't written anything here that given time and common sense one could not conclude on one's own; I am not an academic, nor am I a professional writer, lecturer, or self-proclaimed expert. Nevertheless, I can readily lay claim to having the perfect vision of hindsight described in the old cliché. I am an entrepreneur and professional business manager who has started and managed a number of businesses over my career and made a lot of mistakes in the process. Ranking high among those mistakes are errors in judgment in hiring professionals and subsequent failures to fire them before they did their damage. I have attempted here to combine my years of experience with the accumulated knowledge of many friends, associates, and business acquaintances; mix in some research from existing material; and organize it into a format that lends itself to easy referencing.

My entrepreneurial career began in the 1970s when I joined my parents in a small assembly and packaging business, producing plastic shoe trees my father had invented and patented. I had studied hotel management at Cornell University but entered the family business to assist temporarily and part-time. The company's production had expanded from my parents' basement and garage into a 6,500-square-foot building and continued to grow modestly, but beyond my parents' ability to manage it. So I found myself involved full-time and permanent.

One of my first tasks was to fire the current accountant and hire a new one who could give us better financial information and guidance. This was actually my first experience in dealing with professional consultants. As the business grew from the original 3 my father had invented to more than 25 products and as the markets we were selling to grew from the military and drug chains to include hotels, office suppliers, department stores, discounters; to exporting to Europe and the Far East—so, too, did our need for other service providers. So I found myself hiring graphic artists, lawyers, package designers, and litigators, as well as dealing with bankers and other financial experts.

We then acquired an interest in a plastic injection molding business, and with that came more involvement with lawyers, accountants, and banks. The bankruptcy of the molding business ensued because we made mistakes in negotiating the purchase of our interest in the molding business and because I had not hired advisers who could help us manage the business effectively.

After the company emerged from bankruptcy, I began developing new products and dealing with designers, graphic artists, and patent attorneys. Soon I found myself litigating against infringers of the numerous patents I had been granted. Along the way, I dealt with litigation from and of former employees, arbitration hearings, an acquisition of real estate, acquisitions of other businesses, and an insurance crisis. Meanwhile, the business gradually spread over 85,000 square feet, and the payroll grew from four part-time employees to over one hundred full-time employees. Like many entrepreneurs, I found that after investing much of my heart and soul into the business, there came a time when the business was a success on my terms and I wanted to "cash out" and move on to something new. I was proud of what I had achieved, but I was tired of the day-to-day battle and when the opportunity came to sell, I took advantage of it. Once again, I discovered that I had to turn to professionals—lawyers, bankers, accountants among others—this time to sell the business.

Although I had enjoyable moments in my business ventures, to some extent I seemed to be fighting a constant battle. My experiences, however, reflected a combination of influence: the unavoidable reality of operating a firm in today's business environment, my poor judgment and lack of experience in hiring and managing outside service providers, and to some degree, my style of corporate management.

During the eight years that I lived in Israel, I was involved in several businesses there; I found the same problems and needs existed for careful selection and management of outside service providers. My research, which has included interviewing dozens of businesspeople in all sorts of businesses and professions, suggests that my experiences were not unique either to me or to my business.

Now I have positioned myself on the other side of the relationship by providing consultant services to a wide variety of businesses both in Israel and the United States. I recently advised and guided a major Japanese consumer products company that plans to enter the U.S. market.

This book began innocently enough when I met Professor Deborah Streeter, the Bruce F. Failing Professor of Entrepreneurship and Personal Enterprise at Cornell University. Deborah was interviewing entrepreneurs on video and digitizing the interviews for incorporation into lectures on related topics. Deborah asked what aspect of management I had felt least prepared to handle during my career. The by-product of my reply was a guest lecture in her class on "dealing with professionals." Further discussions with Deborah and others, as well as some research, confirmed there really is a dearth of information on the subject.

Courses, books, seminars, and magazine articles abound on human resource management, purchasing management, business start-ups, development of business plans, and even techniques for getting a book published. But if you talk to any entrepreneur or manager, he or she will soon start telling war stories about unsuccessful attempts to cope with a wide range of service providers while lacking the most basic skills for managing those relationships. Although magazines such as *Entrepreneur* and *INC.* often publish articles (and occasionally whole issues) on dealing with professional service providers, it can be difficult to locate the pertinent information when you need to make a decision unless you are a pack rat and save every magazine you receive and catalog the articles of interest. Therefore, I have tried to organize this book in an easy-to-use format.

I am not a lawyer, and the advice offered here is not intended to be legal advice. The forms and checklists are provided as examples. If you decide to use any of the information here, please be certain to verify that the language meets the requirements of the jurisdiction in which it will be interpreted.

Part I

THE RIGHT PERSON
FOR THE RIGHT JOB

1

BEGINNING THE SEARCH

Buying a professional service you are getting a promise, an expectation, and that uncertainty can be somewhat reduced by careful selection.

Milan Kubr[1]

This chapter supplies the basic guidelines for initiating a search for a professional service provider regardless of the profession, method of compensation, or skill level. The chapter includes techniques for developing lists of candidates, discusses the importance of understanding the language and the idiosyncrasies of the profession, and provides pointers on evaluating candidates as well as caveats for the use of references.

General selection criteria for professional service suppliers include: professional integrity, professional competence, rapport with the client, capability to deliver, ability to mobilize further resources, and delivery of services at a fair price.[2]

Perform a *needs assessment*, that is, define your capabilities, requirements from outside service providers, immediate needs, and anticipated future needs. The needs assessment will define the range of skills and level of competency of your outside service provider.

RESEARCH THE FIELD OF CANDIDATES

I began my business career as a marketer. At varying points in my business life, I also engaged in purchasing products and services. The fundamental principles for learning about a new market or a new product or service are essentially the same as for the selection of a professional adviser. A marketer interested in a new geographic market or an unfamiliar industry will *engage in market research.* A purchasing agent will survey all possible resources including the competition, the Yellow Pages, *Thomas Register,* trade magazines, and other business associates before actually making a purchase from a particular vendor.

One of my best starting points for initiating research has historically been and continues to be the Yellow Pages. While you might have trouble imagining how you would select a real estate attorney from the Yellow Pages (I agree it would be highly unlikely), you could probably find a real estate agent with little difficulty. Also, advertisements in the Yellow Pages sometimes trigger connections or provide key words. If you are computer literate and Internet literate, there are World Wide Web sites and professional forums on many of the provider services (e.g., America On-Line, CompuServe, Expert Marketplace).

Another source for basic information is the business press. Many local business newspapers, trade publications, and magazines run special issues on different professions. If you are like me and save these issues, you can search back and perhaps locate an article that focuses on the profession in which you have interest. Trade publications often include articles highlighting local professionals describing their successes. Some of these publications offer regular and guest columns written by professionals. A truly compulsive manager or entrepreneur may be inclined to establish a "professions file" and insert articles written by or about professionals, for possible future reference.

INVEST TIME IN YOUR SEARCH

All entrepreneurs and managers suffer from lack of time. We all tend to allocate more time for the things we like to do and invest as little time as possible in those things we do not like or do not understand. Unless you are prepared to make the commitment of time on the search and selection process, all the advice accumulated here is worthless. So the next element of the process is *commit to investing the time.*

LEARN THE VERNACULAR

An important element in purchasing services is *learning the vernacular.* For example, if you want to talk intelligently to a graphic artist, you ought to learn the difference between 60 lb. paper and 80 lb. paper and appropriate uses for each weight (yes, 80 lb. paper is heavier than 60 lb.). If you are intending to automate your bookkeeping operations, you should know the difference between a hard disk and a floppy diskette. Again in these areas, trade journals can be very educational. Also, the public library can be an important resource, and the librarians will assist you in tracking down information. Most of the references cited at the end of the various chapters are profession specific and if reviewed will provide you with much of the vernacular; some even have glossaries. (In Chapter 6, I have included several dictionaries of graphic terms in the reference list.)

Talking to people in related businesses is another effective tool for not only learning vernacular but also developing a list of candidates. For example, if you are looking for a graphic artist, talk to a commercial printer. Request a tour of the printer's facility and ask questions without fear of seeming stupid (e.g., what is the difference between offset and lithography; what is the difference between process and PMS?). If you want to learn about architects, talk to a builder. Ask other businesspeople about their patent attorney or accountant. Ask those same associates if there is anyone you should avoid. If I am pleased with someone with whom I am working, I am happy to share my positive experience with associates and sometimes even with strangers who ask. Because it is human nature to want to share experiences—both good and bad—word of mouth can be a valuable source of information.

DEVELOP A LIST

Conventional wisdom suggests building a list with at least 10 names. That may depend on the available pool of professionals. If you are situated in a town of 35,000 people some distance from a major metropolitan area, developing a candidate list of 10 graphic artists may be impossible. On the other hand, you may have a knowledgeable friend who provides you with the names of the three best real estate lawyers within 150 miles and you don't need to waste time on evaluating 10 candidates. Later chapters of this book will provide the names and addresses of professional organizations that can supply lists of members in your geographic area. Try to collect information about candidates. Many law firms have developed informational pieces that provide background on the partners, their specialties, and other general information. An architect or builder not only may have an informational brochure but should provide a list of projects. A graphic artist or advertising agency will have a portfolio. Gather any and all written information about your candidates, including articles they may have written and awards they have won.

OBSERVE THE CANDIDATES OR THEIR PRODUCTS

It is much easier to observe a bankruptcy attorney or a litigator in action than a real estate attorney or an estate counsel. Ask the litigator to give you a list of dates he or she anticipates being on trial. You may not receive a positive response, but ask a real estate attorney if you can be an observer at a closing. You can examine a graphic artist's portfolio or an architect or builder's finished work easier than a computer consultant's projects. But the more thoroughly you can observe a given candidate or inspect his or her product, the more likely you will have confidence in your final selection.

MEET WITH THE CANDIDATES

In some instances, this is easier to say than it is to do.

> *War Story.*   Some years ago I was involved in litigation in Chicago although I was still living in Israel. The case involved temporary restraining orders, letters of credit (L/Cs), and required immediate action by a local attorney. I didn't have time to go through a lengthy selection process. I asked several sources for recommendations and took the advice of my general counsel, retaining an attorney with whom a member of his firm had collaborated. Your general counsel can be as important as your family doctor and serve the same function when you need a referral to specialists.

If time allows, however, you should never hire an outside consultant without meeting with the candidate, just as you wouldn't hire an employee without a personal interview. It is advisable to have this meeting early on in the hiring process, in the consultant's own environment. This will give you the opportunity to:

- Observe each candidate's taste.
- Note aspects of neatness and order.
- See the interaction within the organization.
- Meet the individual's associates and note their interaction.

Encourage a second meeting at your place of business, so the candidates can see how you operate and you can note the candidates' questions and observations. I have found it very revealing to take a candidate on a tour of my production facility and observe him or her observing my operation. You can usually tell how intent a person is in trying to understand what you do by the questions asked and comments made.

OBTAIN REFERENCES

I repeatedly counsel my clients to place limited faith in information received from references. Nevertheless, it can be a useful element in the selection process. Here is an approach to try: Ask the candidate to supply you with one or two references who were not satisfied with his or her work. A candidate who has enough confidence in his or her ability should be willing to share his or her failures as well as successes. A refusal probably will not tell you much. When calling references, be prepared with a list of questions. This serves two purposes: (1) It enables you to compare responses to the same questions, and (2) it is courteous to avoid wasting someone's time. Organize your questions to include issues such as "What didn't you like about the candidate's work?"

ASK QUESTIONS OF THE CANDIDATES

This may seem to be obvious advice, but many first-time entrepreneurs are too timid and even too intimidated to ask probing questions. Prepare a list of 10 or 12 pertinent questions relating to your specific business or project. The candidates will appreciate that you have come prepared and aren't wasting their time with idle chat. You will have the basis for a fair comparison if you evaluate answers to the same questions. And this way, you won't end the interview without having asked everything you wanted to ask. Questions should cover the individual's background, experience in your industry or problem, strategy, and compensation. Lists of questions are included throughout the book for a wide range of professions. There is also a list of general questions in Appendix I to assist you in developing your own set of questions, and guidelines for managing the interview process.

EVALUATE CANDIDATES' EDUCATION, CONTINUING EDUCATION, AND CERTIFICATION

Attending a prestigious college and attaining a high grade point average (GPA) may have little bearing on a person's professional expertise.

My accountant, who is a first-rate professional as well as my loyal adviser and friend, jokes about his performance in high school and college. I have also worked with advisers who did not finish college, and I have met incompetent consultants who were unable to think despite a stellar academic performance. Nevertheless, questions about academic background are among those you should be asking. There are many advertisements for mail-order degrees and while I have never had an experience, good or bad, with someone touting such a degree, I am cynical about their educational value.

Jay G. Foonberg, in *Finding the Right Lawyer*, observes that the law school a lawyer attended should not be a factor in judging his or her competence, but class standing is an important indicator of an effective lawyer. "Good class standing is, in my opinion, indicative of excellence. High standing indicates that the lawyer learned well."[3] I agree with Foonberg, with the reservation that academic learning cannot substitute for practical experience. In some areas of law, common sense and wisdom are more important than knowledge. And the ability to negotiate and compromise may be more valuable to you than your attorney's assurance of being on sound legal ground.

Foonberg discusses the value of the state licensing process and the significance of the bar exam. He notes that in some states 90 percent of those tested pass and in other states less than 50 percent pass.[4] Foonberg's description of the process suggests it is not a very good indicator of competency in the practice of law, but simply a measure of knowledge of law.

On the other hand, *continuing education* is one of those subjects that you should probe deeply during your search. My prized accountant frequently attends courses, seminars, and workshops to update his knowledge and widen his expertise. No matter how busy advisers may be, they must stay on the cutting edge in their field. The practice of medicine illustrates this necessity. When you think about all the developments taking place in medicine constantly, you are unlikely to seek treatment from a physician who practices the same medicine he or she did 20 years ago. In the same pattern, tax laws change every year; trends in how courts interpret laws change, technology is constantly in flux. Every profession discussed in this book is under a constant state of attack from new, improved, and changing conditions. Unless your advisers are up to date, they cannot possibly serve you well. I suggest you ask any and all candidates for any position to provide you with a list of the courses, seminars, and workshops they have attended during the past 12 months. Many professionals such as accountants are required to take courses to maintain their certification. Others have no requirements, but people who take their professions seriously will continuously try to improve their skills.

Certification is a more difficult issue in certain professions. Lawyers have to pass the bar exam; certified public accountants (CPAs) have exams to pass and continuing education requirements to maintain their certification; real estate agents have a state certifying exam (dependent on state). But many professions do not have a formal certifying procedure. In Chapter 5, the Resources section includes notations on some of the consultant organizations that have developed certification programs. I have not evaluated those programs and cannot offer an opinion as to their efficacy. However, if the profession you are considering, such as law or accountancy, is known to have a certifying or qualifying program, be certain to ask for confirmation from your candidates. Where the profession does not have a formal program but certification is offered by a professional association, be skeptical until the candidate offers evidence that such a certification is meaningful.

EVALUATE EXISTING RELATIONSHIPS

In any discussion of effective management, it is simply impossible to exaggerate the importance of decisions about consultants:

> The act of moving an account is inefficient, slowing or possibly even halting marketing momentum, and it is expensive in money and particularly, in time. Devoting considerable effort to making a wise first choice is the superior method.[5]

The focus of this book is the finding, hiring, and managing of outside service providers. If you already have advisers in place and are unhappy with them, you will have to determine whether their lack of performance is a function of incompetence or a lack of leadership and direction by you. Here are some guidelines for reviewing and evaluating an existing relationship.

The initial step in an audit of an existing relationship is a *needs assessment.* Does the problem revolve around your business or your having outgrown the capabilities of the professional? In going through this process now (as opposed to before retaining the professional), you may see that the individual or firm was inadequate from the outset. A needs assessment will consider the following elements:

- In-house skills and knowledge of the field.
- Expectation of the size and requirements of the company five years out.

The next step is to evaluate the capabilities of the service provider. For the moment, put aside any concerns about being over-charged or problems in communication. Look at whether the service provider can fulfill your needs based on your needs assessment. If your answer to this basic issue is unsatisfactory, then the other issues are irrelevant. If your analysis suggests that, with proper management, the basic skills are there to do the job, you may be able to salvage the relationship. To evaluate an in-place service provider, I recommend you turn to the appropriate chapter in this book and review the material and compare your individual against the standard. You can also interview other professionals. This serves two purposes: It will provide a benchmark to measure the current professional, and if the current professional does not stand up to this scrutiny, you will have a list of potential replacements.

Assume your professional fulfills your needs assessment and has satisfactory skills. However, you aren't happy with one or several elements of the relationship. As unpleasant as you may find the prospect, you will have to confront the problems and renegotiate the relationship. For this to be effective, you ought to prepare a Request for Proposal (RFP). An RFP is simply a document that defines what you want to be accomplished by the engagement; a statement of what you expect (see Exhibit 5–3, a sample Request for Proposal). Using many of the tools provided in later chapters in this book (see, e.g., Chapter 10), develop an outline of how you think the relationship should be structured. Finally, you will have to meet with the professional, lay out your concerns, and offer the new revised method as your approach to salvaging the engagement. Although some readers may feel this advice is obvious, inertia prevents many entrepreneurs and managers from doing the obvious. Other readers may fear a negative response. Keep in mind that a good lawyer, accountant, or other professional is not necessarily a savvy businessperson or may be savvy when it comes to *his or her own profession* but not when it comes to managing *your business.* Everyone, however, has a bit of salesperson inside and no one likes to lose a sale, a customer, or a client. If a professional confronted with your serious well-thought-out approach is not responsive, then you should move your account to someone else. Whenever I have replaced an inadequate employee, a manager or an outside service provider; the replacement has always been a better performer than the predecessor, in part because I was more savvy in the selection process the second and third time.

If you determine that you need someone else after conducting a needs assessment and evaluation or after presenting your concerns to an unresponsive service provider, Chapter 13 will provide useful information on terminating a relationship.

THE THREE RS: THE SEARCH

RECAP

- Perform a needs assessment—review your capabilities and your needs now and in the future.
- Engage in market research—developing lists of candidates is a process.
- Commit to investing time—you cannot hire quality employees or consultants without investing time and energy.
- Learn the vernacular—each industry and profession has its own terminology, effective management of professionals includes understanding them.
- Talk to people—ask friends, business associates, anyone who may be a source of a recommendation.
- Develop a list—don't work with less than 3 or more than 10 candidates.
- Observe the candidates—either review their work (portfolios) or watch them in court.
- Meet with the candidates—evaluate their place of business, observe how they evaluate your place of business.
- Obtain references—talk with the references, ask questions.
- Ask questions—don't be shy either with candidates or with references.
- Evaluate education, continuing education, and certification— depending on the function being fulfilled, education and continuing education can be important elements.
- Evaluate existing relationships—don't change for the sake of change, examine the costs to your business and you.

RESOURCES

- Yellow Pages.
- Computer—World Wide Web sites, provider forums.
- Trade and professional journals, business newspapers, and magazines.

(continued)

THE THREE Rs *(continued)*

- Linked professions (e.g., builders for architects, printers for graphic artists).
- Friends and business associates.
- Professional trade associations.

REFERENCES

- *Choosing and Using a Consultant**   This is a good basic primer on the process of choosing consultants and then managing the relationship. Although out of print, it may be available in your library as the author is well-known. Look for other books by Herman Holtz published by John Wiley & Sons.
- *How to Select and Use Consultants*****   You may have some difficulty in obtaining this book because it isn't actually distributed in the United States. I have provided the mailing address of the publisher in the Bibliography and recommend it. I found it in a business school library.
- *How Clients Choose.*
- *How to Select and Manage Consultants*   Shenson was one of the best known and respected authors on the subject. This book may or may not be out of print; there may be a later edition. It should be available in your local library.
- *When and How to Choose an Attorney.**

2

ATTORNEYS

The professional man is in essence one who provides a service. He has no goods to sell, no land to till. His only asset is himself. It turns out that there is no right price for service, for what is a share of a man's worth? If he does not contain the quality of integrity, he is worthless. If he does, he is priceless. The value is either nothing or it is infinite.

The Honorable Elbert Tuttle, Federal Appellate Judge[1]

There is no shortage of "how-to" books for incorporating your business, resolving disputes, writing contracts, negotiating deals, preparing patent applications and other legal documents, and generally managing your legal affairs on your own. Although I do not want to cast aspersions on fellow authors, I think it is not only ingenuous but even *irresponsible* to suggest to someone with no legal training that it is feasible to "do it yourself" without sound legal advice. No matter how modest your success may be, *at some point in your business career you will require the services of a lawyer.* You may need an agreement crafted, litigation handled, laws interpreted, or any number of a multitude of services that will require legal counsel. It is nice, but naive, to imagine you can avoid lawyers during a business career. This chapter begins with a consideration of the self-evaluation necessary before engaging in the search process and then describes the search process itself. There is a discussion of qualifying references, suggestions for the interview and evaluation stage, and a review of the initial consultation. The balance of the chapter is divided into discussions of specialties, with an emphasis on the most common and often required specialties such as general counsel, litigation, and patents.

DECIDE WHETHER YOU WANT A LARGE OR SMALL LAW FIRM

General practitioners today seldom treat serious heart problems; medicine has become a profession of specialists. So too is the practice of law. There is perhaps one obvious difference between the two professions. Large law firms may have departments that deal with a wide range of legal specialties, while medical practices tend to be specialty focused. Even though the trend in law is away from sole practitioners, boutique firms appear to be thriving and should be included in your search.

One of the first decisions a businessperson has to make is whether to retain the services of a large multiservice law firm or of a smaller, less versatile law practice. Large law firms tend to be more expensive although that is not a rule. Large versus small is more a function of the nature of your business and what you anticipate or expect it will become. It may also be a function of your personal preference and to some extent your location (a small town may not offer many options of legal counsel). If you are starting up a high-tech manufacturing business that will have to raise large sums of money from venture capitalists and at a later stage from the public, you ought to consider a large, high-profile law firm, or a boutique firm, from the outset. If you are planning to open up a small retail or service business, a local small firm or sole practitioner will probably serve your needs. On the other end of the spectrum, almost all communications law (radio and television) is practiced in Washington, DC, in proximity to the Federal Communications Commission (FCC). So, if you are planning to acquire or develop a federally regulated business, you may find yourself seeking primary counsel in Washington, even if your company is in Wyoming.

The business you are opening or operating may have some idiosyncrasies that will require you to lean toward firms with a strong focus in a specialty. If your product or service has a high product liability exposure, you will want your general counsel to be competent in dealing with personal injury, insurance issues, and litigation. There are other specialties, such as patent law, you should seek outside your primary firm. If I were planning to get into the real estate business, I would certainly want my law firm to have a strong real estate department. If my long-term goals were eventually to own a building, I don't think the size or depth of the real estate department of my general business counsel would be particularly important. I would look outside the firm at the time I was negotiating to acquire or lease a property. The choice of a law firm should take into consideration the everyday needs of your business and your needs as well. No two firms are exactly the same in terms of size or depth within departments, but if you define your needs, you will find more than one firm that can fulfill them.

The following is a partial list of specialties or areas of the law. You may want to estimate the number of times you might use each specialty in the course of a year to see which specialties you would want your general counsel to be able to handle:

- Business or corporate law:
  —Contracts.
  —Employment and labor.
  —Mergers and acquisitions.
  —Real estate.
  —Government relations.
  —Environment.
  —Bankruptcy.
  —Collections.
  —Taxation.
- Intellectual property law:
  —Patent applications.
  —Copyright registrations.
  —Trademark registrations.
  —Patent infringement litigation.
  —Licensing and technology transfer.
- Litigation:
  —General litigation.
  —Product liability.
  —Personal injury.
- Personal and family:
  —Estate planning.
  —Domestic relations (includes divorce).
  —Immigration.
- Others (communications, admiralty, equipment leasing, commercial and industrial leasing, sports and artistic representation, innkeepers law, etc.).

The list is by no means all-inclusive, I haven't listed every specialty, but keep this rule in mind: If your business needs specific legal advice on an ongoing basis, it is preferable the candidate firms you evaluate have strong experience and depth in those areas. If the general counsel you want and trust does not have the depth within his or her firm to meet the majority of your needs, be certain that you have the firm's agreement and commitment to assisting you in filling the gaps in coverage from outside counsel.

You may feel you require the services of a large law firm but cannot afford to pay their fees. Many large and small firms will make allowances for your capability to pay their standard rates. If your business has the potential to evolve into a major client that can be billed at the firm's published rates, a good firm is not likely to want to lose you as a client because you are unable to pay the going rate in the early stages.

The hiring of legal counsel is not a marriage for life. At the same time, making the effort to select the right firm can save you exasperation and frustration later on in your business career.

Getting Recommendations

Obtaining a referral is probably one of the best methods of identifying candidates. Ask friends who are in business, your banker, your accountant. Anyone who has regular contact with local attorneys and is willing to speak well of an attorney or a firm is likely to be a good source for building your candidate list. If you need an attorney for a specialized limited purpose, your present counsel should be able to recommend one or more candidates. However, be cautious about recommendations. The friend who recommends legal counsel may have had few or no actual dealings with the firm, or may not be a good judge of performance and billing practices. Also, be leery of recommendations by those who have personal ties of friendship or family involving the law firm. Finally, "Be aware . . . that a lawyer who is right for someone else may not be suited to work with you or your legal problem."[2]

The process of evaluating potential legal counsel is not very different from seeking any other vendor. Be skeptical of references a candidate offers; someone interested in getting you as a client is unlikely to provide negative references. A lawyer will rarely suggest you call someone whose negotiation he botched or whose litigation he did not win. He is also not likely to tell you about the clients he lost due to excessive billing.

Do not use a friend as your legal counsel. However, a friend who is an attorney should be an excellent source of recommendations. Using a friend as legal counsel or as a supplier of any other service may damage your friendship. I have discussed this observation with many professional friends who would prefer that I not include this caveat. I also have friends who have successfully worked with friends on a professional basis without problems. This is a subjective issue, and I am simply stating my personal opinion. I value personal friendships, and I lost a friend of over 40 years as a result of engaging in a business transaction with him. If you develop a friendship as an outgrowth of a business relationship, that is fine. However, I have seen many good friendships and family relationships destroyed because of disputes over business issues.

Interviewing and Evaluating the Candidates

Interviewing is considered by many to be an art. There are scores of books, seminars, and courses for developing good interviewing techniques for human resources management. Universities run workshops for seniors prior to graduation to prepare them for job interviews. I have no intention of providing an extensive discussion of interview techniques in this book although Exhibit 2–1 illustrates a general interview format. In addition, I have provided basic interview information in Appendix I to guide management of the process. Here are five key elements to keep in mind:

1. *Don't let the candidate "interview the interviewer."* Entrepreneurs love to talk about themselves and their inventions. It is, in part, what makes them so disingenuous. A smart candidate will ask a lot of questions; knowing full well that if you do all the talking, you will feel it was a good interview. In much the same way as you must manage the relationship when you hire professionals, you must manage the interview. You must direct the process, moving it at your pace.

2. *Be prepared.* The Boy Scout motto is as much on target as it is a cliché. If you have obtained background information on the candidate beforehand, read it. Make notes, and ask for clarifications of unclear items. If you don't want to work from a form such as the one shown in Exhibit 2–1, develop your own. Prepare a list of pertinent questions in advance. Be certain that your questions relate to the specific responsibility or project for which you are considering the candidate.

3. *Listen.* This is a difficult task. Listen to the candidate's questions. Listen to the candidate's answers to your questions. Listen to the tone of the questions and answers and observe body language. When a lawyer prepares a client to testify, there are some rules that every lawyer goes over with their clients:

   —*Listen to the question.* Whether in a courtroom or in conversation, people tend to jump to conclusions about questions rather than allowing the questioner to complete the sentence.

Exhibit 2–1   Interview Questions for General Counsel and All Lawyers

1. What specialties are regularly practiced at your firm? _____
   _____

2. In which departments or specialties does your firm have strength? _____
   _____

3. Which departments or specialties are not strong? _____
   _____

4. Who else in your firm will be involved in my case/account? _____
   _____

5. What are the possible outcomes of the litigation/matter? _____
   _____

6. In addition to your fees and expenses, what other costs should I
   anticipate? _____
   _____

7. What can I do to hold down expenses? _____
   _____

8. If you and I get into a dispute over something, how will we resolve
   it? _____
   _____

9. Please describe the process you utilize to analyze a problem and
   give advice. _____
   _____

10. Are there any clients of your firm that may create a conflict of
    interest? _____
    _____

11. What business experience have you had? _____
    _____

—*Make sure you understand.* Don't assume or try to interpret the question, sometimes questions are purposely framed in an ambivalent way.

—*Pause for three seconds before answering* (to give the lawyer a chance to object). This also gives you time to formulate your answer so you don't fumble through it.

—*Answer only the question.* Don't volunteer any additional information.

These guidelines for giving testimony are equally useful when interviewing candidates. Beware of the person being interviewed who applies Rule 3 (you want interviewees to elaborate on their answers).

4. *Take notes.* If you are not comfortable scribbling during the interview, take time afterward to record your observations. The advantage of using a form like the one shown in Exhibit 2–1 and asking all candidates the same questions (see sample questions in Appendix I and by profession throughout the book) is that you will have a consistent framework for comparison. Your careful preparation also sends a strong message to the candidates that you take these interviews seriously.

5. *Don't make hasty decisions.* Unless there is an emergency, you should carefully evaluate each candidate individually and then in comparison with the other candidates. And if you are not thrilled with the candidates, start the process all over. Don't compromise or you will be left with a nagging doubt that will erode your confidence in the relationship.

Years ago there was a popular movie entitled *Paper Chase*, which later was expanded into a TV series. Lawyers will tell you it was a reasonably accurate portrayal of law schools and the life of law students. Understanding how lawyers are trained may provide some insight into their personalities and through that awareness, an ability to deal with them. Law schools are very competitive environments. Most law students have been top students both in the secondary school and as undergraduates. Being placed once again among high achievers engenders even more competition especially since class standing and grades are the keys to opening the doors to the very best law firms. Professors in law schools often use a kind of confrontational Socratic approach—they seldom actually lecture but instead ask questions. Students answer based on readings of the case law and must defend their argument, or position.

The Bar exam that comes after law school requires further intensive study and preparation. Meanwhile the fledgling attorney serves an internship in a firm where again competition is intense for a position first as an associate and later on as a junior partner. The process by which someone becomes a lawyer is a kind of intellectual and emotional "survival of the fittest." The people who survive this process tend to be confrontational, with a strong desire to win.

The following are characteristics to consider when evaluating candidates.

Accessibility

This is central to an executive's needs. Will the attorney give you his or her home and cellular phone number? Do the secretary and the receptionist for this attorney understand that when you call you do not want to be ignored for half a day? More and more firms are installing voice mail, which may somewhat ameliorate the issue of accessibility. On the other hand, voice mail can be frustrating and I might even lean toward a firm that has a live person to answer my call.

Entrepreneurs tend to be impulsive, a characteristic that has both advantages and disadvantages. "Things happen" effectively describes the day-to-day operations of a business. Many times, for lack of internal resources, a businessperson will look to advisers for advice; nothing is more frustrating than needing a quick fix or answer and not even getting to speak with that adviser. Often, if entrepreneurs can explain their problem, they will feel they have transferred it to someone else, even if the answer is delayed.

Many attorneys do not understand this dynamic and unintentionally alienate their clients by not being more accessible. Since these attorneys do not realize the significance of "instant gratification" or service, their organizations make no effort to meet this need. In some large firms, however, a senior partner will involve an associate with a specific client. The associate can field the call and at least give the entrepreneur a comfort level that the problem is being attended to. An efficient support staff can, at times, be just as effective as a brilliant lawyer.

Find out what the firm's policy is on returning telephone calls. Try to get a written commitment from the attorney handling your account that all calls will be answered within a mutually acceptable time. Does the secretary have sufficient independence and expertise to refer you to an associate or another partner if the boss is unavailable? Does the secretary run interference for the boss or act as the client's advocate at the firm? Passing on your questions to a competent secretary who understands the need to obtain answers from the boss can be an efficient way of working with a busy and often unavailable adviser.

Billing Practices

I was once represented by a firm where the partner responsible for my account generated a bill once a year. It not only drove me crazy but I understand it also vexed his partners to no end. So, once a year I would see a bill that would choke a horse, and I had very little or no recollection of the details billed. Most firms bill monthly. Do they "nickel and dime" you on telephone calls, faxes, photocopies, and courier charges? You may be able to negotiate these expenses out of the billing process (for more information, see Chapter 9). You should also obtain, in writing, the costs and billing policies on those expenses you cannot negotiate out. Don't make unfair billing requests: You'll pay for them one way or another.

You should request and your attorney should agree to itemize each bill by the project or issue and by the attorney(s) involved. Breaking out these issues may be difficult. Often in the course of a half-hour telephone call or a two-hour meeting, you may discuss several issues. However, it is important to control these costs, and in the case of litigation, itemized expenses could be germane to recovering your legal expenses. It is not unusual for agreements to provide for the loser paying all legal costs in the event of a dispute. There is also a movement to incorporate this provision into tort law.

Another option is to ask the attorney to supply a billing summary (see Exhibit 9–2). These internal documents are generated by the partner in charge of each account and summarize all interactions with or on behalf of each client by file number.

Many attorneys bill by either 10- or 15-minute intervals. So a 5-minute conversation may cost you as much as a 15-minute conversation. Find out the firm's practice before you get the first bill. Think about it; an attorney who can hold six 5-minute conversations in an hour can bill one and one half hours for a half hour of work. Also, some attorneys round up to the nearest full billing unit. Be sure to obtain the firm's billing policies in writing. In Chapter 9, I will discuss ways of controlling these costs.

Appearances

There are two schools of thought about appearance (e.g., the firm's decor, the attorney's manner of dress, the car he or she drives): One school holds that success breeds success, the other wonders, "Why am I paying for this?" There is no harm in asking the source of the luxury. Perhaps the landlord, as an inducement for a long-term lease, agreed to make luxury improvements or maybe the previous tenant underwrote the improvements. I have a friend whose firm has been representing insurers of companies that produced asbestos. His firm has lived in the lap of luxury from this part of their practice for years. Their other clients do not pay any extra. The firm that represented my company in a patent infringement case received contingency fees of over $1,000,000, whereas their out-of-pocket expenses and reimbursement of billable time may have run $500,000. I have not seen their offices since the settlement, but I would not be surprised if some of the settlement paid for redecoration.

I do worry when all the partners are driving a Lotus or Maserati and they all wear designer suits. If you are a conservative individual, you may not be comfortable with a firm that presents a flashy or expensive image. Appearance also relates to the firm's profile within the community or your industry. If your business serves conservative institutions, such as hospitals, you may find it problematic to be represented by a law practice engaged in ambulance chasing. Therefore, you need to be aware of what the other partners in the firm are doing and what type of law they are practicing.

The Other Partners

Whether you are dealing with a small firm or a large firm, it is important for you to meet at least some of the other partners. You should feel comfortable with the partners to the same degree you feel comfortable with the partner handling your account. This is particularly true for those specialties you anticipate calling on for service. It is also useful to meet a second or third person in the department in the event you want an opinion when your contact is unavailable.

The Secretarial and Reception Staff

I have a friend and business associate who recommends interviewing the attorney's secretary. His or her attitude is a reflection of the firm's leadership. Being able to transmit your questions and concerns to a competent secretary can be an efficient way of working with a busy attorney. Foonberg suggests that the way you are received by the receptionist is an indicator of a caring or an uncaring firm.

You should insist that candidates for representing your company make at least one pilgrimage to your office. It is important that they see and understand your business and its product or service, meet your team, and become acquainted with your company culture. Again, distance may preclude such a meeting but, where possible, this is important.

Meeting with Lawyers

I consider the initial consultation to be your first meeting after selecting the candidate. Therefore, the preliminaries such as compatibility should already have been resolved to your satisfaction. This meeting should finalize issues of compensation, address specific needs of your business, and include a general legal review. It should also be the time to establish ground rules for your working with other members or departments within the firm.

Foonberg discusses the first meeting as one where you may still be evaluating the attorney. He suggests you evaluate courtesy, work habits, personality, philosophy and beliefs, availability, confidentiality, gender, and conflicts of interest.

According to Cliff Robertson, author of *The Business Person's Legal Advisor,* the initial appointment should be a screening process for both of you to decide if you want to continue the association. Prepare for your appointment much like you would prepare for a job interview. . . . Look for personal compatibility, good judgment, legal expertise, a habit of thorough preparation, prompt response to your needs, and reasonable fees in the attorney you eventually select.[3]

Here are some suggestions:

- Ask about the lawyer's experience and area of practice.
- Ask who will be working on your case.
- Ask about fees and costs.
- Ask about possible outcomes of the case.
- Ask how you can participate.
- Ask about resolving potential problems.[4]

Another suggestion from Foonberg: While you are waiting, listen to how the receptionist answers calls and passes them on to the attorneys in the firm. Can you hear the names of clients or is the receptionist discreet? "Mentioning clients names in front of non-clients can be a serious breach of ethics."[5] Foonberg's book ought to be read by attorneys, so much of what he writes is on target. I have experienced many arrogant and indifferent receptionists at law firms and their bad manners are a reflection of the partners' attitudes.

THE THREE Rs: ATTORNEYS

RECAP

- Define your requirements and consider size—anticipating the range of your legal requirements over three to five years will help to profile the size and depth of candidates.
- Collect recommendations—ask friends, business associates, your accountant, other lawyers, and anyone else who can help you build a list of candidates.
- Explore accessibility—overly busy counsel with poor support staff can be very frustrating.

(continued)

- Understand billing practices—be sure all billing issues are discussed at the beginning of the relationship.
- Be comfortable with appearances—if your tastes are modest, avoid firms with overly fancy offices.
- Get to know the other partners—can you work with them if need be?

RESOURCES

- American Bar Association, Division for Public Education, 541 North Fairbanks Court, Chicago, IL 60611-3314, Tel: 312-988-5735, Fax: 312-988-5032, E-mail: abapubed@attmail.com, WEB site: http://www.abanet.org. The ABA produces a lawyer referral services directory and publications directory with some worthwhile books; both are available on their Web site.
- Your local or county Bar association and/or its referral service (usually listed in the telephone white pages as "Lawyer Reference Service" or "Lawyer Referral & Information Service).
- Local business press.
- Local specialty Bar association (if one exists you should be able to obtain the name from the Lawyer Reference Service).

REFERENCES

- *The American Lawyer*****   This great little monograph will introduce you to the subject.
- *The Businessperson's Legal Advisor.*
- *Finding the Right Lawyer*****   The ABA has performed a community service by publishing this book.
- *Martindale-Hubbell Legal Directory*   It can be found in most public libraries and is also available on-line for a fee through Lexis-Nexis.
- *Save Your Business*****   This is a primer for people facing bankruptcy but has useful insights into the legal profession.
- *The Small Business Legal Advisor.**
- *Taming the Lawyers*****   This superb book is well written, informative, and entertaining. It provides an in-depth discussion of the hiring process.

GENERAL BUSINESS COUNSEL

Many law specialties are incident or transaction specific—real estate attorney for handling a real estate deal, patent attorney for filing a patent application, litigator for suing somebody. In all likelihood, you would seek out the specialists if or when you required their services. A general business attorney should be sought at the very beginning of the process of establishing a company or a new business. Despite the new self-help software and all the self-help books on the shelves of bookstores and libraries—which offer advice on incorporating on your own, preparing forms, and even settling disputes without counsel—entrepreneurs should seek out general counsel for the start-up of a business. You can use those books and programs to make you a better consumer of legal services and to save money on resolving minor matters. Not only is it naive to think you can operate anything but the most primitive business without access to legal counsel in today's environment, it is downright dangerous. Note that this is the only specialty where I have used the term "counsel." By definition, a counsel is an adviser. Viewed in this context, you should look to your general business counsel to provide you with legal advice. It makes no difference whether that advice relates to how to set up your business (partnership, corporation, etc.), or how to negotiate the best contract for services from a vendor or with a customer. Entrepreneurs have enough anxiety starting a business as it is, without adding more worries about whether what they are doing is within the law.

The *function* of your general business counsel includes these tasks:

- Review all legal documents presented to company (leases, purchase contracts, etc.).
- Prepare agreements and contracts (e.g., employment contracts, licensing agreements, leases if applicable).
- Advise management (i.e., *you*) and render opinions on matters such as potential legal issues, conflicts, and liability, as required.
- Recommend solutions to legal problems and potential legal problems.
- Assist in negotiations, if called on.
- Perform annual or periodic legal audits (review purchase orders, invoices, employment manuals, advertising).

Starting up a business is an anxiety inducing and exhilarating experience. You should give the maximum amount of attention to selecting an attorney or a firm to handle general business matters. You may only deal with your patent attorney once a year, but your general counsel is likely to be involved with you on a week-to-week basis. A good general counsel is comparable to a doctor who is a general practitioner. The individual has to be able to diagnose the problem, suggest some alternatives, and recommend a specialist if necessary. Many lawyers seem to feel compelled to give instant advice. Maybe they sense the client wants an instant answer or believe they must seem to be omniscient in their legal knowledge to avoid being viewed as incompetent.

So why should I expect my attorney to know it all? When meeting with a candidate, it might be a useful exercise to present a legal problem and see what process he or she goes through to offer advice.

You also should consider whether the attorney you are considering has experience in your particular business. If you are in manufacturing, has he or she represented other manufacturers? If your business is retailing, who are his or her clients? Also, you may need to confirm the engagement will not be a conflict of interest in the future, with vendors, customers, or competitors. You might consider asking about his or her biggest professional success and what he or she thinks was his or her biggest error.

The central issue is to feel comfortable. If you do not trust the judgment of the candidate, then do not hire the person; if you have already hired unreliable counsel, replace him or her. I have made the mistake too many times of suffering in silence after I had lost confidence in an attorney.

A good attorney is not necessarily a savvy businessperson. I will apply variants of this dictum time and again to all your service providers. While you shouldn't assume that your general counsel is a knowledgeable businessperson, look elsewhere if he or she cannot grasp the fundamentals of your business. You don't make decisions or reach conclusions in a vacuum, they are tempered by your experience and knowledge. Similarly, your general counsel's advice is tempered by experience and personal prejudices. Ask counsel, to distinguish between the legal issues surrounding an event and his or her business opinion when offering advice. You may be interested in hearing your counsel's personal opinion about a business issue, but both parties should understand that it is an opinion and not legal advice. In trying to select your firm's general business counsel, think about your needs—your weaknesses and strengths as a manager, your comfort level in reviewing documents and in negotiating agreements. Be sure the person or firm you select complements your management style.

Evaluate your in-house capabilities. Review the skills already present within your team and yourself. How comfortable are you or a member of your team with generating a simple employment agreement? How valuable is your time: Is it more productive for you to have counsel do it and pay the price or would you rather save the $250 and do it yourself?

What about compatibility? From a personality perspective, how well does your proposed general counsel mesh with your team? In general, people attracted to the law have very strong personalities. My experience suggests that lawyers are, as a group, very opinionated. That makes them good poker players, good negotiators, and good litigators. Entrepreneurs, on the other hand, seem to be full of self-doubt even if they believe wholeheartedly in their business. So, the demeanor of lawyers frequently intimidates entrepreneurs, and business decisions are colored by a lawyer's conviction of the correctness of his or her ideas and not by the entrepreneur's instincts, which have made the business successful.

THE THREE RS: GENERAL BUSINESS COUNSEL

RECAP

- Define your company's present needs and anticipated future needs—be sure you won't grow out of the firm's capabilities to support you in a few years, or that you won't always be going outside the firm for advice.
- Invest the time and energy at the outset to locate and identify the right general counsel for your business—general counsel is so very important to all businesses; be thorough in your search.
- You must feel comfortable with your counsel—you must be comfortable with your choice on a personal level and a professional level.
- A good lawyer is not necessarily a good businessperson—don't mistake business advice for legal advice.

RESOURCES

- Your state or local Bar association (Lawyer Referral Service in White Pages).
- American Bar Association, Division for Public Education, 541 North Fairbanks Court, Chicago, IL 60611-3314, Tel: 312-988-5735, Fax: 312-988-5032, E-mail: abapubed@attmail.com, WEB site: http://www.abanet.org. The ABA produces a lawyer referral services directory and a publications directory with

(continued)

THE THREE RS *(continued)*

---

some worthwhile books; and both are available on their Web site.

- Practicing Law Institute, 810 Seventh Avenue, New York, NY 10019, Tel: 212-765-5700, Fax: 800-321-0093.

REFERENCES

- *Finding the Right Lawyer**** This is an excellent and easy-to-read book. I haven't seen it in bookstores, but it can be ordered directly from the American Bar Association.
- *Growing Your Own Business* This is an okay overview of business management.
- *Martindale-Hubbell Legal Directory* It can be found in most public libraries and is also available on-line for a fee through Lexis-Nexis.
- *The Small Business Legal Advisor.**
- *Taking Care of Your Corporation, Volume 1* If you have decided to set up a board of directors, this will be a handy reference. It also includes a diskette with many of the forms necessary for proper management of your board of directors.
- *Taming the Lawyers**** It contains good solid information on selecting and hiring lawyers.

PATENT ATTORNEYS (INTELLECTUAL PROPERTY LAW)

If your business is based on or engaged in the production of a product, service, software, or technology that you believe to be new and innovative (e.g., you design a better mousetrap or a more effective shoe tree, develop the latest net navigator, or solved the problem of an artificial heart), then you will want to establish a relationship with a patent attorney. Trademarks and copyrights are also the bailiwick of patent attorneys. Registering a trademark is normally a fairly straightforward proposition and can be handled without patent counsel. Trademark litigation is also pretty straightforward, but I wouldn't recommend trying to litigate without counsel. Patent matters are more complex, dealing with issues of prior art, patent searches, and the rather vague definition of "new, useful, and nonobvious."

The *function* of a patent attorney includes these tasks:

- Perform patent and trademark searches.
- Prepare and file patent applications, as well as trademark and copyright registrations.
- Advise of possible infringement on your part.
- Provide appropriate language and agreements for licensing your products and/or processes.
- Review language and advise you on licenses and technology transfers offered to you.
- Participate in negotiations and litigation over patent and trademark infringement.
- Advise during the development of potentially patentable products and processes.

This specialty is a sort of fraternity with its own handshake and initiation rite. Many patent attorneys have an undergraduate degree in engineering, a law degree, and then several years of service as a patent examiner in the Patent Office in Washington, DC. Patent firms tend to be relatively small, although there are a few large organizations. Even in the small firms, however, partners tend to specialize. The division of labor will often fall along lines of their undergraduate degrees; the electrical engineer handling computer-related patents, the chemical engineer dealing with compounds, and so on. An adequate patent attorney for filing applications, and negotiating licenses, may not necessarily be someone you want to represent you in patent infringement litigation. However, since a patent is a *license to litigate,* one should consider this factor even when seeking a patent attorney for filing applications.

Patent attorneys generally have fixed rates for patent searches, patent application filings, and trademark registrations. It is relatively easy to control costs when dealing with these professionals. Patent attorneys are always busy. The worse the economy is, the busier they are. One attorney told me that the Great Depression was one of the busiest times in history for patent attorneys, and during each recession their volume of business increases.

Some large general firms have patent departments. In such cases, treat the patent department as if it were an independent office and evaluate it apart from the general firm's evaluation.

When trying to decide which patent firm to use, keep in mind that the average patent attorney deals with hundreds of inventors and hundreds of patents every year. Also, you aren't hiring a patent

Exhibit 2–2   Interview Questions for Patent Attorneys

1. How many patent applications have you prepared? _____

2. Please share with me some examples of patent applications you filed that were rejected by the Patent and Trademark Office (PTO). _____

3. How many patents have you worked on that were challenged either by competition or by existing patents? What were the outcomes? _____

4. Please describe several patents on which you worked that are similar to my invention. _____

5. How much litigation experience have you? _____

6. Please describe your most recent success in either litigation or negotiation. _____

7. What information will you require from me in order to prepare my application/case? _____

8. What is a reasonable time line for this application/case? _____

9. Have you tried any cases before the International Trade Commission (ITC), Patent Appeals Court? Please describe. _____

10. What is your experience in dealing with foreign patent matters?

Exhibit 2–2 *(continued)*

---

11. May I review some patents, in similar areas, that you have filed? _____

_____

12. May I have the names of several inventors with whom you haveworked?

_____

_____

13. Do you have a schedule of fees; if not, what will your services cost? _____

_____

14. What can I do to assist you in controlling costs? _____

_____

---

attorney because of his or her creativity. Patent attorneys often do not understand the value of the invention for which they are preparing a patent. Their role is to "translate," or describe, your invention so that the patent office, and particularly the patent examiner, will agree that your idea is "inventive" enough to justify being issued a patent. Patentability does not mean marketability. Too often, would-be inventors assume that they have a great product because the patent attorney counseled they could obtain a patent. Thousands of patents are granted each year that never get marketed.

You should be certain that the patent attorney you are considering has experience in filing applications for products or processes in the same industry group. You should also learn about the firm's successes in negotiating and/or litigating on behalf of patents they have prepared (see Exhibit 2–2).

I have examined several how-to books offering advice and direction on filing patent applications without the assistance of an attorney. I dislike paying attorneys as much as you. I have been an active participant in obtaining patents for many low-tech consumer products. Yet I would never attempt filing an application without the assistance of a trained experienced patent attorney. Exhibits 2–3, a sample utility patent and 2–4, a sample design patent, show how complex these applications are: It would be difficult if not impossible to complete these forms without the assistance of an experienced patent

Exhibit 2–3　Utility Patent (First Page)

United States Patent [19]
Bisk et al.

[11] E

Patent Number:　**Re. 32,269**

[45] **Reissued**　Date of Patent:　**Oct. 28, 1986**

[54] **PLASTIC CLIP**

[75] Inventors: **Leonard Bisk,** Elkins Park; **Gunther Rogahn,** Lansdale, both of Pa.

[73] Assignee: **Independent Products Company, Inc.,** West Point, Pa.

[21] Appl. No.: **587,343**

[22] Filed: **Mar. 8, 1984**

Related U.S. Patent Documents

Reissue of:
[64] Patent No.: **4,335,838**
Issued: **Jun. 22, 1982**
Appl. No.: **137,930**
Filed: **Apr. 7, 1980**

[51] Int. Cl.⁴ **A47J 51/095; A47J 51/14; D06F 55/02**
[52] U.S. Cl. **223/91;** 24/501; 24/511; 24/562; 24/564; 223/93; 223/96
[58] Field of Search .... 24/137 A, 346, 489, 24/499, 501, 507, 508, 511, 530, 536, 562, 564; 223/91, 93, 96, DIG. 4; 211/115; 248/341; D6/253, 254

[56]　　　　**References Cited**

U.S. PATENT DOCUMENTS

1,151,556	8/1915	Barney	24/564 X
1,684,721	9/1928	Wood	24/501
2,496,109	1/1950	Terry	24/530
2,583,784	1/1952	Maccaferri	223/91
2,666,240	1/1954	Maccaferri	24/501
2,723,786	11/1955	Martin	223/91
3,227,334	1/1966	Samuelsson	
3,239,902	3/1966	Cohen	223/91 X
3,456,262	7/1969	Coon	24/501
3,963,154	6/1976	Schwartz et al.	
4,009,807	3/1977	Coon	223/96
4,074,838	2/1978	Blasnik et al.	

FOREIGN PATENT DOCUMENTS

1159796	2/1958	France	24/511
1210426	9/1959	France	223/96
348684	8/1937	Italy	24/564
7306492	11/1974	Netherlands	24/562
243567	1/1947	Switzerland	223/91
278907	2/1952	Switzerland	24/508
352309	4/1961	Switzerland	24/501
302326	1/1928	United Kingdom .	
477118	12/1937	United Kingdom .	
576423	4/1946	United Kingdom .	
593125	10/1947	United Kingdom .	
624783	6/1949	United Kingdom .	
697866	9/1953	United Kingdom .	
714990	9/1954	United Kingdom .	
715188	9/1954	United Kingdom	223/91
731906	6/1955	United Kingdom .	
916481	1/1963	United Kingdom .	
925386	5/1963	United Kingdom .	
1360965	7/1974	United Kingdom .	

Primary Examiner—Robert R. Mackey
Attorney, Agent, or Firm—Caesar, Rivise, Bernstein & Cohen

[57]　　　　**ABSTRACT**

A molded plastic hanger and a clip for use therewith or with other members. The hanger includes a body portion having a diverging pair of arms including slots therein and a crossbar for mounting garment holding clips. A plastic swivel hook is connected to the body portion at a stem. The stem includes a shaft having an annular locking recess in its periphery which is adapted to be received within a mating socket of the hook to connect the hook and body portion to each other while enabling them to be swiveled readily with respect to each other. The clip is arranged for securement to the crossbar of the hanger or to any other rod-like element and is formed of a three piece construction comprising a pair of plastic jaws and a resilient U-shaped member, also formed of plastic, but having a higher tensile strength and resiliency than the plastic of the jaws.

8 Claims, 5 Drawing Figures

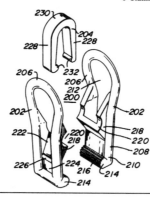

Note: Full patent form appears in Appendix III.

Exhibit 2–4   Sample Design Patent

United States Patent [19]

Bisk et al.

[11]   **Des. 265,156**

[45]   ** **Jun. 29, 1982**

[54] **HANGER**

[75] Inventors: Leonard Bisk, Elkins Park; Gunther Rogahn, Lansdale, both of Pa.

[73] Assignee: Independent Products Company, Inc., Lansdale, Pa.

[**] Term: 14 Years

[21] Appl. No.: 148,896

[22] Filed: May 12, 1980

[51] Int. Cl. .... D6—08

[52] U.S. Cl. D6/253; D6/254; D6/256

[58] Field of Search D6/113, 247–257; 211/113, 118, 119; 223/85, 87, 88, 91–96; D32/61, 65; D8/394, 395

[56] **References Cited**

U.S PATENT DOCUMENTS

D. 251,345	3/1979	Bigelow et al.	D6/257
1,358,560	11/1920	Kennison	24/252 R
1,750,905	3/1930	Schipp	223/91
2,569,371	9/1951	Cohen	24/137 A
2,782,482	2/1957	Baril et al.	24/252 R
2,877,939	3/1959	Dolnick	D6/254
3,456,262	7/1969	Coon	24/137 A
3,710,993	1/1973	Collin	223/91
3,950,829	4/1976	Cohen	223/91

FOREIGN PATENT DOCUMENTS

724710	5/1932	France	D6/256

Primary Examiner—B. J. Bullock
Attorney, Agent, or Firm—Caesar, Rivise, Bernstein & Cohen, Ltd.

[57]   **CLAIM**

The ornamental design for a hanger, substantially as shown and described.

DESCRIPTION

FIG. 1 is a front elevational view of the hanger showing our new design;
FIG 2 is a top plan view thereof;
FIG. 3 is a bottom plan view thereof;
FIG. 4 is a side elevational view thereof taken from the right side as seen in FIG. 1;
FIG. 5 is a side elevational view thereof taken from the left side as seen in FIG. 1.

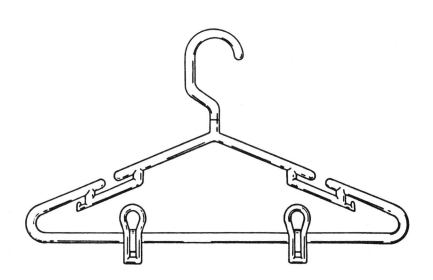

attorney. Exhibit 2–3 is the first page of a seven-page utility patent I was granted on a simple plastic clip (the balance of the patent is in Appendix III). The patent is full of detailed descriptions and illustrations using a very specific language and style of writing. Even if you want to attempt to write the patent application yourself, you ought to have a patent attorney review, coach, and audit your work.

Exhibit 2–4 illustrates a design patent I was granted and again shows how a simple consumer product becomes complicated when viewed in the context of a patent.

If you are on a very tight budget, you can suggest to your patent attorney that you will do some of the work yourself. Your patent attorney will likely utilize the services of a patent searcher in Washington to do the search.[6] If your counsel has the search done, he or she will likely tack on a 15 to 25 percent markup. Since patent attorneys don't get rich from patent searches, your attorney may be willing to accept a search performed by an independent searcher or you. However, you should factor into the process that you will have to locate a qualified searcher who will be acceptable to your counsel.

Most of the Patent Office's files have been computerized, making searches much easier although some search categories have not yet been completely loaded into the government's database.

Some business lawyers may tell you they can handle work relating to your intellectual property rights. Accepting their offer is a foolhardy risk. The world is full of poorly written patents that will not hold up under scrutiny: *A well-written patent is a valuable asset.* As I mentioned earlier, a patent is a license to litigate, a subject that will be explored later in this chapter.

THE THREE RS: PATENT ATTORNEYS

RECAP

- Look for an attorney with appropriate experience—your patent counsel should have some experience with the product or process category in which your invention falls.

- A well-written patent is a valuable asset—check out some of the attorney's work and ask for references where the patent was successfully defended.

- A patent is a license to litigate—it is easier to defend a well-written patent than a poorly written one.

THE THREE Rs *(continued)*

RESOURCES

- Office of Enrollment and Discipline, Patent and Trademark Office, Department of Commerce, Washington, DC 20231.
- National Council of Intellectual Property Law Associations, PO Box 2974, Greensboro, NC 27402. (an association of associations; see if there is a local or state association of patent attorneys in your area).

REFERENCES

- *Eureka! The Entrepreneurial Inventor's Guide* This is a good general reference with good forms and examples.
- *Patents, Copyrights and Trademarks***** This is an excellent primer on the whole process.
- *Martindale-Hubbell Legal Directory* It can be found in most public libraries and is also available on-line for a fee through Lexis-Nexis.

INTERNATIONAL PATENT ATTORNEYS

A patent, trademark, or copyright issued in the United States will afford you protection of your idea only in this country. If your product, service, or idea has the potential to satisfy the needs of or appeal to markets such as Europe, Asia, or South America, you will want to consider obtaining protection in each country where it may be sold or even produced. I have applied for and been granted more than a dozen foreign patents for improvements on plastic clothes hangers and plastic clips. I have obtained those patents two ways: having my U.S. attorney handle the work, and dealing directly with patent attorneys abroad. Most U.S. patent law firms do not handle the foreign applications themselves. They work with associates and generally mark up the services of the associates by 20 or 25 percent. There are several *advantages* to this approach:

- Since you may not know whom to contact abroad and may not be in a position to evaluate their capabilities, it may be more convenient to have the local counsel handle matters.

- Local counsel undertakes some ethical, legal, and moral obligation if counsel acts as intermediary.
- All your intellectual property issues have one address.

On the other hand, you will pay more, and it is a lot like "whispering down the lane." You work with your local attorney, he or she writes to the offshore attorney, he or she writes back. Local counsel sends you a cover letter to overseas counsel's letter and the process produces more paper and longer lead times.

War Story. In Felix Zandman's book *Never the Last Journey,* he shares with us a highly instructive story dealing with international patent infringement and violation of license agreements. (From the book's dust jacket: "Felix Zandman is known on Wall Street as the brilliant scientist–entrepreneur whose billion-dollar Fortune 500 company, Vishay Intertechnology, reshaped the electronic component industry.") The incident deals with a French licensee of Felix's Vishay Intertechnology that first violates its contractual obligation, which precipitates litigation in France. Then Vishay learns that the French firm copied a patented resistor. To make matters worse, the copying was accomplished with the help of a former employee who left Vishay after signing a nondisclosure agreement. Felix writes, "Monsieur André Netter was our patent attorney in France—the same man who many years before had helped me take out the patent on Photostress without charging a fee. When I told Netter the story he said, 'It's very simple. You have a patent in France. I can go to the judge and get a court order. Then we'll take the police to Sfernice, collect the documents and samples, and prove the case.'

"That kind of straightforward approach wasn't possible under American law, but we were not in America. When our attorney went in and presented the court order to the Sfernice management, they stopped all work in the plant so that he and the photographer couldn't see the process in action. Meanwhile, Sfernice's Schirmer ran to a judge to get a cease-and-desist order. But by the time he got back, we had collected all the evidence we needed to show that not only was the product a copy, but also that the methods of fabrication were our methods. We now had a case against Sfernice not only for patent infringement but for theft of trade secrets.

"Once we had proof, a difference emerged among our attorneys as to how best to handle the case. One opinion was to attack Sfernice in U.S. Federal Court on grounds of patent infringement and theft. Another was to proceed against them in front of the International Trade Commission. The preponderance was to take the ITC route. A federal patent case might drag on for four or five years, but the ITC was obligated by law to render a decision within twelve months."

This story goes on with settlement negotiations with Sfernice who threatens to counter with an antitrust action. Vishay's principal attorney (not a litigator) counsels settlement, "another of our attorneys took the opposite view. 'Never,' he said. The law was clear, and our evidence couldn't be more conclusive. Now was our chance to nail the bastards to the wall and get them out of the United States altogether.

"I decided to nail them to the wall—a major mistake, as it turned out. Napoleon said many times that if you win a battle, keep a door open so the enemy can get out. If you close the door completely, you don't know how he might fight or what might happen. I should have listened.

"Instead I listened to the aggressive lawyer and my bruised ego." Vishay sued in the ITC and Sfernice brought an antitrust suit in federal court. Vishay's lead counsel "made a serious mistake early on. Given the merits of the case, he decided it was unnecessary to be present in the courtroom himself. Instead, two of his younger associates handled the actual trial work. And they did not do it well."[7]

This international patent war story is instructive, first, because it describes the option of filing an action in federal district court or with the International Trade Commission. This is something only a domestic patent attorney knowledgeable about litigation on international infringement would know. Second, the French attorney knew what he could do according to French law. This relates to any foreign litigation and the importance of having good local counsel. Finally, this is an example of how successful resolution can depend on proper preparation for trial and delivery in the courtroom.

An interesting phenomenon I have discovered is that all the foreign patent counsel with whom I have worked supply printed price lists for their services—whereas U.S. firms do not. I have included as Exhibits 2–5 and 2–6 the Schedule of Fees of attorneys I have worked with in Europe and Japan. They may be useful when you obtain a quote from a U.S. attorney for overseas patent work, or from another foreign counsel, and certainly for budgeting purposes. U.S. patent attorneys do not normally publish a schedule of fees. Each engagement will require obtaining a quotation.

After your first few attempts at obtaining foreign patents through your local counsel, you should consider dealing directly with overseas counsel. I started moving away from local counsel as intermediary by suggesting to local counsel that I would deal directly and pay overseas counsel myself but would copy local counsel on all correspondence and instruct overseas counsel to do the same. This way we kept local counsel in the information loop. Eventually, I dropped even that pretense when I realized that local counsel really didn't have much to offer when dealing with overseas work.

Exhibit 2–5   Foreign Counsel Schedule of Fees, United Kingdom

BRITISH PATENTS	GOV'T FEES £	OUR FEES £	TOTAL £
1. Preparation and filing of an application comprising full description, claims, abstract and filing request for search (includes one hour of professional work)	155	476	631
2. Preparation and filing of an informal application comprising description, claims and abstract (includes one hour of professional work)	25	238	263
3. Filing request for search	130	238	368
4. Filing of priority documents (if not filed with application)		60	60
5. Preparation of formal drawings		From 60	
6. Filing request for substantive examination	130	96	226
7. Dealing with official actions		From 96	
8. **RENEWAL FEES**			
5TH YEAR	110	42	152
6TH YEAR	120	42	162
7TH YEAR	130	42	172
8TH YEAR	140	42	182
9TH YEAR	150	42	192
10TH YEAR	170	42	212
11TH YEAR	190	42	232
12TH YEAR	210	42	252
13TH YEAR	230	42	272
14TH YEAR	260	42	302
15TH YEAR	280	42	322
16TH YEAR	310	42	352
17TH YEAR	340	42	382
18TH YEAR	370	42	412
19TH YEAR	410	42	452
20TH YEAR	450	42	492

NB The official fees for renewal are reduced by one half if the Patent is endorsed 'Licences of Right.

FINE FOR LATE PAYMENT - UP TO 6 MONTHS	24 PER MONTH	21	

EUROPEAN PATENTS

	GOV'T FEES £	OUR FEES £	TOTAL £
1. Preparation and filing of an application (includes one hour of professional work):-			
- filing (not including claims in excess of 10)	276	1020	1296
- payment of search fee	874	-	874
- payment of designation fee (per country)	161	-	from 161
2. Filing of priority documents (if not filed with application)	-	60	60
3. Filing request for exam and payment of the fee	1288	567	1855
4. Dealing with official actions	-	From 96	From 96

Note: Courtesy of Lawrence Shaw & Associates, used with permission.

Exhibit 2–5   *(continued)*

		GOV'T FEES £	OUR FEES £	TOTAL £
5.	Lodgement of claims translation and payment of grant and printing fees (up to 35 pages)	644	180	824
6.	**Activation of British national phase of a European patent:-**			
-	filing English translation of claims	35	60	95
-	becoming address for service only	-	55	55
-	filing English translation of claims and becoming address or service	35	86	121
-	filing English translation of text, entering onto our renewal register and becoming address for service	35	91	126
-	filing English translation of text without entering onto our renewal register and becoming address for service	35	120	155
7	**EUROPEAN APPLICATION MAINTENANCE FEES**			
	3RD YEAR	345	87	432
	4TH YEAR	368	87	455
	5TH YEAR	391	87	478
	6TH YEAR	644	87	731
	7TH YEAR	667	87	754
	8TH YEAR	690	87	777
	9TH YEAR	874	87	961
	10TH YEAR and each subsequent year	920	87	1007
	FINE FOR LATE PAYMENT - UP TO 6 MONTHS	10%	44	

PCT PATENT APPLICATIONS

		GOV'T FEES £	OUR FEES £	TOTAL £
1.	Preparation and filing of an application (including one hour of professional work):-			
	Filing	55	1020	1075
	Search Fee (European)	1104	-	1104
	Basic fee (up to 30 pages)	419	-	419
	Designation Fee (per country - up to 9 countries)	102	-	From 102
	Designation fee (10 or more countries)	1020	-	1020
2.	Filing of priority documents (if not filed with application)	-	60	60
3.	Preparation of formal drawings	-	From 60	From 60
4.	Filing request for preliminary exam. (demand under Chapter II)	1488	567	2055
5.	Dealing with written opinions	-	From 91	From 91

Exhibit 2-6   Foreign Counsel Schedule of Fees, Japan

A 1. PATENTS   (Including PCT National Stage Work)
(application filed on or after January 1, 1988)

	Attorney's Fee(yen)	Official Fee(yen)
APPLICATION PROCEDURES		
101. Application for patent (application filed on or after January 1, 1994)	165,000	21,000
102. Application for patent (application filed from January 1,1988 to December 31, 1993)	150,000	21,000
103. Application for registration of extension of patent term	165,000	74,000
104. Claiming Convention priority or internal priority		
A) Basic charge ; and	8,000	—
B) Charge per claiming Convention priority or internal priority	6,000	—
105. Preparation of abstract	4,200	—
106. Application for exception to loss of novelty of invention	47,000	—
107. Late filing of formal documents	12,000	—
108. Request for examination for patent application		
A) Basic charge ; and	13,000	84,300
B) Charge per claim	4,000	2,700
109. Bookkeeping for the request for examination per case per year	6,000	—
ELECTRONIC FILING PROCEDURES (excluding PCT National Stage Work)		
111. Electronic filing of application and any other document to be filed at JPO by on-line transmission or submission of flexible disc	8,500	—
112. Payment for the designated Information Processing Organization in case of paper filing for the electronic filing procedure		
A) Basic fee ; and	—	4,300
B) Fee for specification per page	—	800
EXAMINATION PROCEDURES		
121. Preference examination		
1) by applicant	160,000	—
2) by third party	270,000	--
122. Accelerated examination	150,000	—
123. Argument	85,000	—
124. Amendment	85,000	—
125. Additional charge for each claim exceeding the number of current claim(s) in case of amendment	4,000	2,700
126. Interview	65,000	—
127. Extension of period or change of date	10,000	2,000
128. Presentation of information to the Patent Office by third party	140,000	—
OPPOSITION PROCEDURES		
131. Opposition including a first claim	280,000	11,000
132. Answer to opposition including the first claim	200,000	—
133. Additional charge for each additional claim added to the first claim in case of opposition or answer to opposition	6,000	—
APPEAL AND TRIAL PROCEDURES		
141. Appeal against final rejection including a first claim and see Item 150	260,000	55,000
142. Appeal against final rejection combined with a complaint against decision of dismissal of amendment including a first claim and see Item 150 (applicable to the patent application filed on or after January 1, 1994)	280,000	55,000
143. Appeal against decision of dismissal of amendment including a first claim and see Item 150 (applicable to the patent application filed on or before December 31, 1993)	150,000	55,000
144. Accelerated appeal examination	95,000	—
145. Trial for invalidation including a first claim	360,000	55,000
146. Intervention in trial for invalidation	300,000	55,000

Note: Courtesy of Kohno & Co, used with permission.

Exhibit 2–6   *(continued)*

B 1 . UTILITY MODELS   (Including PCT National Stage Work)
(application filed on or after April 1, 1994)

APPLICATION PROCEDURES	Attorney's Fee(yen)	Official Fee(yen)
301. Application for registration of utility model		
A) Basic charge including a first claim	160,000	14,000
B) Additional charge for each claim added to the first claim	4,000	—
302. Claiming Convention priority or internal priority		
A) Basic charge ; and	8,000	—
B) Charge per claiming Convention priority or internal priority	6,000	—
303. Preparation of abstract	4,200	—
304. Application for exception to loss of novelty of invention	47,000	—
305. Late filing of formal documents	12,000	—
306. Conversion of application		
A) utility model application (filed on or before December 31, 1993)		
→utility model application filed under new Utility Model Law	140,000	0
B)patent application		
→utility model application filed under new Utility Model Law	140,000	14,000
C) design application		
→utility model application filed under new Utility Model Law	160,000	14,000

ELECTRONIC FILING PROCEDURES (excluding PCT National Stage Work)

	Attorney's Fee(yen)	Official Fee(yen)
311. Electronic filing of application and any other document to be filed at JPO by on-line transmission or submission of flexible disc	8,500	—
312. Payment for the designated Information Processing Organization in case of paper filing for the electronic filing procedure		
A) Basic fee ; and	—	4,300
B) Fee for specification per page	—	800

PROCEDURES AFTER FILING APPLICATION

	Attorney's Fee(yen)	Official Fee(yen)
321. Amendment	85,000	—
322. Request for search report for the utility model including a first claim	17,000	42,000
323. Additional charge for each claim contained in the request for search report	—	1,300
324. Request for correction of specification and/or drawing of the registered utility model	38,000	1,400
325. Presentation of information to the Patent Office by third party	140,000	—

APPEAL AND TRIAL PROCEDURES

	Attorney's Fee(yen)	Official Fee(yen)
331. Trial for invalidation including a first claim	360,000	55,000
332. Additional charge for each additional claim added to the first claim in the invalidation trial	6,000	5,500
333. Intervention in trial for invalidation	300,000	55,000
334. Request for correction during the course of procedure of the invalidation trial	120,000	55,000
335. Additional charge for each additional claim added to the first claim in case of request for correction	6,000	5,500
336. Re-trial including a first claim	300,000	55,000
337. Attendance of oral examination, examination of evidence, preparatory proceedings, hearing, etc.	140,000	—
338. Motion for preservation of evidence or taking of evidence	300,000	—
339. Demand for official opinion on technical scope	300,000	40,000
340. Demand for decision on establishment of non-exclusive license in case of non-working, etc. (Demand for an arbitration)	240,000	55,000
341. Administrative appeal	240,000	—
342. Refutation or reply to refutation in trial case	90,000	—

Finding Overseas Counsel

The question arises as to how to find an overseas counsel (general and litigation) if you don't wish to go through local counsel at the outset. If you are seeking patent protection in a given country, you can usually obtain a list of patent attorneys by contacting the consulate, embassy, and/or binational chamber of commerce. You will receive names without any qualification. If you can identify candidates through personal references, that is preferable. You can then contact the attorneys and request references and their Schedule of Fees (price list).

Time and financial limitations may preclude the in-depth research you ought to perform and prevent a face-to-face evaluation of the candidates. In fact, you may end up selecting and then working with foreign counsel for years before actually meeting. Nevertheless, the technique in evaluating the candidates is essentially the same. The references you request from foreign counsel should be U.S. inventors and businesses that have worked *directly* with counsel. If the work has been performed through a local patent attorney, it may be difficult to evaluate what added value the local counsel provided. It is not unusual for foreign counsel to fulfill a more or less clerical role, filing the patent as is, or arranging for a technical translation and then filing the application. Your research should reveal signs that foreign counsel has made a contribution to the process and not simply been a cog in the mechanism. There are jurisdictions such as Japan and Germany, where the local intellectual property rights laws have certain idiosyncrasies. In these situations, there may be more options and choices and you should expect to hear from foreign counsel regarding the options. Your discussions with references should delve into this issue.

Contact the U.S. Department of State, specifically the Office of Emergency Services, Office of Citizens Consular Affairs, or the Country Desk.[8] If you contact the U.S. embassy or consulate in the target country, it may have a list that will very likely be free of attorneys about whom the American government has received complaints.

Obtaining samples of foreign counsel's work, especially if it has been translated into a language you do not read, will be of marginal value at best. Also, the foreign applications will be based largely on your domestic application. So here again, your discussions with references ought to take a different tack and you should be exploring foreign counsel's contributions.

Language skill is a major element to consider when evaluating candidates. Unless you or a member of your staff speaks the language of the foreign country fluently, you will have to rely on foreign counsel's command of English to provide good communication. Foreign counsel's staff's language skills should also be confirmed. You don't want to discover you have hired a very successful and busy sole practitioner in Japan, only to find every time you call you reach a secretary who doesn't speak English.

> *War Story.* For many years I utilized the services of a Japanese patent attorney referred by my U.S. patent attorney. When I began developing the Japanese market and products that could be patented in Japan, I began to work directly with him and met with him several times during visits to Japan. I ultimately developed a very nice personal friendship with my Japanese patent counsel and found him to be invaluable in some very delicate negotiations I had with a Japanese firm that had infringed our patents. Through those negotiations we signed a license agreement with the Japanese infringer. I later became good friends with the Managing Director of the Japanese firm and have worked with the company for many years.

THE THREE RS: INTERNATIONAL PATENT ATTORNEYS

RECAP

- Obtain references that are U.S. based—clarify whether or not the client had an offshore subsidiary manage the relationship.
- Determine added value provided by candidate—be sure the U.S. counsel did not perform the bulk of the work and foreign counsel merely appeared as local counsel.
- Confirm candidate's language skills—not only candidate's but his or her office staff.

RESOURCES

- Your domestic patent counsel.
- Consulates and embassies—commercial attaches.
- Binational chambers of commerce.
- U.S. embassy or consulate in target country.
- Eurolink for Lawyers, Tel: 44-113-242-2845, leads England based network of small to medium-sized law firms worldwide.
- Globalex, Tel: 414-271-2400, four major law firms with offices on three continents.

(continued)

THE THREE Rs *(continued)*

REFERENCES

- *Finding the Right Attorney***** You will discover good insights about finding foreign counsel.
- *Martindale-Hubbell Law Directory* It can be found in most public libraries and is also available on-line for a fee through Lexis-Nexis.
- *The Practical Guide to Patents Trademarks Copyright Designs* This may be difficult to obtain but offers insights about European patent law.

LITIGATION ATTORNEYS

It is my sincere hope that you will never require the services of a litigator. If you do, it means that either you wish to sue someone or that you are being sued. Litigation is a frustrating, time-consuming, and expensive proposition. Rarely do the participants find that the ends have justified the means. If you are being sued, you really have no choice but to consult with a litigator unless you simply allow the case to proceed unopposed. Even if you are willing to admit wrongdoing and compensate the other party, you will probably require the services of a litigator to avoid having to pay excessive damages. On the other hand, if you are contemplating filing suit against someone, I advise you to examine carefully all the costs associated with litigation—your time, your anxiety and frustration, and your out-of-pocket costs as well as the attorney's fees. You can add to that the risk of losing, no matter how good your case is and the related risk of paying damages. In retrospect, I have to wonder why I ever pursued some of the litigation I have been a party to over the years.

The *function* of a litigator includes these tasks:

- Prepare, file, and litigate all cases whether you are plaintiff or defendant.
- Negotiate settlements before, during, and after litigation.

From my experience you do not want your litigator to be a nice guy. You want someone who has a large ego, is very competitive, and does not like to lose. Find a person you would not want to play tennis opposite (this may detract somewhat from the "rapport with client" noted in the general selection criteria). But you also want a lawyer who cares more about clients winning the war than about his or her battles with other competitive egomaniac lawyers.

The best reference for a litigator is someone who sat opposite him or her. I sought someone to represent me in a patent infringement case that required counsel in another jurisdiction. Someone spoke highly of a patent litigator who had represented the opposition in another suit. When I met with the prospective counsel, I too was impressed and my confidence was rewarded with a successful prosecution of the infringer (even though it took seven years). The product was a plastic women's suit hanger, known in the trade as "The Swiveler," we had developed and for which we had obtained utility and design patents and a trademark. The initial product prompted the development of a wide range of products that fueled significant growth of my company. It was an instant success in the marketplace and our competitors were anxious to develop competitive products.

If the anticipated litigation is likely to come to trial in the near future, you certainly want to be sure that your litigator has the necessary time and sufficient support staff. Depth in the litigation team is important—who else in the firm will be conversant on the case?

You should try to get the attorney to commit to high-side and low-side estimates of legal costs. Ask about the odds of success and what that success will mean in monetary terms. Litigators are like surgeons. Surgeons will almost always recommend cutting, even when there is an alternative. Some litigators will rarely recommend negotiated settlement, and when you are angry, you want to get even. However, litigation can end up being expensive, time consuming, and emotionally demanding. By the time the case comes to trial (assuming you win), you may find yourself with a Pyrrhic victory as I did in one case where my patent was upheld as valid but not infringed. A litigator who counsels the track of negotiation and settlement, and can draw the correct line in the sand as well, is someone to whom you should listen. You want a lawyer who loves to litigate and is confident of his or her trial skills but is more interested in doing a good job for you, including settling cases quickly and cheaply. If you have the time to invest, it would be worthwhile to arrange to observe a candidate representing a client at trial.

You can also discuss contingency fees with litigators or some blend of flat fee and contingency. There are two schools of thought about litigation on contingency, putting aside your capability to finance the litigation. One school holds that an attorney who has a vested interest in the outcome will fight harder. The other school argues that litigators

Exhibit 2–7   Interview Questions for Litigation Attorneys

1. Of the last 10 cases you handled, how many were settled out of court, in court? _____

_____

2. Of the negotiated settlements, for how many did you initiate the settlement discussion? _____

_____

3. How many cases do you have pending at present? _____

_____

4. Please describe the case you handled that most closely resembles my situation? _____

_____

5. What is the high-side/low-side estimate of costs for this matter? _____

_____

6. What do you feel are the odds for winning this case or resolving it favorably? _____

_____

7. Will you provide a written opinion outlining the strengths and weaknesses of the case? _____

_____

8. What is your estimate for length of time until the matter is resolved?

_____

_____

9. How much of my time or my staff's time will be required to successfully resolve this matter? _____

_____

Exhibit 2–7   *(continued)*

10. If we win what are the high-side/low-side estimates of the settlement/ decision? _____

    _____

11. If I compromise on a settlement, how much will it cost and how much will I receive? _____

    _____

12. Would you consider some form of contingency or combination of fee and contingency? _____

    _____

13. What can I do to keep expenses down? _____

    _____

prioritize their time toward the cases that cover overhead, and the contingency business may get shortchanged. If a litigator won't take a case on a contingency basis, it may be a weak case. At the very least I recommend obtaining a written opinion outlining the strengths and weaknesses of your case and projected costs, time, and outcome.

When *talking with references,* be sure to ask about:

- *Preparation.* How well did counsel prepare the client for the case, how well was counsel prepared?
- *Budget.* How close to the projected costs did case end up costing?
- *Surprises.* Did things happen that counsel had not prepared reference for?
- *Negotiation.* How effective was counsel during negotiation stage?
- *Overall.* Would reference use counsel again?

Litigation can be prosecuted at the local, county, state, or federal level. Often the litigation capabilities of an attorney may be less important in certain jurisdictions than their friendships, affiliations, and associations. Keep this in mind when evaluating candidates. Exhibit 2–7 provides a list of questions you should ask litigators before retaining one.

THE THREE RS: LITIGATION ATTORNEYS

RECAP

- A good litigator is not necessarily a nice guy—you can be certain the other side's attorney won't be a nice guy either.
- Confirm time—make sure that the attorney and/or firm has time available to prepare and prosecute your case; you don't want to be faced with a filing deadline while your attorney is stuck in court on another matter.
- Obtain a high-side and a low-side estimate—counsel will probably insert caveats, such as subject to appeals; however, you should know your likely financial exposure in advance and not six months into the case.
- Get it in writing—ask for a written evaluation of your case and possibility of success.
- Discuss fees—ask about the possibility of contingency fee or a combination of fee for service and performance-based compensation.
- Observe the candidate on trial—this way you can observe courtroom demeanor and degree of preparation.

RESOURCES

- Association of Trial Lawyers of America, 1050 31st Street NW, Washington, DC 20007, Tel: 202-965-3500, Fax: 202-625-7312 (there may be a local or state trial lawyers association).

REFERENCES

- *Martindale-Hubbell Legal Directory* It can be found in most public libraries and is also available on-line for a fee through Lexis-Nexis.
- *Saving Your Business***** Read Chapter 2; in some ways a bankruptcy proceeding is not unlike litigation due to the adversarial nature of the process.
- *Taming the Lawyers***** It has an excellent chapter on managing a litigation attorney.

OTHER SPECIALTIES

There are specialty areas of the law where we do not require representation on a regular basis. These areas include real estate, estate planning, mergers and acquisitions, labor law, bankruptcy, and taxation. When we do need a specialist, there is often an urgency, therefore even thoughtful and prudent businesspeople will often take the first firm recommended by general counsel. It may be reasonable to trust the judgment of your general counsel in these matters, but it would not hurt to do some comparison shopping. Time constraints may not permit a careful review, but you can do a quick survey.

REAL ESTATE LAWYERS

The leasing of a small office or even a basic commercial or industrial location may not require the services of a lawyer specializing in real estate law. However, there are many factors to consider (see Exhibit 2–8). Most reputable leasing agents will supply a fairly standard lease agreement. While you may be able to negotiate some minor clauses out of a standard lease, a start-up or early stage business leasing a limited amount of space would not have much leverage to negotiate out potentially problematic clauses—you should engage a real estate lawyer when you are selling or purchasing real estate or signing a lease for a significant amount of space. You may also call a real estate lawyer if you have problems with a landlord. Finally, if your business is real estate intensive then your general counsel may also be a real estate lawyer.

The *function* of a real estate lawyer includes these tasks:

- Assist in negotiating the best price and advising about issues to be considered.
- Prepare and/or review all documents relating to the transaction.
- Advise and recommend courses of action, alternatives, and pros and cons of each condition of an agreement.
- Oversee all necessary documentation for closing and for conformity to law and to your needs.
- Represent clients in developing property, rezoning, and similar matter.

An excellent source for a recommendation of a real estate attorney is a real estate agent or a banker as these people deal with real estate attorneys on a daily basis. Some readers may take exception to that

Exhibit 2–8   Industrial Building Lease Checklist[9]

_____ 1. Parties to agreement identified.

_____ 2. Premises described.

_____ 3. Commencement and termination dates noted.

_____ 4. Description of improvements provided by landlord prior to occupancy and definition of satisfactory completion.

_____ 5. Use defined with compliance to local zoning code.

_____ 6. Rental terms described with provisions for increases.

_____ 7. Clarification of responsibility for all taxes—federal, state, county, local. Provision for tax deposits, appeals.

_____ 8. Clarification of responsibility for insurance, limits, waivers, subrogations.

_____ 9. Responsibility for repair or rebuilding in the event of damage.

_____ 10. Conditions for termination in the event of condemnation.

_____ 11. Maintenance of exterior of premises assigned, responsibility for mechanical equipment, responsibility for doing alterations required by government agencies.

_____ 12. Conditions under which tenant can make alterations or additions. Ownership of additions, landlord liability.

_____ 13. Right of tenant to assign or sublease with or without landlord's permission.

_____ 14. Conditions, if any, for tenant-created encumbrances or liens.

_____ 15. Assignment of responsibility for payment of utilities.

_____ 16. Indemnification of tenant by landlord or landlord by tenant.

_____ 17. Landlord's right to inspect and show premises.

_____ 18. Tenant's right to "quiet enjoyment."

_____ 19. Provisions for tenant's possession in the event of foreclosure and subordination or superiority of lease to mortgage.

_____ 20. Define condition of premise at end of lease, right to remove fixtures, repair of damages.

_____ 21. Landlord's remedies in event of default.

_____ 22. Tenant's obligation to provide financial information.

_____ 23. Recording of lease.

_____ 24. Payment of brokerage commissions, entitlement to commissions, landlord protection from other claimants.

_____ 25. Dispute resolution and payment of other side's legal fees.

_____ 26. Extent of signage permitted.

_____ 27. Option to extend, terms and conditions.

_____ 28. Option to purchase, terms and conditions.

_____ 29. Right of first refusal to purchase.

_____ 30. Security deposit, terms and conditions.

advice, observing that a recommendation from an agent opens you to cronyism and kickbacks. Therefore, keep in mind that obtaining a recommendation from an agent is *not a substitute for performing your own due diligence* (see Exhibit 2–9). To date, I have had only positive experiences with referrals provided by real estate agents.

Real estate attorneys should be able to give you a fairly firm price for their services. If you are contemplating a real estate transaction in one county, township, or definable jurisdiction, be certain that your

Exhibit 2–9   Interview Questions for Real Estate Attorneys

1. May I see a copy of a sample closing checklist you have used for a similar transaction? _____

2. How many transactions have you completed in the geographic area in the past year? _____

3. How many transactions, similar to ours, have you completed in the past year? _____

4. What do you anticipate your charges will be for completing this transaction? _____

5. What can I do to keep costs down? _____

6. Have you worked with the counsel representing the other parties to this transaction? Bank? _____

7. What is the lead time I should anticipate to reach closing? _____

counsel is well connected in that area. Many zoning boards, planning agencies, and local politicians are chauvinistic and the stories of real estate deals going afoul because the wrong attorney was retained, are legend.

> *War Story.*   My wife and I acquired an industrial building that was to house my business. The plastic hanger mentioned in the previous chapter pushed us from our original 20,000 square foot building to lease another building across the street with an additional 25,000 square feet. After a few years we were out of space there as well. Finally, I found an 85,000 square foot building I thought would contain us and our growth for a while. I was sitting at the closing in Philadelphia and my wife was summering in Israel. The attorney for the lead bank discovered that the notarization on the power of attorney my wife had signed was incorrectly executed and would not authorize the closing to proceed. We had to fax a set of powers of attorney to my wife. She had to go to the U.S. Embassy to get the power notarized and arrange for a courier to bring them to New York. The real estate agent went to New York to the airport to retrieve the powers. We lost several days and several thousand dollars because my attorney had not reviewed every document for its accuracy. I also have to accept responsibility for this screwup. I should have reviewed every document myself and managed the relationship and the transaction in a more proactive way.

THE THREE RS: REAL ESTATE ATTORNEYS

RECAP

- Talk to bankers and real estate agents—they can supply names of candidates.
- Be sure the attorney has had experience in the specific type of real estate transaction you contemplate—an attorney who has only performed residential closings may not be effective in a complicated commercial transaction.
- Confirm that the attorney has closed transactions in the jurisdiction—being well connected is often more important than legal competency in matters of zoning and licensing.

THE THREE RS *(continued)*

RESOURCES

- American College of Real Estate Lawyers, 733 15th Street NW, Washington, DC 20005-5710, Tel: 202-393-1344, Fax: 202-783-3780.
- American Industrial Real Estate Association, 345 South Figueroa, Suite M-1, Los Angeles, CA 90071, Tel: 213-687-8777, Fax: 213-687-8616.

REFERENCES

- *How to Hire a Home Improvement Contractor Without Getting Chiseled* This is a consumer guide to working with contractors. It offers some useful ideas regarding potential legal issues.
- *Martindale-Hubbell Legal Directory* It can be found in most public libraries and is also available on-line for a fee through Lexis-Nexis.
- *Real Estate Fundamentals* Primarily a textbook or reference for real estate professionals, it nevertheless touches on many legal issues relating to acquisition and sale of real estate.

ESTATE PLANNING LAWYERS

This is a specialty not necessarily associated with business law. However, many entrepreneurs' estates consist primarily of their businesses. Many businesses are family owned, and as such there may be issues of succession. Most start-up businesses are one- or two-person operations, and when seeking outside financing, these businesses must provide evidence of a contingency or succession plan. Banks and venture capitalists may want more than just key man insurance. A good thoughtful lawyer may be able to recommend methods to reduce or even avoid probate fees and the costs of estate administration.

The *function* of an estate planning lawyer includes these tasks:

- Advise that your estate provides adequately for your children and spouse, handle probate matters, reduce probate fees and estate administration fees.

- Prepare your will, estate plans, trusts, and so on.
- Assist you in developing a succession plan for your business.
- Prepare prenuptial agreements.

A good estate planning attorney should have a strong knowledge of the tax laws and various vehicles for preserving an estate, and should be a top-notch mediator. The mediator role is especially important where an estate may have to be divided. Your accountant may be one of the best sources for referrals, especially since he or she will most likely have to work with the estate planning attorney. Also, a friend who has survived a difficult estate settlement may be able to direct you to a good attorney. The very nature of estate planning may be a barrier to obtaining solid references. Estate settlements tend to be private and just as you would want your counsel to preserve and maintain your privacy, he or she may be reluctant to provide references, as that may invade someone else's privacy. However, you can ask for references of other attorneys and accountants who can vouch for performance without revealing clients' identities. References provided should include people who have been involved in the disposition of an estate and not just people for whom the attorney has prepared estate plans. This is an important distinction; mistakes may only reveal themselves *after* a person has died and the estate faces all the problems of probate, taxes, and division.

A significant element of estate planning relates to the laws of the state in which you reside. Your interview of candidates ought to include a discussion of recent changes in local laws, if any; what the attorney

---

THE THREE RS: ESTATE PLANNING LAWYERS

RECAP

- Get recommendations—talk to your accountant and general counsel.
- Ask candidates to discuss recent changes in tax laws—observe the response because someone not conversant in this issue may not be up to date.
- Try to determine the attorney's experience in succession issues—if succession is one of your concerns, you must consider candidates who have not only designed but implemented a succession plan.

THE THREE RS *(continued)*

- Request examples of mediations in which the attorney has participated—you want to confirm the candidate's capability in dispute resolution.

RESOURCES

- American College of Estate Planning Counsel, 3415 South Sepulveda Boulevard, Los Angeles, CA 90034, Tel: 310-398-1888, Fax: 310-572-7280.
- National Association of Estate Planning Councils, PO Box 801226, Dallas, TX 75380-1226, Tel: 214-788-1561, Fax: 214-788-1561.

REFERENCES

- *Guide to Wills and Estates* It will be more beneficial in learning the vernacular than in assisting in the selection of estate planning counsel.
- *Martindale-Hubbell Legal Directory* It can be found in most public libraries and is also available on-line for a fee through Lexis-Nexis.

---

has done to stay current; and what impact pending changes may have on your estate planning.

MERGERS AND ACQUISITIONS ATTORNEYS

How early in the life of a business you will require the services of a mergers and acquisitions (M&A) attorney will largely depend on your plans for your business. If you anticipate being a one-store retail operation or a professional corporation, you may never need the services of an M&A attorney. On the other hand, an early stage start-up of a high-tech business that will require large infusions of capital may require an M&A attorney at the outset. The reason this type of business ought to retain an attorney experienced in mergers and acquisitions is structuring the business early in its development avoids the need to make major changes later on when it can be very expensive, and it also projects a more professional image. The utilization of a M&A attorney will occur when you are beginning negotiations for either the sale of your business or the purchase of another business.

The *function* of an attorney specializing in mergers & acquisitions includes these tasks:

- Assist in negotiations of the merger or acquisition.
- Prepare and/or review all documents.
- Provide advice, act as a buffer, be sure that the client gets the best deal available.

Attorneys who deal in "M&A" probably have the highest profile after criminal litigators. However, there are many excellent M&A attorneys who are low profile and are competent to handle the sale of your business or your acquisition of another privately held business.

Sales of businesses usually involve a variety of legal specialties, I think it is safe to counsel that you want someone in a fairly large firm. Frequently, business sales include real estate, employment contracts, estate planning, intellectual property rights, and complex negotiations. A friend (an attorney) once observed, *"The best way to [screw]-up a deal is to get two attorneys involved."* There is a contradiction here: On the one hand you want a strong negotiator (specially if you are not), yet you do not want someone so strong that he or she will end up killing the deal. A large firm, with departments providing input on various aspects of a deal, would appear to be more manageable and cost-effective than three or four independent specialists.

In searching for the right M&A attorney for you, talk with friends and associates who have bought or sold businesses. If you are buying or selling a gas station, a small retail shop, or some other modest sized business a good general business lawyer will probably suffice. On the other hand, even small businesses where there are employees or estate issues involved can represent complicated enough transactions that you may want someone with a lot of experience. In this situation, obtaining references from candidates who have been involved in similar business sales is a sound approach. Although the problem mentioned earlier still applies (an attorney will not give you a bad reference), you should ask probing questions:

- In what areas was the attorney weak? An otherwise satisfactory attorney may not be able to handle certain aspects of the transaction. Even if you hire the individual, you should be aware of those weaknesses in advance.

- What were his or her strengths?
- How was the other side's attorney (if you get a positive response, try to get the attorney's name)? If the other side had an aggressive attorney and yet your candidate still extracted a satisfactory settlement for his or her client, this reflects effective representation.
- Would you use the attorney in another transaction? References sometimes speak in vague and oblique ways about candidates, for fear of creating a problem. A frank answer to this question reveals what the reference really thinks about a candidate.

THE THREE Rs: MERGERS AND ACQUISITIONS ATTORNEYS

RECAP

- Get recommendations—talk to people who have sold or bought other businesses.
- Seek out a strong negotiator—negotiation skills are more important than legal knowledge. There is no such thing as a fixed price, everything is open for negotiation.
- Legal knowledge is also important—you won't be well served if after a successful negotiation, the deal is so poorly written, you lose what was gained in the negotiation.

RESOURCES

- Your accountant.
- Your corporate counsel.
- Friends and associates.
- Local Bar association referral service.
- Local business press articles.

REFERENCES

- *Martindale-Hubbell Legal Directory* It can be found in most public libraries and is also available on-line for a fee through Lexis-Nexis.

BANKRUPTCY LAWYERS

I have included this section with the hope and maybe even a small prayer that you never have to retain a bankruptcy attorney. However, the mortality rate of small businesses within the first five years of their existence suggests that a not insignificant number of readers will have to consult with a bankruptcy attorney at some point during the business growth cycle. If your business is losing money on a consistent basis, if creditors are putting pressure on you to pay bills and you are unable to satisfy them, and if you seem unable to make the business a going concern, then you ought to consider talking with an attorney who specializes in bankruptcy.

There is another side to engaging a bankruptcy specialist and that relates to a major customer who owes you a significant sum of money and appears to be unable to pay.

The *function* of a bankruptcy lawyer includes these tasks:

- Preserve as much of your business and estate as possible.
- Prepare and file all pertinent documents.
- Insulate you from the creditors and their lawyers.
- Assist in collection of large accounts receivable, especially from bankrupt customers.

If patent law is a small fraternity, then I guess I would categorize bankruptcy attorneys as a tight gang. These are the legal advisers who feed on carrion and often they are the only participants in a bankruptcy who profit. Hateful as they might seem, you may one day need one to handle your bankruptcy or to try to retrieve some bad debt from a customer. In personal injury law, firms tend to specialize, some representing the insurance companies and defendants and other firms representing the injured party or plaintiff. In bankruptcy law, you will see attorneys handling the interests of a debtor in one case and a creditor in the next case on the court docket. If you can find someone who will offer a good word about a bankruptcy attorney, hire the person!

In researching for this section of the book, I discovered in my local library what I consider to be required reading for anyone contemplating taking a company through bankruptcy, *A Feast for Lawyers, Inside Chapter XI: An Expose,* by Sol Stein. Mr. Stein, sometimes a little too passionately for my taste, does an otherwise excellent job of describing the world of bankruptcy law. He personally went through the process and, for the most part, I found his descriptions on target.

The following provide a sampling of Stein's blunt wisdom:

Most lawyers in commercial or criminal practice know little or nothing about the subject of commercial insolvency, let alone the intricacies of operating under the bankruptcy laws.

If you wouldn't ask to marry somebody on a first date, why hire a bankruptcy lawyer under the same conditions?

Lie Number 6. You are the client. The lawyers are working for you. . . . [instead] You will find lawyers calling the shots. The lawyer representing the Creditor's Committee, instead of providing advice, will start making decisions. Attorneys are generally not good businessmen . . . lawyers are not businesspeople. Many bankruptcy lawyers think they can solve business problems. That's not true in a large number of instances.

Let this serve as a warning: The CEO must find out what types of businesses this prospective lawyer has represented. It is crucial for the CEO to obtain a list of the attorney's success stories, if any, and check them out.

Again and again I heard from CEOs of companies in distress that they had to hire somebody on the run because filing had become an emergency.

A debtor has to find a bankruptcy lawyer who is turned on by the excitement of helping a company pull out of the hole . . .[9]

Suzanne Caplan, author of *Saving Your Business,* Chairman and CEO of Pittsburgh Glove Manufacturing Company, and a survivor of a Chapter 11 bankruptcy and reorganization, offers another viewpoint:

The practice of bankruptcy law has been growing steadily during the past five years, and virtually all types of lawyers can be found in this specialty. Somewhere between the high-priced "too busy to take time" variety and the slightly sleazy bankruptcy-mill type is a growing cadre of bright, professional, and responsive lawyers joining the field.[10]

Exhibit 2–10 provides a list of questions to help you interview bankruptcy lawyers before you retain one.

Exhibit 2–10   Interview Questions for Bankruptcy Attorneys

1. What types of businesses have you represented and are currently representing? _____

   _____

2. Please provide me with a list of five success stories—clients who emerged from Chapter XI. _____

   _____

3. How many financial restructuring cases have you handled? _____

   _____

4. What do you anticipate this case will cost, your fees, creditor committee fees, and so on? _____

   _____

5. Please discuss possible conflicts of interest. _____

   _____

6. What experience do you have in business? _____

   _____

7. How many cases have you handled before this judge? _____

   _____

8. Based on the information you have, what sort of strategy do you anticipate? _____

   _____

THE THREE Rs: BANKRUPTCY LAWYERS

RECAP

- Try to obtain a recommendation—most people who have gone through bankruptcy do not have a fondness for attorneys; any recommendation is a good one.
- Talk to people who have gone through the process—there are hundreds of thousands of bankruptcies every year. Locate businesspeople who have survived the experience, not only for procedural advice, but also to find out what and who to avoid.
- Seek out a specialist, not a general business attorney. The bankruptcy Bar is very cliquish, don't be the guinea pig for someone who wants to get into bankruptcy practice.
- Observe candidates in court. You will learn a lot about their courtroom demeanor, caseload, and preparation.

RESOURCES

- American College of Bankruptcy, 510 C Street NE, Washington, DC 20002-5810, Tel: 202-546-6725.
- Local Bar referral service.
- Visit bankruptcy court.
- Businesspeople who have gone through a bankruptcy.

REFERENCES

- *A Feast for Lawyers** If you can locate a copy of this out-of-print book, it makes good reading with some valuable information.
- *Martindale-Hubbell Legal Directory* It can be found in most public libraries and is also available on-line for a fee through Lexis-Nexis.
- *Saving Your Business***** Anyone contemplating bankruptcy should read this book.
- *Taming the Lawyers***** You will find good basic information on attorneys and how to evaluate them.

TAX ATTORNEYS

In the section on bankruptcy, I expressed the wish that you never have to engage a bankruptcy specialist. In contrast, I open this section with the wish that *everyone* reading this book feels compelled at some point in his or her business career to retain an attorney specializing in taxation. I never minded paying income tax because it meant I was making money. At the same time, I would much rather pay as little tax as I can. Although the minimizing of tax consequences is primarily the responsibility of your accountant, a good tax attorney can contribute significantly to that effort. Tax attorneys must work very closely with your accountant, estate planning attorney, and your real estate attorney. Often estate planning attorneys perform the function of advising on tax issues, especially if the situations are not complex. The proper structuring of a real estate transaction or trusts for your spouse and children will often impact current and future tax liabilities.

The *function* of your tax attorney includes these tasks:

- Assist in minimizing federal, state, and local tax burden on business.
- Review potential transactions and advise on tax consequences.
- Work in tandem with accountant regarding tax matters.

Usually, a taxation attorney is called in to advise on a specific transaction (e.g., sale of a business, sale of commercial real estate, estate planning, IRS audit). Most large firms will have someone in-house. Smaller firms will generally have someone they use on a regular basis. Unless you are constantly engaging in a business that requires ongoing tax advice, you would not normally search out and establish a relationship with someone in this specialty.

Local, state, and federal tax laws are in a constant state of revision, amendment, and change. You should focus a portion of your questioning on the candidates' participation in seminars and workshops that update participants on the changes.

Given the choice between two otherwise apparently equally qualified tax attorneys, I would choose the one who is also a certified public accountant (CPA). Accountants, as a rule, are very analytical and conservative. An attorney who has arrived at this specialty without the accounting background may be less conservative.

If you are generally satisfied with your cooperate counsel and counsel does not have in-house capability, you may be reasonably safe with using the tax attorney recommended by your corporate counsel. If

THE THREE Rs: TAX ATTORNEYS

RECAP

- Tax counsel tend to be transaction specific—they are usually retained for a short-term engagement with a periodic review.
- Contact your corporate counsel—this may be an in-house service provided by corporate counsel or estate planning counsel.
- Tax counsel must be up to date—try to determine whether candidates regularly update their knowledge of ever-changing local, state, and federal tax laws. Can they explain how anticipated legislation may affect you?

RESOURCES

- Your corporate counsel.
- Your accountant.

REFERENCES

- *Martindale-Hubbell Legal Directory* It can be found in most public libraries and is also available on-line for a fee through Lexis-Nexis.

you have an estate planning counsel, you should explore with counsel his or her comfort level in advising you on tax avoidance.

LABOR LAW

Too many companies fit the cliché of "closing the barn door after the horses have escaped." Unless you are a one-person or two-person business, there are some good sound reasons to periodically review your personnel policies and procedures with a knowledgeable attorney. Much of the information on the legal aspects of personnel administration can be obtained from other sources. Whatever method you use to obtain the information, this is one area on which you need to focus.

The *function* of a labor lawyer includes these tasks:

- Provide preventive legal guidance in hiring, firing, and making personnel policies.
- Make sure you conform to Occupational Safety and Health Administration (OSHA) and Department of Labor regulations.
- Help you develop policies and procedures to minimize unemployment compensation claims.
- Help you deal with labor unions including unionization efforts and contract negotiations.
- Represent your firm in all labor-related administrative and legal hearings.

An article in the March 1993 issue of *INC,* reported a very important reason for working with a labor lawyer: "New laws have made employer-employee relationships more of a mine field than ever. Well thought out company policies can go far to prevent future litigation." It appears that the current climate for sexual harassment complaints is worse than for infractions of the OSHA standards at the agency's zenith.

Well-crafted personnel policies can save a company significant sums in state unemployment compensation tax. The rate your company pays is directly related to the amount of claims and the amount of money drawn down from your account at the bureau.

Well-defined personnel policies and procedures are a must in this era of affirmative action, OSHA, and local as well as federal regulations. Many trade groups offer off-the-shelf packages of human resource management materials to their members. This material may be too generic and you may need an attorney to customize it to your company's situation.

When evaluating candidates for handling your labor law matters, credentials and experience are essential. Be sure the candidate is up to date with the labor laws. Ask what the person has done over the past six months in the areas of cases, research, and so on. Talk to references about general advice and about counsel's handling of specific matters.

A good labor lawyer should have a variety of formats of all the documents and policies necessary for your business in his or her word-processing files and should charge only for necessary changes to meet your needs. In fact, he or she should be able to provide you with a fixed price for setting up your policies and procedures.

THE THREE Rs: LABOR LAW

RECAP

- Check out candidates specialty qualifications—ask about their efforts to remain current with the case law and pending legislation.
- If you are more than a two-person firm, you should obtain input on personnel issues—too many companies are being crippled by avoidable conflicts with employees because they haven't anticipated problems while in a growth mode.
- Review your personnel policies—well-crafted policies can save you money and maybe your business.

RESOURCES

- Corporate counsel.
- Your trade association or local business support group.
- Local business press.

REFERENCES

- *Martindale-Hubbell Legal Directory* It can be found in most public libraries and is also available on-line for a fee through Lexis-Nexis.

3

ACCOUNTANTS

An entrepreneur is likely to seek the services of an accountant before he or she retains the services of an attorney. While the plethora of accounting software, and tax preparation software may lead one to believe accountants will be an anachronism in the not-too-distant future, my own sense is that we will be dependent on these professionals for a long time to come. Based on that premise, as well as the need to be open and candid with your accountant, the selection of a qualified person or firm to handle your accounting requirements can be a daunting affair. This chapter discusses the steps in preparing yourself for the search, the development of the list, and the interview and evaluation process.

You may be asking yourself, "If I ought to hire an accountant before I hire an attorney—why isn't the chapter on accountants before the chapter on attorneys? And, if they are so important—why is this chapter so much shorter?" My own experience and my research suggests that working with attorneys gives entrepreneurs and managers more problems than working with accountants. Also, the accounting profession does not have the broad range of specialties as does the practice of law.

The *function* of your accountant includes these tasks:

- Help you set up your accounting system (e.g., cost controls, billing procedures, and payroll) and meet record-keeping and report filing requirements.

- Provide auditing services on an as-required basis (monthly, quarterly, semiannually, or annually).
- Prepare and submit all appropriate local, state, and federal tax returns, and help you pay the lowest possible taxes.
- Advise management (i.e., *you*) on issues of debt and equity financing, financial controls, financial record keeping, business insurance, cash management, and corporate structure, and on operating as a public company if appropriate.
- Periodically review financial controls, cash flow, costing procedures and other elements of financial management that may affect profitability.

"A good accountant is the most important outside adviser the small-business owner has."[1] One source suggests that it is easy to save in taxes what you pay your accountant. I submit to you that your accountant will cost you more than the $400 in their illustration and that a good accountant, whatever he or she charges, will save you far in excess of what you pay for the accountant's advice.[2] I have also seen how a bad or indifferent accountant can cost a company large penalties and substantial aggravation.

DECIDING ON AN ACCOUNTING FIRM

The choice between a small firm and a large one for a start-up business may in large part be determined by the plans for the business. A high-tech start-up seeking to raise funds from venture capitalists and later from the public ought to be looking at a large high-profile firm. For other situations, there are many small firms that can deliver high-quality work. There are not as many sole practitioners today as there were 20 years ago. Most probably serve the needs of their clients as well as the largest firms.

In more than 20 years as a business owner, I have had only three accountants. I hired the first accountant after a modest search effort to replace my parents' accountant. They had used him more because he was a friend than because he was competent. My new accountant eventually obtained a law degree and turned over his practice to someone else—thus my second accountant. When I was ready to replace this person, I shopped very carefully and remained with my choice for over 15 years. Before making my selection, I invested considerable time in obtaining recommendations from business associates and from my banker. I interviewed all candidates and obtained references.

The firm I selected was a small father-and-son partnership recommended by my banker. The father was the source of wisdom and good advice and the son handled our business on a day-to-day basis. They were always accessible, their fees were fair, and the quality of their work was excellent.

My biggest fear with sole practitioners is continuity and succession. If this person dies, what happens to my records? You can probably insulate yourself from this possibility by arranging to get copies of the accountant's worksheets each year or even each quarter. This is a good idea even with the largest firm.

> *War Story.*   When I changed accountants, I did not know it was customary for the outgoing accountant to withhold the client's files until he is paid in full. I didn't know the risks, costs, and issues of making a change. You should ask your new accountant to provide guidance for structuring a smooth transition. My old accountant had done a very bad job of maintaining worksheets from year to year, and before he could turn over the files, he had to virtually reconstruct them from memory. My new accountant could not file our returns until he had the historical data. The old accountant was facing professional embarrassment with his peer and tried to put us off for months. Finally, after threats and cajoling, he allowed the new accountant to come to his office to see what he had. It took a long time to get the problem resolved. I was as much at fault as the accountant because I had failed to manage the relationship effectively.

A private business owner's relationship with his or her accountant is an intimate one. This person knows how much you make, how much you save, how much you skim. He or she is in your personal affairs almost to the degree of your spouse and may know more about your finances than does your spouse. The accountant will prepare your business returns and your personal returns and can either cost you a lot of money or save you a lot of money. The results will depend on this consultant's knowledge of the tax avoidance opportunities permitted by law, the ever-changing tax laws, and the idiosyncrasies of your business.

Unless your financial records are a complete mess and need to be sorted out, the costs associated with public accounting should be straightforward. Your accountant can advise you of the appropriate costs of setting up books, doing the quarterly returns and reports, and performing the end-of-the-year audit and filing all necessary returns. Generally, IRS audits and specific financial advice are billed separately and by the hour. I did not hear even one war story about excessive accountant fees from the people I interviewed for this book. That is not to say it hasn't happened, wouldn't happen, or that you should not be concerned with the accountant's fees and charges.

A known and well respected accountant will give you a great deal of credibility with your bankers and even venture capitalists. Accountants can also be excellent sources for a wide range of financial advice, as long as you keep in mind being an accountant is not a guarantee the individual is a savvy businessperson. My accountant has introduced me to a wide range of other first-rate service providers, including bankers, lawyers, real estate agents, and stockbrokers.

GETTING RECOMMENDATIONS

I had a good working relationship with my banker. I asked him to recommend an accounting firm. If you have outside investors or advisers, they can also be good sources for candidates. Someone in your industry may also be an excellent source of recommendations. Generally, there are not as many conflict of interest issues as may exist with an attorney, so using the same accounting firm that a competitor uses may not be a problem. However, this is something that should be discussed with candidates.

Consider the accountant's standing in the local business community. If you are a member of local business and philanthropic and/or service organizations, these can be resources for names of candidates and resources to obtain opinions about candidates you have identified.[3]

The National Society of Professional Accountants (NSPA) offers a series of brochures that can assist you in your search. In one brochure, titled "Choosing Your Professional Accountant and Tax Practitioner," you are advised that because of ". . . the ever-changing complexities of the tax laws and developments in business methods and practices, the accountant must be alert to the value of continuing study in their field."

INTERVIEWING AND EVALUATING THE CANDIDATES

Many of the same issues apply to selecting an accountant as were mentioned earlier for selecting an attorney. To save you from flipping between chapters, here are some of the key characteristics:

- *Accessibility.* Be sure your accountant is not a 9-to-5 type of person and that he is willing to give you his home phone and car phone numbers.
- *Reasonable fees and costs.* Even with a friend this should be a frank and candid discussion.

- *Time and motivation to handle your account.* Who will be working on your account?
- *Experience and skill.* What experience has the firm had with similar businesses?

My accountant and close friend (the friendship evolved from the business relationship not the other way around), Howard Stredler—who happens to be a sole practitioner—suggests asking yourself several questions.

How Large Is Your Business?

What is your industry and who regulates it? What are your plans? If you are going to be faced with raising large sums of money at some stage in your business plan, you will probably be better served by selecting a firm with auditing capabilities who will be acceptable to the investment community.

Do You Need an Opinion Audit?

(This is necessary for a private placement memorandum—a device for the sale of equity in a company by offering the shares to a limited number of investors.) A small accounting firm may not be insured. If the firm does not regularly perform opinion audits (frequently required with loan documents) it does not require on-site peer review (Exhibit 3–1 is a sample Peer Review Letter and it outlines the conditions a firm must meet in order to satisfy the requirements of the profession).

There are three distinct levels of financial statement preparation or presentation which you can request from an accountant—*Opinion* (Opinion Audit or Audit), Review, or Compilation. All publicly held and traded companies and many privately owned companies have *Opinions* performed every year. The published annual statements of publicly traded firms always include a letter from the auditors with language such as: "We have audited the accompanying. . . . We conducted our audits in accordance with generally accepted auditing standards. . . . In our opinion . . . ." When an Opinion Audit is performed, the accountant will actually count inventory, send out letters to suppliers and customers for confirmation of balances, and perform a detailed analysis of the company's books.

A *Review* consists of taking the company's data and reviewing it and perhaps testing some of the numbers, such as going out into the warehouse and counting several items to see if they match the inventory

Exhibit 3–1   Sample Peer Review Letter

Firm in the Private Companies Practice Section*

[State CPA society letterhead for a "CART Review"; firm letterhead for a "Firm-on-Firm Review"; association letterhead for an "Association Review"]

August 31, 19XX

To the Owners Smith,
Jones & Co.

or

To John R. Smith, CPA

We have reviewed the system of quality control for the accounting and auditing practice of *[Name of Firm]* (the firm) in effect for the year ended June 30, 19XX. Our review was conducted in conformity with standards established by the Peer Review Board of the American Institute of Certified Public Accountants (AICPA). We tested compliance with the firm's quality control policies and procedures to the extent we considered appropriate. These tests included a review of selected accounting and auditing engagements.

In performing our review, we have given consideration to the quality control standards issued by the AICPA. Those standards indicate that a firm's system of quality control should be appropriately comprehensive and suitably designed in relation to the firm's size, organizational structure, operating policies, and the nature of its practice. They state that variance in individual performance can affect the degree of compliance with a firm's quality control system and, therefore, recognize that there may not be adherence to all policies and procedures in every case.

In our opinion, the system of quality control for the accounting and auditing practice of *[Name of Firm]* in effect for the year ended June 30, 19XX, met the objectives of quality control standards established by the AICPA and was being complied with during the year then ended to provide the firm with reasonable assurance of conforming with professional standards in the conduct of that practice.

[Name of Firm] is a member of the private companies practice section of the AICPA Division for CPA Firms (the section) and has agreed to comply with the membership requirements of the section. In connection with our review, we tested the firm's compliance with those requirements to the extent we considered appropriate. In our opinion, the firm was in conformity with the membership requirements of the section during the year ended June 30, 19XX, in all material respects.

John Brown, Team Captain
[or *Name of Reviewing Firm*]

* Pursuant to the membership requirements of the private companies practice section, a copy of this report, the letter of comments, if any, and the firm's response thereto will be placed in the public files of the AICPA Division for CPA Firms, along with the letter from the state CPA society accepting those documents. Copyright © 1996, American Institute of Certified Public Accountants, Inc. Used with permission.

numbers provided by the company. The American Institute of Certified Public Accountants (AICPA) defines Review as:

> Performing inquiry and analytical procedures that provide the accountant with a reasonable basis for expressing limited assurance that there are no material modifications that should be made to the statements in order for them to be in conformity with generally accepted accounting principles (GAAPs).

An accountant's cover letter to a Review will normally include the following kind of disclaimer: "A review is substantially less in scope that an audit, the objective of which is the expression of an opinion . . . , accordingly, no such opinion is expressed."

For a *Compilation* the accountant takes the information provided by the company and organizes it into a financial statement. Good bookkeeping software can provide you with an equivalent to a compilation. The AICPA defines Compilation as:

> Presenting in the form of financial statements information that is the representation of management (owners) without undertaking to express any assurance on the statements.

An accountant's cover letter to a Compilation will include language such as "We have not audited or reviewed the accompanying financial statements and, accordingly, do not express an opinion or any other form of assurance on them."

The sample letter in Exhibit 3–1 illustrates how the accounting profession monitors itself. Not every accountant or firm has clients requiring opinion audits. If the accounting firm does perform annual opinion audits then their in-house procedures are reviewed by their peers—other accountants—to be certain that they have the capability and integrity to provide an opinion that can be trusted.

The accounting profession, through the AICPA peer review, is the only profession discussed in this book that monitors itself. Peer review is also applied to firms performing Review audits, and there is discussion within the profession about making peer review a condition of recertification along with continuing education.

Understanding these differences relates to your review of your needs from your accountant not only in the present but also in the future. If your business will require going public or raising large amounts of capital from outside investors, you can be assured you will require an opinion audit. It doesn't make sense to hire an accountant today whom you will have to replace two or three years from now. Evaluating a candidate's peer review will confirm he or she is qualified to perform an opinion audit.

What Is Your Capability In-House?

If you have a bookkeeper you may only require a once a year visit, or at most quarterly visits. Even if you know how to do the books, you may be too busy to properly maintain them, so you may want your accountant to come in more frequently.

Here are some questions to ask prospective firms:

- Describe the type of practice. Do you have any specialties? You will see from the answer how much experience the accountant has with your type of business.
- What is the staff turnover in your office? A high staff turnover reflects poor management and will mean seeing many new faces each time you require service. A major concern with medium size and large size firms is seeing a different face every year for the on site work. And as a result, paying for the learning curve to bring the new faces up to speed each year.
- What would be the staffing you anticipate for my business? It is useful to understand how many people will be running around your office at any given time. It will end up costing you more as the team size increases. Exhibit 3–2 is a list of these and other questions to ask accountants before you retain them.

Here is a piece of advice I think has some merit: When hiring a new accountant, never permit him or her to bring you any proposals, business investments, or business opportunities. It clouds the accountant's judgment and affects his or her impartiality.

Unless you or someone in your business is sufficiently knowledgeable and has the time to monitor the way rising costs of material, labor, and other needs affect revenue growth and profitability, you can find your business in trouble. If you cannot justify that in-house capability, you ought to make sure that your outside auditor is not only able but willing to render that service. You should prearrange for the review to take place at least once a year. Accountants not only perform year end analysis and tax preparation, they can also periodically review financial controls, cash flow, and costing procedures.

According to Cliff Robertson: Your accountant should become an integral part of your business. His or her expertise should not only help you establish and maintain an accounting system, but conduct periodic reviews of the system to ensure that it is being properly maintained, provide advice to help you identify the true costs of your products and determine those products that are not making a profit, assist you in raising capital, and provide tax management. Consequently, you will

Exhibit 3–2   Interview Questions for Accountants

1. Describe the nature of your practice. Do you have any specialties? _____

_____

2. What is the staff turnover in your office? _____

_____

_____

3. What do you anticipate to be the staffing requirement for my account?

_____

_____

4. How many clients do you have? What kinds of clients? _____

_____

5. How much time is spent with owner/managers versus audit and tax work? _____

_____

6. Who in the firm will actually perform my work? _____

_____

7. How many hours per month is anticipated for my account? _____

_____

8. What will your services cost me? How will I be billed? _____

_____

9. How do you stay up to date on trends and developments in the tax field?

_____

_____

10. How do you communicate important trends and developments to your clients? _____

_____

Exhibit 3–2   *(contniued)*

11. What do you see as your role in helping me to manage my business?

_____

_____

12. May I see a copy of your most recent peer review? _____

_____

_____

want to choose an accountant with whom you are personally compatible and who has good judgment, expertise, promptly responds to your needs, and charges reasonable fees.[4]

Invite the accountant you have identified ". . . to conduct an initial diagnostic review of your business's finances. Then ask for a proposal letter to find out what kind of work needs to be done and what it will cost to do it."[5]

The American Institute of Certified Public Accountants (AICPA), Private Companies Practices Section (PCPS) will supply you with copies of your candidate's most recent peer review. The candidate must provide you with permission to obtain a copy; if the firm refuses, it should be a red flag.

THE THREE Rs: ACCOUNTANTS

RECAP

- Determine your needs, large versus small—evaluate where you anticipate your business will be in five years. Will you be borrowing from financial institutions?
- Consider your in-house skills—if your spouse works with you and is a great bookkeeper, you may not require much in the way of service.
- Develop a list—talk to bankers, lawyers, and friends.
- Evaluate candidates—be comfortable on a personal level as well as a professional level. It won't be sufficient that the candidate is technically competent if you cannot develop a good personal rapport.

(continued)

THE THREE RS *(continued)*

- Consider accessibility of candidates—how easy are the candidates to reach; how have they instructed their staffs to handle clients' inquiries.

RESOURCES

- American Institute of Certified Public Accountants (AICPA), 1211 Avenue of Americas, New York, NY 10035-8775, Tel: 212-575-6200, Fax: 212-575-3846. The Private Companies Practices Section (PCPS) will provide a member list of the 6,500 member firms that primarily serve private companies and will supply a copy of the most recent peer review of firms you may be considering. You can call their toll-free number: 1-800-272-3476.
- National Society of Public Accountants, 1010 North Fairfax Street, Alexandria, VA 22314-1574, Tel: 703-549-6400, Fax: 703-549-2984. The NSPA offers a referral service of members in your area and produces several brochures such as *How Accountants Set Fees, Accountant Banker Client: The Relationship.* The NSPA requires its members "to adhere to a strict Code of Ethics and high standards for professional performance."
- HLB International, Tel: 44-171-334-4783. This company is based in London and represents accountants and business advisors in more than 90 countries.

REFERENCES

- *Small Business Advisor*   This is not specifically a reference on accountants; however, it has some good advice about accounting relationships

4

BANKS AND BANKERS

Many entrepreneurs begin their businesses with their own savings or with financial assistance from friends and family. In some cases, that may be all the capital necessary to finance a small business. Others may be fortunate enough to have access to venture capital and even the public equity markets. At some point, however, most businesses need to turn to the banking industry for short- or long-term financing.

In this chapter, I have distinguished between banks and bankers. The chapter discusses the issues you should consider when evaluating *banks* as well as the criteria you should review when determining which *commercial loan officer* will work best with you. The chapter is divided into two main sections. The first section describes the functions of a bank and criteria for choosing one. The second section focuses on commercial loan officers. It provides insights into identifying the individual who will serve you and your business most effectively and what you should do to cultivate the relationship.

This group of service providers gets a lot of negative press, especially in business journals. I have had my share of war stories, but along the way I learned how to deal with banks and bankers and even have gained some lasting friendships.

The *function* of your *bank* includes these tasks:

- Process cash receipts, payments, letters of credit (L/C), wire transfers, and so on.

- Loan money, finance equipment acquisition, finance real estate acquisition, provide receivable and inventory financing.
- Help you gather credit information and manage your cash flow.
- Provide services such as lockbox, management of float, issuance of L/Cs.

The *function* of your *banker* includes these tasks:

- Facilitate your firm's interactions with the bank.
- Be your advocate to the loan committee.
- Assist you in utilizing and maximizing services provided by the bank.
- Recommend and advise you on proper etiquette in dealing with the bank.

FINDING A GOOD BANK

Many entrepreneurs probably categorize banks and bankers along with lawyers, life insurance salespeople, and used car dealers as their least favorite people. Understanding the perspective of the bank and the mind-set of the banker can go a long way to alleviating the stress and frustration businesspeople often experience in their banking relationships. The old cliché "banks are only willing to lend you money when you don't need it" could be restated as "only borrow when you don't need the money," which is to say develop your banking relationship before you need to borrow. This then ought to be the basis for your strategy regarding developing a banking relationship.

I utilized advice from a professor in college when I began managing our family business, which was to build up my company's creditworthiness with my bank. I started out by borrowing small amounts of money ($5,000–10,000) for short periods (90 days) and repaying the loans before the due date. The "cost"—the interest expense and nominal service charges—were tax deductible and I viewed those costs as the price of establishing a credit history.

Here are some advantages of borrowing from banks:

- Banks charge one of the lowest interest rates of any of the institutions that make loans.
- Banks can give you expert advice about businesses related to yours and about general business and economic trends.
- Borrowing from banks, as opposed to government sources, is more beneficial for your credit rating.

- Banks offer a wider variety of loans than other sources.
- Banks offer many other services that are helpful in running your business.
- After granting you a loan, banks will do *everything they can* to keep your business afloat.

Here are some of the disadvantages:

- Banks are very conservative and are one of the most difficult loan sources.
- Banks want more information and more precise information than other lending sources.
- Personnel turnover in banks is high and developing long-term relationships may be difficult.
- Banks monitor loans they make more closely than other institutions.[1]

If you aren't anticipating a borrowing relationship with your bank, then the selection process is simpler. A major component to look at is *convenience*. Take into consideration all the elements of convenience, not only the location of the nearest branch but also its capability of offering the services you will require. For example, if your business is engaged in exporting and/or importing, and as a result is constantly working with L/Cs (letters of credit), a full-service international department is a must.

The next component to evaluate is the *cost of services*. Ask each bank to provide you with its schedule of charges (see Exhibit 4–1) so that you can compare and establish which bank has the most reasonable rates. Also, you can request a list of the charges that will be used in your account analysis. This information may be significant if you have a very large and active account. You may want to compare the account activity you anticipate with that list and with the bank's published list of charges.

Quality is one of the vaguer measures of banks. If the commercial loan officer and his or her secretary are working on your behalf, sometimes even a bank with a reputation for being unresponsive may be good for you. However, if you hear too many negative comments about a specific institution, especially from businesspeople in similar businesses or circumstances, it would be wise to drop that bank from your list.

If you anticipate having a borrowing relationship with your bank, you should consider other issues in your search. All banks have lending histories. You can speak to other borrowers in your community and obtain a fairly accurate picture of how aggressive or nonaggressive a given

Exhibit 4–1　　Sample of Bank's Schedule of Charges

Analysis Charges

Check printing	$ —	vary by style
Coin rolls sold	.07	per roll
Currency deposited	.10	per $1,000
Deposits	.30	per deposit
Deposit items returned	7.00	per item
Depository transfer check fee	2.00	per transfer
Incoming wire transfers	10.00	
Insurance charge	prevailing FDIC rate	
Items deposited	.15	per item
Items paid	.20	per item
Maintenance fee	15.00	per month
Outgoing wire transfers	15.00	
Outgoing wire transfers (non-domestic)	25.00	
Overdraft/NSF	30.00	per item
Stop payments	15.00	per item
Telephone transfers	2.00	per transfer
Unavailable funds	30.00	per item

Direct Charges

Account research	$ 25.00	per hour
	10.00	minimum
Check collection fee	10.00	
Check withdrawals (to other than accountholder)	5.00	
Counter check	1.00	
Coupon processing	3.00	per envelope
Coupon returned	7.50	
Interim statements	6.00	
IRS levies	100.00	
Photocopy	3.50	per item
Writs, Garnishments, Attachments	250.00	

Special Services

Please consult a bank representative for details and fees:
- Account Reconciliation Program
- Payroll Direct Deposit
- Lockbox Processing
- Merchant Credit Card Program

At Progress, the average monthly investable balance (average collected balance less an adjustment for Federal Reserve Requirements) in your Business Checking Account earns an Earnings Credit. The Earnings Credit rate is calculated and set monthly. The Earnings Credit is applied to offset the Business Checking Analysis Charges. The Earnings Credit cannot be applied to offset any of the Business Checking Direct charges. In the event that the account uses funds which are unavailable on an average basis during the month, Progress Federal Savings Bank will charge the account through Account Analysis for the use of those funds at a rate of Progress Prime plus two percent.

Note: Courtesy of Progress Federal Savings Bank, Plymouth Meeting, PA.

bank is when it comes to making loans. You should avoid basing a decision about a given bank on the positive or negative experiences of one reference. Success of one borrower may be based on criteria that you are not aware of and lack of success may reflect that potential borrower's lack of sophistication rather than the bank's attitude.

Try to determine the bank's attitude toward small business. Even large banks may have a favorable attitude toward loans for small businesses and frequently will maintain independent departments within lending for loans that fit the range of your borrowing needs. Review the stability of the top management. Turmoil at the top does not bode well for borrowers nor for lenders to make decisions or to get loans approved. Look at the stability of your commercial loan officer's manager. Here again, turmoil at this management level can be a source of delay and indicate a lack of leadership within the bank.[2]

A study published by the New York Federal Reserve Bank, based on data gathered in 1993, suggests that the takeover of smaller banks by larger banks does not affect the lending practices of the acquired bank: "The 133 banks with assets of $5 billion or more held 35.4 percent of all commercial and industrial loans under $1 million, a typical small-business loan. Those loans represent 17 percent of the big banks' portfolios. But that is equaled by the loans written by small banks (assets under $300 million). It took the lending power of 9,057 small banks to do it, but this category issued 34.6 percent of small-business loans. Those loans make up 97 percent of the small banks' commercial loans. Small commercial banking didn't decline after small banks were taken over by larger organizations.[3]

Ask the following questions:

- Does your bank see you through adversity?
- Does it save you time?
- Does it treat you as an individual?
- Does it teach and advise?
- Does it do something special for you?
- Does it accept responsibility for you?
- Does it let you borrow against the future?
- Does it find customers for you?
- Does it send you searching?[4]

"The best way growing companies can negotiate for lower rates is by demonstrating their attractiveness as customers, rather than by asking for discounts."[5]

This observation came from a banker, "On lending to business, we bankers take into account the borrower's ability, experience, reputation, character, even his personality, and sometimes his influence."[6]

While I have never had access to a bank board member, other writers about bank relationships discuss the importance of the makeup of the bank's board. Perhaps in a small community or neighborhood, this information may help identify a desirable bank, but my sense is that in most major metropolitan areas the small borrower is unlikely to have access to or the benefit of the influence of a board member. A friend who is a bank board member may have to refrain from voting on your loan approval because of the friendship.

Some observers note that the board—intentionally or not—sets the loan climate within the bank, and the officers you deal with will reflect that climate. A banker adds to this, "Look at the bank's annual report and take note of the professions or businesses of the board members." He cites the example of a local bank that had a $450 million commercial loan portfolio; on closer examination, however, only $50 million was in loans not secured by real estate. The board was weighted heavily with real estate developers and property owners. This bank was obviously *not* as small business commercial loan oriented as it seemed at first glance.[7]

All banks work with *loan-to-deposit ratios*. This ratio reflects the bank's interest in making loans. It is a percentage figure that reflects the total value of the loans the bank has outstanding against the total amount of the bank's deposits. In 1991, the national average was 80 percent. Banks believe that 70 percent is an optimal ratio and that anything over 50 percent reflects a willingness to lend money. These ratios may change from time to time and it is worthwhile to check the loan-to-deposit ratios of the banks in your area. Asking a banker for this information will also establish that you are a sophisticated consumer. Another measure that can be utilized is the bank's commercial loan activity. Ask for a statement with a breakdown of the bank's loan figures (generally available in the bank's annual report; an example is shown in Exhibit 4–2). This statement will reflect the percentage of the total loan figure that consists of commercial loans. Exhibit 4–2 illustrates that the bank has less than 5 percent of its "interest earning assets" in nonmortgage-backed commercial businesses, up only 3 percent of its loan portfolio in 1994. This may reflect a trend by the bank to do more commercial lending.

Banks may have tendencies toward certain kinds of businesses—one may have a reputation for LBOs, another may seek out high technology or retailing. If the market or industry in which your business operates works with a bank that has developed an interest in businesses like yours, you may find dealing with that bank easier, since it will have a better command of the intricacies of your business. Some specialized businesses, such as government contractors, may find banks outside their geographic area that are better suited to serve their needs. For an out-of-state or out-of-region relationship to work, however, the loan must be sufficiently large ($5 million–$10 million) to justify the travel cost and time.[8]

You shouldn't rule out working with a nonlocal bank. Some banks seek commercial loans in markets where they don't have a retailing presence as a precursor to entering that market. Or the bank may look favorably on certain industries even if they are outside the bank's traditional geographic market.

Some banks have, either consciously or unconsciously, established a reputation and a working relationship with the Small Business Administration (SBA). I have had the experience of a commercial lender advising that his bank would not make a loan to my company but he would work with us in obtaining an SBA-guaranteed loan. If you have discovered that yours is a problematic business for raising funds from banks, you may want to target those banks in your community with whom the SBA has worked and even specific commercial loan officers in those banks. You may be able to call your local SBA office and get a list of banks in your area who work regularly with the SBA.

Exhibit 4–2   Sample Statement of Bank's Loan Figures

The following table sets forth, for the periods indicated, information regarding (i) total dollar amount of interest income on average interest-earning assets and the resultant average yield; (ii) the total dollar amount of interest expense on average interest-bearing liabilities and the resultant average cost; (iii) net interest income; (iv) interest rate spread; and (v) net interest margin. Information is based on average daily balances during the indicated periods. For the purposes of this table non-accrual loans have been included in the appropriate average balance category.

Distribution of Average Assets, Liabilities and Stockholders' Equity

For the years ended December 31,	1995			1994			1993		
	Average Balance	Interest	Yield/ Rate	Average Balance	Interest	Yield/ Rate	Average Balance	Interest	Yield/ Rate
Interest-earning assets:									
Investment securities and other									
interest-earning assets (1)	$ 19,364	$ 1,235	6.38%	$ 16,939	$ 1,029	6.07%	$ 6,090	$ 358	5.88%
Mortgage-backed securities (2)	100,377	6,598	6.57	113,819	6,617	5.81	115,876	6,343	5.47
Mortgage loans (2)	178,979	15,489	8.65	161,339	12,692	7.87	140,984	11,914	8.45
Consumer loans	20,895	1,821	8.72	17,055	1,456	8.54	15,651	1,375	8.79
Commercial business	13,651	1,426	10.45	10,658	1,036	9.72	9,784	834	8.52
Total interest-earning assets	$333,266	$26,569	7.97%	$319,810	$22,830	7.14%	$288,385	$20,824	7.22%
Non-interest-earning assets	18,274			20,304			30,889		
Total assets	$351,540			$340,114			$319,274		
Interest-bearing liabilities:									
Interest-bearing deposits:									
Money market accounts	$ 33,577	$ 1,042	3.10%	$ 41,428	$ 1,138	2.75%	$ 42,128	$ 1,187	2.82%
NOW and Super NOW	26,661	716	2.69	21,932	532	2.43	17,488	418	2.39
Passbook and statement savings	27,290	783	2.87	27,808	820	2.95	21,212	623	2.94
Time deposits	177,972	9,712	5.46	168,250	7,678	4.56	159,973	7,148	4.47
Total interest-bearing deposits	265,500	12,253	4.62	259,418	10,168	3.92	240,801	9,377	3.89
Advances from the FHLB	44,177	2,812	6.37	44,007	2,202	5.00	48,702	2,088	4.29
Subordinated debt	3,000	270	9.00	1,508	135	8.95	—	—	—
Total interest-bearing liabilities	$312,677	$15,335	4.90%	$304,933	$12,505	4.10%	$289,503	$11,465	3.96%
Non-interest-bearing liabilities	24,516			21,528			18,841		
Total liabilities	$337,193			$326,461			$308,344		
Stockholders' equity	14,347			13,653			10,930		
Total liabilities and stockholders' equity	$351,540			$340,114			$319,274		
Net interest income:									
Interest rate spread (3)		$11,234	3.07%		$10,325	3.04%		$ 9,359	3.26%
Net interest margin (3)			3.37%			3.23%			3.25%
Average interest-earning assets to average interest-bearing liabilities			106.58%			104.88%			99.61%

(1) Includes investment securities classified as available for sale.
(2) Includes mortgage loans held for sale and mortgage-backed securities classified as available for sale.
(3) Interest rate spread represents the difference between the weighted average yield on interest-earnings assets and the weighted average cost of interest-bearing liabilities, and net interest margin represents net interest income divided by average interest-earning assets.

Note: Courtesy of Progress Federal Savings Bank, Plymouth Meeting, PA.

Another interesting issue to explore when identifying potential banks is their willingness to 'participate' in deals and to either be a second bank or allow a second bank to be involved.

I have experienced a situation where my bank was not interested in lending me additional funds and I had to borrow from another bank in order to fund an equipment acquisition I had determined was necessary for my business. The banker was annoyed by my finding another institution that was willing to lend me asset-based funds to acquire new equipment that my lead bank was not willing to finance or at least not on terms I felt were reasonable. This may be a difficult attitude to uncover; the loan officer may tell you the bank has no problem in principle but when the time comes, the bank is less than cooperative. I took a risk in alienating my lead banker, who eventually got over his unhappiness with me. I also learned from this experience not to allow the bank to try to control the growth of my business. Bankers sometimes take a proprietary attitude about their accounts. They may even view your shopping around as disloyal rather than just good business. They may also be concerned about your overextending yourself and diluting your asset-to-loan ratio.

Exhibit 4–3 lists questions to ask when choosing a bank.

EVALUATING BANKERS AND COMMERCIAL LOAN OFFICERS

Once you have identified the bank or banks with which you would like to work, you then need to target the commercial loan officer or officers with whom you would like to deal day to day. Engaging in an active campaign to identify which loan officer in the target bank(s) will serve your business best is a worthwhile investment of your time. If you are already in a banking relationship and the loan officer is leaving, you do not have to accept the replacement loan officer assigned by the bank. Ask the outgoing loan officer to recommend the best person to replace him or her.

You should be looking for characteristics that are compatible with your business. If your business is on the fast track for growth, avoid a middle-aged loan officer who has been with the bank for 20 years and is still only a loan officer. Target young managers on the fast track. I recommend asking about the officer's lending limits. One banker, however, counsels not asking about lending limits as it may appear to be a put-down of the loan officer.[9] You may want to approach this question diplomatically, if or when you ask. My feeling is that you will have to "disrobe" financially before the loan officer, so metaphorically speaking, you should be able to see the color of your inquisitor's socks.

Try to obtain the names of other clients the loan officer serves and talk with the person in those accounts who manages the banking relationship. You should be able to get a sense from these referrals about the ability of the officer to represent you effectively at loan committees and about the officer's real commitment to the account. Ask about problems they have encountered and the sort of advice and creativity the loan officer has used to resolve the problems.

Exhibit 4–3 Interview Questions for Banks and Bankers

1. Convenience.
   a. Where is the closest branch to my business? My home? _____

   b. What are the hours of operation? _____

   c. How much of our transactional business can be done by phone, computer, lockbox, ATM, depository? _____

   d. Will my commercial officer be on location at the branch? If not, where?

2. Cost of services.
   a. What is the schedule of charges? _____

   b. Are there charges that the bank will waive or provide at reduced levels? _____

   c. Will my account activity credits offset charges? _____

   d. Are there services this bank cannot provide that another can? _____

3. Attitude toward risk.
   a. What is the bank's loan-to-deposit ratio? _____

   b. What are bank's loan figures? Ask to see a breakdown. _____

   c. Does the bank have other customers in my industry? _____

(continued)

Exhibit 4–3   *(continued)*

---

4. What is the lending officer's business background? _____

   _____

5. What is the bank's lending authority? _____

   _____

6. What is the bank's comfort level? _____

   _____

7. What is the bank's turnaround time and what are the steps in approval process? _____

   _____

8. What is the bank's policy for a request going to 1st-level committee? ___

   _____

9. What is the bank's policy for a request going to 2nd-level committee? ___

   _____

10. What does the loan officer know about your industry? _____

   _____

11. If, after opening a relationship, I want to change officers, what is the policy? _____

   _____

12. What is the loan officer's authority to make a loan? _____

   _____

13. What kind of credit arrangements has the bank made for other similar businesses? _____

   _____

14. Does the bank have any specialized services for my industry? _____

   _____

People get into banking the way people get into any other business. Some plan a career as a banker, some go into banking as a good but temporary experience on the way to something else, but most wander into it because they need a job and a banking job is available and respectable.

Bankers are just human beings. Moreover, they have a family, friends, watch television, pursue the American dream, and have trouble paying their bills just like the rest of us.

The one factor common to all bankers, in addition to having a business background or business degree, is that they form rules based on their experience which guides them in their decisions on business loans. They work with businesses every day and they have seen several successful businesses and several failures. Along with their experience they accumulate certain "rules of thumb" as the basis on which they consider all applications for loans. An example of a rule of thumb might be, "If the company's current assets divided by the current liabilities is less than 1, this is unfavorable to making a loan."[10]

Understanding these observations will be very helpful in developing your relationship with commercial loan officers.

One of my most frustrating experiences with banks was the constant turnover of loan officers. This is a complaint echoed countless times by entrepreneurs and managers. The loan officer who sells you on transferring your business to his or her bank is usually attentive and knowledgeable. Almost invariably, six months to a year after you switch your account, your loan officer is either promoted or transferred. He or she will introduce you to a new loan officer who doesn't have the same vested interest in your account. By the time the new loan officer is transferred and you get number three, service and responsiveness may be in the toilet.

> *War Story.*   The preceding chain of events has happened to me at least three times. So at one point, when a banker was courting me to transfer to his institution, I proposed I would transfer my account if the bank would commit in writing that he would remain my loan officer regardless of where he was transferred geographically or department wise, unless he left the bank. Lo and behold, six months later Jim was transferred to the other side of the city, but he continued to handle my account. I think he was moved about five more times and each time the bank tried to pawn off another officer and each time I pulled out the letter.

On the other hand, if the bank officer is leaving the bank to work in another bank in the same market, you may gain from having a personal relationship with someone in two banks.

The important thing to remember about loan officers at all times, but especially when you need to borrow money, is not to treat them as adversaries. When you do need to borrow, you will have built a level of trust and confidence that allows the loan officer to go to bat for you at the bank. It is your responsibility to keep your loan officer apprised of all the important news about your business, not only the good news but also the bad news. Banks are monolithic institutions, even the small ones. If you cultivate the relationship, the loan officer can be the vehicle for avoiding many of the frustrations entrepreneurs normally associate in dealing with banks. Many entrepreneurs are reluctant to share their financial information or to sign personal guarantees. What you should do is view the situation from the other side. As a lender, I would question the credibility of anyone asking me to part with my money or to put my money at risk if he wasn't willing to put his money at risk.

"See all loan officers who call on you." This sage advice comes from Bob Bifolco, who at this writing is Senior Vice President of Commercial Banking at Progress Bank—a midsize bank in the Philadelphia area. Bob is one of two bankers who profoundly influenced my perspective of banks and bankers. He goes on to recommend that you develop a resource file of all potential loan officers. Don't be afraid to ask for a resume from each one. He recommended some criteria to evaluate when considering loan officers:

- *Ability to listen*—entrepreneurs like to talk about their businesses, *but* (and this is good advice for interviewing anyone) while talking, you ought to be observing the candidate's body language. Is he or she really listening—(a good way to check is to ask a question that relates to something you have explained)?
- *Someone who can offer ideas outside the realm of banking*—everybody has to start someplace, but a 24-year-old loan officer who has had the same job since graduating college is not going to provide the perspective of a 35- or 45-year-old who came to banking from another industry.
- *Positive experience*—this is not only a quantitative element but also a qualitative one. An individual who has had a negative experience, such as a bad loan, with another business in the recent past may not be as likely to take a chance of going to bat for an account that isn't rock solid.
- *Good interpersonal skills*—if the individual cannot hold an intelligent conversation with you, cannot ask intelligent and meaningful questions relating to your business, he or she may not engender much respect within his or her institution.

- *Knowledge of your competition/industry*—this can be a double-edged sword. A loan officer who has knowledge of, or at least understands, your industry will require less orientation and convincing than one who doesn't. However, if the individual has an account that is either a competitor or in the same industry, there is some risk that he or she may reveal proprietary information about your company.

Bob Bifolco suggests that, since the lending officer and you both realize that lending drives any decision, you should ask about the bank's loan policies; the following are some considerations, but see also Exhibit 4–3.

- What is the bank's lending authority (its mandated limit per transaction)? This is set by the state or federal agency overseeing the institution and probably won't impact on your lending needs. If your requirement is over the bank's lending authority, the bank may need to bring in a colender.
- What is the bank's comfort level for loans? It may be much less than mandated. A bank may have a technical limit of say one million dollars but only make commercial loans of one-half million.
- What is the turnaround time (i.e., what are the steps in the approval process)? If you need your money "yesterday," you may not want to wait through a 30-day process until the next bank board meeting.
- What is the bank's policy for a request going to 1st-level committee? You should understand the effect of the size of the loan, the officer's lending limit, and the approval process. It may also include issues such as depth of financial information required. (Every banker has a lending limit. The larger the loan, the more likely it has to go through several levels of approval. In a small bank, the board of directors may be the only level. In a large bank, there may be two or three levels of approval before a final okay is issued.)
- What is the policy for determining when a request must go to 2nd-level committee.

And you should be prepared to discuss:

- *What can you offer the bank* (as in deposits)? Remember, your commercial loan officer is your representative to the bank; be prepared to give him or her something he can show to his or her bosses that the bank will value.

- *What are you willing to do about personal guarantees?* The issue of personal guarantees can and does send many entrepreneurs off the deep end. In a perfect world, I would agree that an entrepreneur who has built up his or her business eventually ought to achieve the status of not needing to provide personal guarantees. At the same time, personal guarantees, especially in lieu of liens on other assets, make a statement to any borrower that "this person is for real, he or she is willing to stand behind his or her words and numbers." You can always discuss some sort of staged phaseout of personal guarantees based on achieving mutually agreed-on targets.

Bob Bifolco notes your banking relationship is a fundamental business relationship, which will only work when there is give-and-take. He also mentioned that loan brokers are making inroads in the placement of loans. His final comment is that high bank turnover (i.e., if you change banks frequently) is a red flag for a loan officer. *Banks don't like clients who jump around.* It may be a symptom of something other than seeking a better rate of interest.

An additional element of a successful ongoing banking relationship is occasionally visiting the loan officer at his or her office and being sure that you are introduced to your loan officer's boss.

Many banks offer a wide range of services that they frequently do not promote. The bank may provide services it developed to accommodate certain major customers. Because these services generally are not profit centers, the fees may be attractive. They are not aggressively marketed; however, a good relationship with a loan officer can uncover some of these special benefits.

An additional advantage of a healthy relationship with a loan officer and his or her secretary is the lubricating of the wheels of a sometimes unwieldy bureaucracy. I found my loan officers' secretaries invaluable in getting service charges reversed, expediting the processing of L/Cs and wire transfers, and bending the rules of inflexible technocrats in various departments within the bank.

Here are some questions to ask to get you started thinking about what you want from your banking relationship:

1. Does the loan officer "marketing" the bank to you have the authority to make a loan (of any size)?
2. Does the bank or the officer have any expertise in your industry?

Exhibit 4–4 Robert Morris Associates Sample Statement Study

580 — RETAILERS—RESTAURANTS. SIC# 5812

Type of Statement / Number of Statements

# Postretirement Benefits / Type of Statement	0-500M	500M-2MM	2-10MM	10-50MM	50-100MM	100-250MM	Comparative Historical 4/1/90-3/31/91 ALL	Comparative Historical 4/1/91-3/31/92 ALL
# Postretirement Benefits	38	23	18	9	1	2		
Unqualified	7	18	58	57	15	24	138	144
Reviewed	37	59	53	9	1		173	168
Compiled	322	143	45	4			476	523
Tax Returns	118	43	7		1		26	55
Other	149	129	81	33	10	6	293	304
	344 (4/1-9/30/94)			1085 (10/1/94-3/31/95)				
NUMBER OF STATEMENTS	633	392	244	103	26	31	1106	1194

Financial Statement Data

Item	0-500M %	500M-2MM %	2-10MM %	10-50MM %	50-100MM %	100-250MM %	Hist 4/1/90-3/31/91 %	Hist 4/1/91-3/31/92 %
ASSETS								
Cash & Equivalents	16.7	10.6	11.1	8.6	11.6	6.0	12.2	12.5
Trade Receivables - (net)	3.3	3.8	3.7	3.9	5.9	3.4	4.3	3.6
Inventory	8.5	5.4	4.7	4.2	2.9	3.4	6.8	6.6
All Other Current	2.1	2.2	2.0	2.2	1.4	2.4	2.1	2.0
Total Current	30.6	22.1	21.5	18.9	21.8	15.3	25.3	24.7
Fixed Assets (net)	50.7	59.6	61.1	59.6	64.7	63.3	56.1	55.2
Intangibles (net)	7.5	7.1	6.7	10.6	3.8	9.7	6.8	7.0
All Other Non-Current	11.3	11.3	10.7	10.8	9.8	11.8	11.8	13.0
Total	100.0	100.0	100.0	100.0	100.0	100.0	100.0	100.0
LIABILITIES								
Notes Payable-Short Term	5.4	4.9	3.0	2.4	2.7	.5	6.0	5.8
Cur. Mat.-L/T/D	4.8	5.8	5.8	5.8	2.4	2.5	6.1	6.2
Trade Payables	12.1	11.1	10.6	8.5	8.7	6.4	11.2	11.0
Income Taxes Payable	.6	.3	.4	.3	.4	.4	.7	.8
All Other Current	16.0	11.0	12.7	8.0	8.6	11.0	11.9	12.3
Total Current	38.9	33.1	32.5	24.9	22.8	20.9	36.0	36.1
Long Term Debt	24.3	32.6	31.3	34.8	19.4	25.5	32.1	30.8
Deferred Taxes	.0	.2	.3	.7	.8	1.6	.4	.4
All Other-Non-Current	4.8	4.0	4.9	3.7	5.7	3.2	3.7	3.7
Net Worth	31.9	30.1	31.1	35.9	51.3	48.8	27.9	29.0
Total Liabilities & Net Worth	100.0	100.0	100.0	100.0	100.0	100.0	100.0	100.0
INCOME DATA								
Net Sales	100.0	100.0	100.0	100.0	100.0	100.0	100.0	100.0
Gross Profit	57.0	57.8	55.8	50.3	37.5	39.9	56.3	57.4
Operating Expenses	52.4	53.8	51.5	45.7	30.7	32.1	52.0	52.7
Operating Profit	4.6	3.9	4.3	4.6	6.8	7.8	4.4	4.7
All Other Expenses (net)	.8	1.4	1.6	1.9	1.1	1.9	1.7	1.7
Profit Before Taxes	3.8	2.5	2.7	2.7	5.7	5.9	2.6	3.0

Ratios

Ratio	0-500M	500M-2MM	2-10MM	10-50MM	50-100MM	100-250MM	Hist 90-91	Hist 91-92
Current	1.7	1.1	1.2	1.0	2.0	1.2	1.3	1.3
	.8	.6	.6	.6	.8	.7	.7	.6
	.4	.3	.3	.3	.4	.4	.3	.3
Quick	1.2	.8	.8	.7	1.6	.8	.9	.9
	(625) .4	(388) .3	.4	.4	.7	.4	(1094) .4	(1186) .4
	.1	.1	.2	.2	.2	.2	.1	.1
Sales/Receivables	0 UND	0 UND	0 999.8	1 472.7	3 107.4	2 190.7	0 UND	0 UND
	0 UND	1 639.5	1 330.5	2 178.1	6 64.3	5 66.6	1 629.4	0 736.8
	2 195.0	3 127.7	5 77.8	7 53.5	17 21.8	12 29.7	4 95.7	3 111.7
Cost of Sales/Inventory	6 56.9	7 54.9	7 50.7	6 59.3	5 78.7	6 63.8	7 52.1	7 50.6
	11 32.7	11 33.1	11 33.1	12 30.9	9 40.0	11 34.5	11 31.8	12 30.9
	18 20.8	17 21.1	18 20.7	21 17.3	17 21.8	16 22.3	19 19.4	19 19.4
Cost of Sales/Payables	0 UND	14 26.5	17 21.8	23 16.1	19 19.5	13 27.6	9 41.3	9 39.2
	13 28.2	27 13.4	30 12.3	34 10.7	27 13.6	22 16.5	24 15.2	24 15.4
	30 12.3	44 8.3	51 7.2	53 6.9	48 7.6	29 12.7	43 8.5	39 9.3
Sales/Working Capital	36.6	104.4	71.2	-605.8	14.4	71.6	63.2	56.7
	-71.3	-27.3	-27.3	-22.7	-32.7	-26.9	-36.1	-34.0
	-18.3	-12.5	-10.8	-12.8	-16.0	-12.8	-12.7	-12.9
EBIT/Interest	11.5	6.8	7.2	4.8	20.0	15.3	5.4	6.0
	(476) 3.5	(352) 2.4	(229) 3.0	(98) 2.4	(24) 4.3	(29) 4.7	(972) 2.1	(1056) 2.4
	1.0	.8	1.4	1.2	2.7	1.7	.9	1.1
Net Profit + Depr., Dep., Amort./Cur. Mat. L /T/D	3.9	3.2	5.0	4.4	29.9	22.9	3.7	3.3
	(95) 2.0	(92) 1.6	(89) 2.2	(64) 2.4	(19) 11.3	(11) 13.9	(451) 1.8	(377) 1.6
	.5	.9	1.2	1.0	2.4	5.5	.9	.8
Fixed/Worth	.8	1.3	1.3	1.3	.8	1.0	1.1	1.0
	2.1	3.0	2.8	2.5	1.5	1.6	2.7	2.5
	NM	11.7	9.6	33.8	2.6	2.7	284.5	45.7
Debt/Worth	.7	1.1	1.2	1.1	.4	.5	1.1	1.0
	2.9	3.3	2.9	2.4	.9	1.0	3.2	3.0
	-127.0	16.7	11.2	35.8	2.9	3.2	UND	108.9
% Profit Before Taxes/Tangible Net Worth	106.0	66.1	70.4	36.7	19.8	34.7	71.9	70.4
	(473) 42.9	(317) 23.6	(201) 30.0	(80) 16.4	(25) 14.8	(29) 26.9	(834) 24.8	(908) 26.4
	12.6	6.3	7.8	4.6	7.6	13.4	4.6	6.3
% Profit Before Taxes/Total Assets	32.7	14.6	15.5	10.4	12.4	14.9	17.9	20.2
	13.2	6.0	7.4	5.5	8.2	8.7	5.9	6.3
	.4	.0	1.3	1.1	3.1	4.2	-.4	.6
Sales/Net Fixed Assets	23.2	10.1	7.2	5.3	3.1	2.9	12.5	13.3
	10.8	5.6	3.9	2.8	2.2	2.1	6.1	6.3
	5.1	2.6	2.4	2.0	1.5	1.6	3.0	3.1
Sales/Total Assets	7.4	4.6	3.4	2.4	2.0	1.7	4.9	5.0
	4.9	3.0	2.5	1.8	1.4	1.4	3.3	3.3
	3.2	1.9	1.6	1.3	1.2	1.1	2.0	2.1
% Depr., Dep., Amort./Sales	1.1	1.9	2.3	3.1	3.8	3.5	1.1	1.8
	(556) 2.1	(369) 3.0	(234) 3.1	(98) 4.0	4.4	(14) 4.0	(1005) 3.0	(1104) 2.8
	3.3	4.1	4.0	4.9	5.1	4.7	4.5	4.2
% Officers', Directors', Owners' Comp/Sales	3.2	2.7	1.9	.8			3.0	3.0
	(351) 5.6	(188) 4.5	(75) 3.7	(12) 3.0			(425) 5.0	(529) 5.3
	8.9	7.1	5.5	5.3			8.6	8.6
Net Sales ($)	673147M	1322459M	3046877M	4125684M	3229061M	8498349M	13190157M	15200072M
Total Assets ($)	141091M	394508M	1119899M	2201313M	1863072M	4952096M	6597401M	6864212M

© Robert Morris Associates 1995

M = $ thousand MM = $ million

See Pages 1 through 15 for Explanation of Ratios and Data

(continued)

Exhibit 4–4 *(continued)*

RETAILERS—RESTAURANTS. SIC# 5812   **581**

	Comparative Historical Data				Current Data Sorted By Sales					
	10	38	91	**# Postretirement Benefits**	30	18	8	12	13	10
				Type of Statement						
	163	164	179	Unqualified	4	12	9	17	52	85
	174	131	159	Reviewed	21	43	24	37	25	9
	468	443	514	Compiled	202	208	49	40	11	4
	92	112	169	Tax Returns	78	69	16	4	1	1
	322	327	408	Other	97	121	37	55	57	41
	4/1/92-3/31/93 ALL	4/1/93-3/31/94 ALL	4/1/94-3/31/95 ALL		344 (4/1-9/30/94) 0-1MM	1-3MM	3-5MM	1085 (10/1/94-3/31/95) 5-10MM	10-25MM	25MM & OVER
	1219	1177	1429	**NUMBER OF STATEMENTS**	402	453	135	153	146	140
	%	%	%	**ASSETS**	%	%	%	%	%	%
	12.4	12.3	13.1	Cash & Equivalents	13.7	15.3	11.6	12.4	11.3	8.8
	3.5	3.5	3.6	Trade Receivables - (net)	2.4	3.4	4.6	4.2	4.3	5.4
	6.5	6.9	6.5	Inventory	7.1	7.1	6.9	5.2	5.9	4.4
	2.0	2.0	2.1	All Other Current	2.0	2.1	2.3	2.4	2.0	1.9
	24.4	24.6	25.3	Total Current	25.2	27.9	25.4	24.2	23.5	20.6
	56.6	56.7	56.1	Fixed Assets (net)	57.6	52.4	55.5	57.9	59.0	59.0
	6.6	7.2	7.5	Intangibles (net)	8.3	6.4	8.0	6.9	7.7	8.3
	12.4	11.5	11.1	All Other Non-Current	8.9	13.3	11.2	11.0	9.9	12.1
	100.0	100.0	100.0	Total	100.0	100.0	100.0	100.0	100.0	100.0
				LIABILITIES						
	4.6	4.9	4.5	Notes Payable-Short Term	5.0	4.9	5.4	4.3	3.3	2.3
	5.9	5.2	5.2	Cur. Mat.-L /T/D	4.7	5.1	5.2	6.0	6.2	4.8
	11.6	11.0	11.1	Trade Payables	9.3	12.2	11.9	12.1	12.4	9.8
	.6	1.2	.5	Income Taxes Payable	.5	.5	.3	.3	.5	.3
	13.8	13.6	13.3	All Other Current	13.3	14.7	12.9	12.8	12.2	10.4
	36.5	36.0	34.5	Total Current	32.8	37.5	35.6	35.5	34.7	27.6
	30.3	30.4	28.5	Long Term Debt	31.7	26.0	27.1	30.8	26.4	28.0
	.3	.3	.2	Deferred Taxes	.0	.1	.2	.2	.4	.9
	3.2	4.3	4.5	All Other-Non-Current	4.9	4.6	3.7	3.9	5.7	3.3
	29.8	29.0	32.3	Net Worth	30.6	31.7	33.3	29.5	32.9	40.3
	100.0	100.0	100.0	Total Liabilities & Net Worth	100.0	100.0	100.0	100.0	100.0	100.0
				INCOME DATA						
	100.0	100.0	100.0	Net Sales	100.0	100.0	100.0	100.0	100.0	100.0
	57.4	56.6	55.8	Gross Profit	57.2	58.2	53.0	58.7	54.0	45.6
	52.5	52.2	51.3	Operating Expenses	52.1	54.4	47.8	55.7	49.3	40.4
	4.9	4.4	4.5	Operating Profit	5.2	3.8	5.2	3.1	4.6	5.3
	1.4	1.2	1.2	All Other Expenses (net)	1.7	.8	.8	1.4	1.1	1.3
	3.5	3.2	3.3	Profit Before Taxes	3.5	3.0	4.4	1.6	3.6	4.0
				RATIOS						
	1.2	1.3	1.3	Current	2.0	1.4	1.1	1.2	1.0	1.1
	.6	.6	.7		.7	.7	.7	.6	.6	.6
	.3	.3	.3		.3	.3	.3	.3	.4	.4
	.8	.9	.9	Quick	1.2	1.0	.9	.9	.7	.8
	(1210) .4	(1167) .4	(1417) .4		(396) .4	(449) .4	(133) .4	.4	.3	.4
	.1	.1	.2		.1	.1	.1	.1	.2	.2
	0 UND	0 UND	0 UND	Sales/Receivables	0 UND	0 UND	0 999.8	0 UND	0 925.6	1 409.6
	1 684.0	1 590.0	1 646.5		0 UND	1 716.0	1 320.4	1 651.6	2 197.1	3 121.8
	3 110.8	4 102.7	3 111.8		1 253.6	3 128.1	5 79.7	3 125.8	6 63.2	10 37.8
	7 50.2	8 48.2	7 55.7	Cost of Sales/Inventory	7 55.9	6 56.6	6 59.2	7 50.9	8 47.4	6 58.9
	11 32.3	12 30.1	11 33.0		12 29.6	11 33.8	9 38.6	11 34.1	12 31.1	11 34.7
	18 19.8	20 18.7	18 20.7		19 19.7	17 21.4	16 23.1	17 21.0	19 19.1	17 22.1
	11 34.1	7 51.2	8 44.1	Cost of Sales/Payables	0 UND	7 51.9	14 26.4	16 23.3	20 18.7	17 21.3
	24 15.2	23 16.0	22 16.3		11 34.2	22 16.5	23 16.0	30 12.1	33 11.2	28 13.2
	41 9.0	41 9.0	41 9.0		29 12.6	41 8.9	35 10.5	44 7.4	50 7.3	48 7.6
	75.9	61.1	51.5	Sales/Working Capital	33.6	48.6	77.1	55.7	933.9	111.4
	-34.2	-35.4	-41.0		-57.7	-49.5	-39.7	-33.7	-26.7	-26.5
	-13.1	-13.5	-13.8		-15.7	-14.0	-13.2	-10.9	-13.6	-13.6
	7.3	7.3	8.1	EBIT/Interest	6.9	10.0	9.3	6.2	6.4	10.3
	(1050) 2.8	(1017) 2.8	(1208) 2.9		(305) 2.3	(376) 3.0	(119) 2.9	(135) 2.5	(140) 3.2	(133) 4.1
	1.1	1.1	1.1		.8	1.0	1.6	.9	1.5	1.6
	4.1	3.5	4.8	Net Profit + Depr., Dep., Amort./Cur. Mat. L/T/D	3.4	4.0	5.2	3.1	5.5	13.6
	(350) 1.9	(317) 1.4	(370) 2.2		(54) 1.6	(90) 2.0	(34) 2.3	(50) 1.8	(67) 2.4	(75) 3.8
	1.0	.6	1.0		.1	.8	1.2	.5	1.3	1.6
	1.0	1.0	1.0	Fixed/Worth	1.0	.8	1.1	1.3	1.3	1.1
	2.5	2.7	2.4		2.9	2.2	2.4	2.8	2.3	1.9
	19.8	26.3	16.6		-21.5	26.9	7.3	20.4	6.9	5.4
	1.0	1.0	.9	Debt/Worth	.7	.9	.9	1.1	1.2	.7
	2.9	3.0	2.9		3.4	2.9	2.7	3.3	2.6	1.9
	31.9	54.0	24.6		-27.6	50.5	9.7	26.7	8.2	7.3
	73.1	71.4	76.3	% Profit Before Taxes/Tangible Net Worth	85.9	92.2	80.5	83.1	64.5	38.0
	(951) 25.7	(903) 28.0	(1125) 29.8		(293) 35.6	(357) 30.3	(112) 30.4	(121) 30.0	(124) 27.3	(118) 20.0
	7.8	7.3	8.1		9.7	6.7	6.7	8.9	8.6	9.4
	19.5	17.9	20.9	% Profit Before Taxes/Total Assets	25.4	26.1	23.6	15.7	14.5	14.0
	8.0	7.5	8.3		9.5	8.2	7.3	7.3	7.3	8.0
	1.0	.5	.8		.0	.0	1.6	.2	2.2	2.9
	12.3	12.9	14.1	Sales/Net Fixed Assets	17.5	19.1	13.0	8.7	8.1	6.5
	6.0	6.2	6.3		7.0	8.4	6.7	5.8	5.0	3.1
	2.9	2.8	2.9		3.0	3.8	3.3	3.1	2.4	2.1
	5.0	5.2	5.3	Sales/Total Assets	6.2	6.0	5.4	4.8	4.0	2.9
	3.3	3.2	3.3		3.4	3.9	3.7	3.1	2.6	2.0
	2.0	1.9	1.9		1.9	2.4	2.1	2.0	1.7	1.4
	1.7	1.7	1.6	% Depr., Dep., Amort./Sales	1.4	1.4	1.4	2.1	2.2	2.6
	(1140) 2.8	(1082) 2.8	(1297) 2.8		(349) 2.6	(412) 2.4	(131) 3.0	(144) 3.0	(143) 3.0	(118) 3.8
	4.1	4.1	4.0		4.1	3.7	3.7	3.8	4.1	4.5
	3.1	2.7	2.9	% Officers', Directors', Owners' Comp/Sales	3.8	2.6	2.8	1.8	2.1	1.0
	(524) 5.3	(557) 5.2	(629) 4.9		(225) 6.0	(237) 4.5	(65) 4.8	(53) 3.2	(33) 3.5	(16) 2.4
	8.1	9.0	7.8		9.6	7.3	7.0	5.7	4.9	6.1
	13420103M	16655146M	20895577M	Net Sales ($)	239860M	802300M	525053M	1072420M	2442699M	15813245M
	6701178M	9115615M	10671981M	Total Assets ($)	92444M	277978M	215804M	405808M	1126705M	8553242M

© Robert Morris Associates 1995

M = $ thousand   MM = $ million
See Pages 1 through 15 for Explanation of Ratios and Data

3. What kind of credit arrangements has the bank offered to other businesses in your industry?

4. What is the turnaround time—when will you have an answer?

5. Is your business part of an existing industry the bank services or is it in a new market the bank wants to enter?

6. Has the bank developed any specialized services for your industry?

7. Ask yourself—where is my competition banking?

8. Try to find out the background of the founders or leaders of the bank; is it outside of banking?

There is nothing better than an educated borrower to a loan officer.[11] To that end, one very effective vehicle for being prepared to negotiate with banks is the Robert Morris Associates *Annual Statement Studies* (see Exhibit 4–4). This book lists by SIC (standard industrial classification) code the key ratios and percentages of various industries, and is used by loan officers in evaluating credit risk.

I learned about the RMA Statement Studies many years ago at a workshop on Financial Management for Closely Held Businesses. The workshop was a marketing device of a local bank. We learned that banks look at quantifiable measures of businesses' performance such as key ratios and quick ratios, which deal with the relationship between assets and liabilities, and accounts receivable and accounts payable aging. Each industry group has a different range of these measures, and bankers rely on the RMA Statement Studies to identify benchmarks for industries of clients or potential clients with whom they work. It is a useful exercise to find the SIC code of your business and calculate your ratios and compare them to industry ratios to see how you measure up. Also, as mentioned earlier, learn the vernacular of the business. Books such as *Banking Smarter* or *Banking* are modest investments that will help you "do your homework." Finally, talk with your accountant about key issues to negotiate with your bank. Accountants work with banks and bankers on a variety of levels, and a good accountant can provide excellent guidance on your banking relationship.

THE THREE Rs: BANKS AND BANKERS

RECAP

- Be an educated borrower—learn what banks want from clients. Don't have unreasonable expectations.
- Don't treat loan officers as adversaries—if you treat bankers as the enemy, you cannot expect them to assist you.
- Negotiate with a view of the entire package, not just the cost of money—the number of points above or below prime should not be the singular factor determining where you bank.
- Consider convenience—not just the location nearest you but also the availability and cost of services, and the accessibility of the loan officer.
- Evaluate cost of services—compare cost of services you are likely to use to be certain that the loan rate differential isn't eroded by service charges.
- Explore attitude toward risk—if you will need to borrow money, be comfortable that the candidate banks are predisposed to make commercial business loans to companies like yours.
- Obtain commitment against officer turnover—your best advocate at the bank will be the loan officer who opens your account. Hold onto that person as long as possible.

RESOURCES

- RMA (Robert Morris Associates)—The Association of Lending and Credit Risk Professionals, 1650 Market Street, Suite 2300, Philadelphia, PA 19103, Tel: 215-851-9100, Fax: 215-851-9206. Publishes the *Annual Statement Studies*, which provides analysis of businesses by SIC code, used by bankers to compare your business to your industry norms.
- American Bankers Association, 1120 Connecticut Avenue NW, Washington, DC 20036, Tel: 202-663-5000, Fax: 202-296-9258.
- American League of Financial Institutions, 900 19th Street NW, Washington, DC 20006, Tel: 202-628-5624.

THE THREE RS *(continued)*

- Independent Bankers Association of America, One Thomas Circle NW, Suite 950, Washington, DC 20005, Tel: 202-659-8111.
- National Council of Savings Institutions, 900 19th Street NW, Washington, DC 20006, Tel: 202-857-3100.
- BCS & Associates, PO Box 5108, Scottsdale, AZ 85261-5108, Tel: 800-644-8384 (consultants in managing banking relationships).

REFERENCES

- *Banking*****   This is a good basic primer to learn about the banking business and how to deal with banks.
- *Banking Smarter*   Described as a "Guide to Bank Depository Management," this book offers some insights on controlling costs associated with banking.
- *Business Loans*   This is an excellent discussion of how to obtain loans from banks, in addition to other sources.
- *Learning to Live With (or Without) Your Banker.*
- *Note on Acquiring Bank Credit.*
- *RMA—Annual Statement Studies*   Financial information by industry is presented in a format many bankers use when analyzing companies. If you know your business's SIC code and it is listed in the RMA book, it can be a helpful tool in approaching banks.

5

CONSULTANTS— BUSINESS AND TECHNICAL

Effective selection and use of consultants begins with understanding that you have a problem or see an opportunity and want to solve the problem or capitalize on the opportunity. You may be skeptical about hiring consultants, I know I was until I used the services of my first consultant over 20 years ago.

The decision to retain this consultant stemmed from a sense that I had lost focus on the direction of the company. The consultant was a generalist who came highly recommended by a business associate for whom I had enormous respect. The consultant did help me see many of the weaknesses of my company and me, and provided guidance for managing the development and growth of the company. As with so many other service providers, satisfaction with a consultant depends on your own efforts. Consultants can be an inexpensive way of developing expertise, obtaining input about what to do, solving problems, or providing guidance. If you're lucky, you may end up with a good consultant without performing a thorough search. If you have done your homework, however, there are no secrets in obtaining good counseling from a qualified consultant.

You should *consider* hiring a consultant if:

- You have a problem that you need to solve.
- You have determined that you cannot solve the problem in-house either because of lack of knowledge or lack of time.
- You are prepared to implement the recommendations to correct the problem.
- You are interested in improving the operation of your business, acquiring new technology, or improving management and/or production elements of the business.
- You want to bring knowledge to your organization.

The profession of consultants was the only group of service providers for which I found a body of information on hiring and managing the category. There is one caveat: All the books were written by consultants. I located an obscure piece of university research on the use of consultants by various businesses. It revealed that entrepreneurs were more satisfied with the performance of their consultants when a problem had been identified and a consultant was then sought out to solve the problem. They were less satisfied with the performance of a consultant when they were cold canvassed and solicited.[1]

I draw two conclusions from this anecdote. First, if you don't think or recognize that you have a problem, you will suspect an outsider who tells you that you do have a problem. Second, beware of unsolicited advice. Most businesses are less than perfect. Anyone can come in from the outside and point out all sorts of things that could be improved. In most aspects of life, we have to want to improve before we will accept help.

The assumption in this chapter is that you have identified the problem or opportunity, cannot correct it or capitalize on it yourself and recognize you need help.

THE PRESELECTION PROCESS

"Vague consulting assignments produce vague, unsuccessful results" [emphasis mine].[2] It isn't enough to recognize that there is a problem, that you don't have the resources to solve the problem, and therefore need outside help. Your task is further complicated because, if you want to do the job correctly, you need to define what you expect to accomplish.

Here is a useful list of benefits consultants can provide that will help you to focus on what you ought to expect to receive from your consultant:

1. Finding and providing management and business information.
2. Performing the client's task.
3. Helping the client to focus appropriate attention to specifics, causes rather than symptoms.
4. Delivering systems and methodologies.
5. Demonstrating and teaching how to do a job.
6. Diagnosing the client's condition.
7. Telling the client what to do.
8. Presenting alternatives with recommendations.
9. Presenting alternatives without recommendations.
10. Asking questions to stimulate thinking and action.
11. Focusing attention on the corrective program and a timetable.
12. Observing organizational processes and giving feedback.
13. Acting as a sounding board.
14. Providing moral support and counsel.[3]

Many consulting engagements are problem- or opportunity-specific. Unlike the general business counsel or the accountant or even the graphic artist, consultants are called in to solve a real or perceived problem or to help to develop an opportunity, such as:

- We need to upgrade our information system.
- Our personnel turnover is too high.
- We need to modernize our production line.
- We are losing money.

The problem or opportunity may be highly technical and precisely defined or it may be general and somewhat vague. Finding an appropriate consultant for the precisely defined problem is probably easier than for the general problem. But the evaluation and selection process is essentially the same. For your company to benefit from the consultation, you need to examine and gauge the profile, capabilities, history, personality, and availability of the consultant. You also should consider your company's culture, your personal preferences, the time you and your staff can make available, the cost of the project, and your own mind-set (see Exhibit 5–1).

Exhibit 5-1 What It Feels Like to Be a Buyer

1. I'm feeling *insecure*. I'm not sure I know how to detect which of the finalists is the genius and which is just good. I've exhausted my abilities to make technical distinctions.
2. I'm feeling *threatened*. This is my area of responsibility, and even though intellectually I know I need outside expertise, emotionally it's not comfortable to put my affairs in the hands of others.
3. I'm taking a *personal risk*. By putting my affairs in the hands of someone else, I risk losing control.
4. I'm *impatient*. I didn't call in someone at the first sign of symptoms (or opportunity). I've been thinking about this for a while.
5. I'm *worried*. By the very fact of suggesting improvements or changes, these people are going to be implying that I haven't been doing it right up till now. Are these people going to be on my side?
6. I'm *exposed*. Whoever I hire, I'm going to reveal some proprietary secrets, not all of which are flattering. I will have to undress.
7. I'm feeling *ignorant*, and don't like the feeling. I don't know if I've got a simple problem or a complex one. I'm not sure I can trust them to be honest about that: It's in their interest to convince me it's complex.
8. I'm *skeptical*. I've been burned before by these kinds of people. You get a lot of promises: How do I know whose promise I should buy?
9. I'm *concerned* that they either can't or won't take the time to understand what makes my situation special. They'll try to sell me what they've got rather than what I need.
10. I'm *suspicious*. Will they be those typical professionals who are hard to get hold of, who are patronizing, who leave you out of the loop, who befuddle you with jargon, who don't explain what they are doing or why, who . . . , who . . . , who . . . ? In short, will these people deal with me in the way I want to be dealt with?

Source: David Maister, *How Clients Choose* (Boston, MA: David H. Maister Associates, 1991).

FINDING QUALIFIED CONSULTANTS

Here are four sources for finding qualified consultants:

- Referrals.
- Reading/writing advertisements (place an advertisement in a trade journal appropriate to your business and define the consulting project you require).

- Directories (your local library should have the *Encyclopedia of Consultants and Consulting Organizations. The American Consultants League* annual directory is another source).
- Research for the ideal consultant:
  - —Leading authorities (authors of articles in your trade press).
  - —Trade and professional associations (*National Trade and Professional Associations Directory*—many professional associations will supply a membership list or a referral to members in your area).

Ray Rauth, National Chairman of the International Computer Consultants Association (ICCA), recommends a more contemporary source—the Consultants Forum on CompuServe or other on-line services such as The Expert Marketplace, The Consultants Mall, and ConsultLink.

"Most independent consultants work alone, and very often maintain their offices in their homes. Image and fancy trappings have no bearing on the expert's competence."[4] I used consultants over the years who were sole practitioners operating out of their homes, and I was satisfied with their work.

Don't be skeptical of people who set themselves up as consultants after being early retired or downsized out of larger corporations. While these individuals may lack some of the sophistication of a consultant who has been operating for many years, their hands-on experience can be invaluable. By sophistication, I refer more to the trappings, such as engagement letters, billing, or the follow-up and paper trail, than to the basic skills and ability to contribute to your company's success. One of the benefits of working with an experienced businessperson who has recently hung out a shingle as a consultant is that he or she is less likely to bill for every telephone conversation and piece of advice. Experienced consultants are usually more guarded about providing free guidance.

EVALUATING POTENTIAL CONSULTANTS

"I wish my large corporate clients were more like my smaller entrepreneurial clients. Working with a precise, no-nonsense, frugal client is often more productive than working with casual, often undisciplined, free spending bureaucrats" [emphasis mine].[5]

"There is no college or university that offers a degree in consulting. Nor does any state license consultants."[6] In addition, even those professional associations granting members a certification don't monitor performance of the certified members to any significant extent. It is difficult to imagine how such a monitoring system could work. So, we are left to relying on references and our ability to evaluate people.

As in the process for hiring staff, selecting a consultant will bring you inevitably to an interview. The candidate should be interviewing you as much as you interview the candidate. Here is a checklist of issues you should raise during the interview:

1. What do you regard as our principal need or problem?
2. What can you offer us that other consultants have not been able to provide?
3. How will we measure or evaluate your success in meeting our needs?
4. Are you willing to work on a performance basis?
5. What related experience have you had in working with similar situations?
6. Whom may we contact as references?

You should obtain clarification on the following issues: measurable objectives, business arrangements, experience and references (see Exhibit 5–2).[7]

Knowing how long the consultant has been in business is important. You want someone with whom you can develop *rapport*. You should be certain they have the *time* to devote to your project.[8] This caveat is very important and speaks to a problem of working with sole practitioners. My own experience as a consultant is that it is either feast or famine. When working alone, it is difficult to turn down business and even more difficult to subcontract out work. On the one hand, clients like to believe the consultant who is busy reflects competence and success. On the other hand, you don't want to contract with someone who does not have the time to give you the personal attention you need. I have run into the situation where a college professor operates a consulting practice and uses students to do most of the work. The clients are paying prices that reflect the professor's tariff, while he is paying minimum wage to the real consultants. By the way, using students who are supervised by a professor can be a rewarding and economically worthwhile exercise, but you ought to know the arrangement up front.

You should request the consultant provide a job specification (you may have to pay for this as it will take considerable effort for the consultant to prepare).[9]

Your interest should be in the consultant's current professional activities as they relate to your specific problem. In sum, you want an experienced specialist with appropriate credentials.[10]

Exhibit 5–1 ought to be required reading for every professional service supplier you engage: I am inserting it in this chapter because it

Exhibit 5–2   Interview Questions for Consultants

1. How long have you been in business? _____

    _____

2. Please discuss what other projects you currently have and how you will
   provide adequate time for our project. _____

    _____

3. What do you regard as our principal need or problem? _____

    _____

4. What can you offer us that other consultants have not been able to
   provide? _____

    _____

5. How will we measure or evaluate your success in meeting our needs? __

    _____

6. Are you willing to work entirely or in part on a performance basis? ____

    _____

7. What related experience have you had in working with similar situations?

    _____

8. Whom may we contact as references? _____

    _____

9. Will you provide a job specification and what will that cost? _____

    _____

10. Who will actually be working on my project? _____

    _____

11. What can I do to keep costs under control? _____

    _____

describes the range of emotions experienced by clients when faced with the need to hire a consultant.

I would wager that more managers have had unhappy experiences with information management consultants than any other specialty. I refer to suppliers of customized software. My own war story is typical of the stories I have heard from other entrepreneurs.

> *War Story.* In the early 1980s when my business was growing rapidly and I already had a controller and a general manager working for me, both with experience in moving from manual to computerized accounting, we undertook to computerize our bookkeeping. Feeling the complete idiot as far as computers, I relied entirely on my manager's and controller's judgment. They narrowed their choice based on off-the-shelf software and hardware that most closely met our requirements. Due to the unique characteristics of our invoicing history, it was determined that we would have to have the off-the-shelf software customized. Using recommendations of both the software vendor and the hardware vendor, we selected a customizer.
>
> My after-the-fact analysis of the situation was we *bought* a blackmailer when we signed on with the consultant. He changed the operating system and we did not have the program. So every change, every need to download the system, every glitch, required us to call him in. That first required tracking him down, arranging a convenient time and of course paying for several hours of work. I even began to suspect that he had some way of entering our system and triggering a problem any time he needed a little extra cash. So, with all our care in trying to select a system that would serve us well for many years, we ended up with a white elephant that we served.

If you are fortunate enough to know someone who has used a consultant, was satisfied, and will give you a recommendation, you are a long way toward identifying the right consultant for you. Be sure to understand exactly what problem was solved by the consultant and consider how it relates to your needs. On the other hand, there are sufficient consultants in the marketplace to locate one or more who have the specific skills and experience to help you solve your specific problem. There is absolutely no excuse for compromising on the consultant right for you.

USING A REQUEST FOR PROPOSAL (RFP)

More sophisticated users of consulting services (primarily government agencies and large corporations) use a Request for Proposal (RFP) as a standard operating procedure. Even a small business or a start-up can work with an RFP. It is an excellent vehicle for assisting you in defining your problem and clarifying the scope of the engagement for the candidates. It can also be used to measure the success of the engagement. Exhibit 5–3 shows a sample RFP.

Preparing a RFP should not be such a daunting task. It doesn't have to be a complicated or detailed document, unless you want it to be. An RFP consists of three essential elements:

- A description of the company, its product(s) or services, its industry or market, and its size.
- A definition of the problem that the company wants solved or the opportunity explored.
- The expectations from the consultant (i.e., time frames, basic skills).

A proposal is a key element in the paper trail mentioned frequently in this book and speaks to your professionalism as a manager:

- People forget. Both you and the consultant will not remember everything discussed at the beginning of an engagement.
- People make mistakes. If there is an error in a written proposal, you are more likely to recognize it and correct it.
- People leave their jobs after making commitments. If you are part of a larger organization, or the consultant is part of a firm, one of you may not be there at the end of the engagement.
- People tend to hear what they want to hear. You or the consultant may misinterpret what the other is saying or implying.
- Some people will try to take advantage of any misunderstandings.
- In general, things change.
- Proposals provide a documented record.[11]

RFPs can be dozens of pages long or one page. If you cannot define your company in one page and define your problem in one page, then you probably will have difficulty in communicating with a consultant, or anyone else for that matter. Don't try to define the consultant; most consultants will not invest their time and energy in responding to an RFP unless they have the skills to match. A financial consultant will read the outline of the company's problem and if it is a personnel issue or a technical issue will automatically pass over it.

Exhibit 5–3   Sample Request for Proposal (RFP)

The Company

Widgets International is a manufacturer based in the Ivory Coast. The company has two manufacturing facilities in the Ivory Coast and one facility in Madagascar. The Madagascar plant is a joint venture with a publicly traded firm. Widgets International generated revenues in 1995 in excess of ninety million dollars and is one of the dominant manufacturers in the widget market. The Madagascar operation was established three years ago in order to provide a low-cost alternative manufacturing location for the company's expanding market in the Ivory Coast.

The Madagascar facility currently employs five hundred employees. Widgets International has embarked on an active effort to export production from its Madagascar facility to other markets in Africa.

Widgets International has targeted the market and is in the process of determining which of its products can compete in the market.

The Market

This is a $54 billion industry. Widgets International's product line is a category within the market. Within the widget category, the dominant companies are General Widgets, International Business Widgets, and American Wudgets and Widgets.

The company has targeted Belize for its initial market. There is one major trade show each year. Sales are generally made through independent sales representatives.

The Products

Widgets International's marketing consultant has identified fifteen of the products within the company's existing product line that are going to be initially offered to customers. Samples of the products will be provided with this RFP. The company intends to offer these products in limited markets. The current packaging as configured for the Ivory Coast market is inappropriate for the Belize market.

Scope of Project

This project has several elements to it.

1. Develop a corporate identity.
2. Develop individual packaging for each product.
3. Develop catalog sheets and selling materials.
4. Design, build, and install a 20-foot trade show booth.

(continued)

Exhibit 5–3   *(continued)*

1. Develop a corporate identity.

The company is desirous of establishing an overall 'look' for its packaging and advertising materials. This look should incorporate the company's Ivory Coast origins but establish itself as a quality product line designed for the market. The corporate identity development will precede the other elements of the project.

2. Develop individual packaging for each product.

Samples of products have already been sent to sales reps and potential customers. During the course of this exercise, some products may be dropped. However, the company wishes to have prototype packaging on display in its booth at the Widget Show. Packaging should reflect the high quality of the product line and be effective point of purchase (POP) sales elements. Packaging design should consider the need for durability during shipping, requirements of the environment, and provide the necessary information to make an intelligent purchase decision.

3. Develop catalog sheets and selling materials.

Product catalog sheets must incorporate full-color photographs of the product in use and packaged. Also, information must be included for the buyers and merchandisers indicating master carton pack, individual unit pack, stock-keeping numbers and codes, ordering information, and a description of the product. Samples of catalog sheets will be provided. This phase of the project will include price list formation, presentation folio development, and guidelines for print advertising.

4. Design, build, and install 20-foot display booth.

The vendor is requested to quote on this element both as a complete package and broken down in stages. The booth should consist of slat wall elements for displaying product, seating, storage, and graphics.

Timing

Widget International wishes to introduce its product line at the Show. The booth will have to be shipped the first week of January. Prototype samples should be shipped with the booth. Catalog sheets can be delivered by the last week in November.

Formal quotations should be provided to Widget International by June 15 for budget approval.

Exhibit 5–3 *(continued)*

Personnel

This project will be managed by the marketing consultant to Widgets International. However, approvals will be required from the company's Managing Director. Therefore, all sketches, rough drafts, layouts, copy, etc. will have to be provided in a form that can be easily transmitted by facsimile.

Reporting

The company is desirous of receiving updates and status reports twice a month. These reports may be memos or more detailed reports and should be delivered to the marketing consultant prior to the first and the fifteenth of each month.

The downside to RFPs is that they are time consuming to prepare and administer and they require a five-step procedure:

1. Develop the solicitation package (the RFP plus supporting elements).
2. Compile a list of prospects.
3. Read, review, evaluate and cull the proposals.
4. Hold conferences or interviews with some or all the candidates.
5. Negotiate a contract.

EVALUATING THE PROPOSAL

Whether or not you provide an RFP to the candidates, you should expect a written proposal from anyone who wants to be seriously considered for the engagement. "Look for clear, concise writing and the avoidance of endless purple, turgid prose."[12] I agree, and I would add *sloppy writing reflects attitude.* If the proposal writer is unable to produce a clear coherent proposal, he or she likely will have difficulty communicating recommendations and assisting in implementation. On the other hand, there are geniuses who are dyslexic, and there are problems we can get solved without detailed written communications. I have met consultants whose hands appear to be attached backward, whom I would be pleased to have come in and solve some computer malfunction or to straighten out a production problem.

The proposal should reflect an understanding of the problem that you outlined either verbally or through the RFP; however, it should not simply be a restatement of your description of the problem. The proposal should describe, in some detail, the steps and the process the consultant anticipates will be necessary to achieve a positive result. In addition, the proposal should set forth the consultant's fee structure, including anticipated out-of-pocket expenses, and should describe *your* responsibilities.

The proposal will describe the goals to be achieved, but will never promise to fulfill them. This is because the consultant cannot be certain that:

- You have described the problem accurately.
- You will fulfill your responsibilities in a cooperative manner.
- His performance is not dependent upon that of a third party.

The consultant will not expose himself to nonfeasance liability in this regard.[13] The following war story illustrates the third point just mentioned.

> *War Story.* A consulting engagement that I participated in as a subcontractor to another consultant addresses the issue of performance being dependent on a third party. The primary consultant had originally been retained by the client to assist in identifying a COO for his business. In the end, the client hired someone that the consultant recommended not hiring. In the subsequent engagement, which I worked on, we were trying to mold a program around the limitations of the COO, rather than build on the strengths of the COO. At one point, the client complained to me about the cost of the engagement, and I candidly observed that had he followed the advice of my associate at the outset, he would probably not have even needed us at this point. Here we were, spending the client's money to make his choice work out, rather than focusing on assisting the CEO and COO in building the company.

A good "proposal will not limit itself to a specific time frame for the completion of the project for the same reason."[14] Both the consultant and you are not sitting around with nothing to do except deal with your problem. The ability to complete a project in a timely fashion may depend a great deal on your ability to focus attention and resources. This is even more relevant where the consultant is engaged in the implementation of his or her recommendations and not just recommending a solution.

CONTRACTS

There are four types of contracts with consultants—oral, signed proposal, formal written contract, and letter of intent. I would recommend avoiding, at all cost, an oral contract. Unless the engagement is a simple one-day (or less) affair involving little or no preparation or follow-through, I believe in a paper trail. I also don't make a major distinction between a signed proposal and a letter of intent. In Chapter 10, you will find the "Engagement Bill of Rights" (Exhibit 11–2). If you add the EBR to a proposal or a letter of intent, I believe you have effectively converted either of those two documents into formal contracts.

Although I don't want to digress too much here, I have heard it said that contracts only come into play when one party is unhappy. Another observation I have heard is that a dishonest person can get around any contract. Formal written contracts properly prepared by one attorney and reviewed by another attorney can be very expensive insurance policies. If the value of a project is so large as to justify the expense to both parties to engage lawyers to reach agreement, I recommend breaking the project down into segments. Enter into signed proposals or letters of intent for each segment and avoid the expense and consumption of time that will inevitably go along with a formal written contract.

Exhibit 5–4 is a checklist of issues to consider when drafting a contract with a consultant.

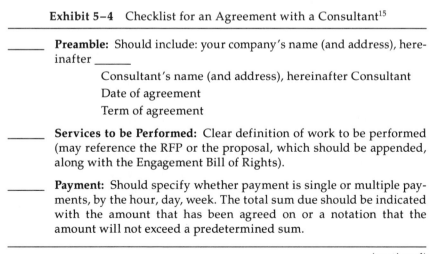

Exhibit 5–4   Checklist for an Agreement with a Consultant[15]

_____   **Preamble:** Should include: your company's name (and address), hereinafter _____

Consultant's name (and address), hereinafter Consultant

Date of agreement

Term of agreement

_____   **Services to be Performed:** Clear definition of work to be performed (may reference the RFP or the proposal, which should be appended, along with the Engagement Bill of Rights).

_____   **Payment:** Should specify whether payment is single or multiple payments, by the hour, day, week. The total sum due should be indicated with the amount that has been agreed on or a notation that the amount will not exceed a predetermined sum.

(continued)

Exhibit 5–4   *(continued)*

_____ **Terms of Payment:** Should indicate frequency of payments. Or if payment is to be made against certain performance requirements (i.e., upon delivery of final report), upon submission of an invoice.

_____ **Expenses:** If you have agreed to reimburse for out-of-pocket expenses, it should be noted. If consultant must obtain prior approval above certain sums, it should be noted. If all expenses are the responsibility of consultant, it should also be noted.

_____ **Independent Contractor Status:** Contract should include language such as:

Consultant is an independent contractor. Consultant has the right to perform services for others during the term of this Agreement. Consultant has the right to perform the services required by this Agreement at any place, location, or time.

_____ **Intellectual Property Ownership:** Language should clearly establish your ownership:

Consultant assigns all rights in all designs, creations, improvements, original works of authorship, formulas, processes, know-how, techniques, inventions, and all other information or items created by Consultant during the term of this Agreement. The rights assigned include title and interest in all patent, copyright, trade secret, trademark and other proprietary rights.

_____ **Confidentiality:** Include clear and concise language obligating consultant, his or her employees, and subcontractors to maintain confidentiality, such as:

Consultant will not disclose or use, either during or after the term of this Agreement, any proprietary or confidential information of without prior written permission except to the extent necessary to perform services on Contractor's behalf. Upon termination of Consultant's services, Consultant shall deliver all materials in Consultant's possession relating to the project.

_____ **State and Federal Taxes:** To avoid potential exposure as an employer, you should include a disclaimer: Company will not withhold FICA (Social Security and Medicare taxes) from Consultant's compensation contributions on Consultant's behalf, or withhold state or federal income tax from Consultant's payments. Consultant shall pay all taxes incurred while performing services under this Agreement—including all applicable income taxes.

Exhibit 5–4 *(continued)*

_____ **Terminating the Agreement:** Be certain to include well defined reasons for termination:

With reasonable cause, both parties may terminate this Agreement, effective immediately upon giving written notice. Reasonable cause includes:

   —A material violation of this Agreement, or

   —Any act exposing the other party to liability to others for personal injury or property damage.

_____ **Exclusive Agreement:** No other agreements between the parties.

_____ **Severability:** If any part of this Agreement is held unenforceable, the rest of the Agreement will continue in effect.

_____ **Applicable Law:** Indicate which state's jurisdiction will apply.

_____ **Signatures**

Name: (Yours) _____

By: _____
                 (Signature)

_____
         (Typed or Printed Name)

Title: _____

Date: _____

Name of Contractor: _____

By: _____
                 (Signature)

_____
         (Typed or Printed Name)

Date: _____

THE THREE Rs: CONSULTANTS

RECAP

- Recognize you have a problem—if you do not acknowledge that you have a problem, you will not buy into the consultant's recommendations. In all likelihood, you will not implement the recommendations either.
- Realize you can't solve it yourself—it is insufficient to admit you have a problem unless you also acknowledge you cannot solve the problem yourself, either because of lack of time, human resources, or skill.
- Define what you want done—to obtain measurable results, you need to determine what you expect from the engagement.
- Develop a list of candidates—only after you have defined what you want done. Ordering events this way also narrows the search field.
- Request a proposal—in writing, if possible, and expect a formal proposal in return after the initial meeting.

RESOURCES

- National Association of Personnel Services, 3133 Mt. Vernon Avenue, Alexandria, VA 22305, Tel: 703-684-0180, Fax: 703-684-0071 (awards the Certified Personnel Consultant [CPC] designation).
- Association of Executive Search Consultants, 230 Park Avenue, Suite 1549, New York, NY 10169-0005, Tel: 212-949-9556, Fax: 212-949-9560.
- Institute of Management Consultants, 521 Fifth Avenue, 35th Floor, New York, NY 10175, Tel: 212-697-8262, Fax: 212-949-6571 (awards the Certified Management Consultant [CMC] designation).
- National Bureau of Professional Management Consultants, 3577 Fourth Avenue, San Diego, CA 92103, Tel: 619-297-2207, Fax: 619-692-0351. Operates certification program (Certified Professional Management Consultant [CPMC]), will provide referrals in geographic area and specialty required.

THE THREE RS *(continued)*

- American Consultants League, 1290 North Palm Avenue, Suite 112, Sarasota, FL 34236, Tel: 941-952-9290, Fax: 941-379-6024. Supplies inquiring clients with a list of members in their geographic area and specialty being sought. Annual directory available for $39.00 and a how-to book for potential clients for $96.00 (see references).

- International Association of Professional Security Consultants, 13819-G Walsingham Road, Suite 350, Largo, FL 34644, Tel: 813-596-6696, Fax: 813-596-6696.

- Independent Computer Consultants Association, 11131 South Towne Square, Suite F, St. Louis, MO 63123, Tel: 314-829-1675, Fax: 314-487-1345 (network of independent computer consultants).

- National Association of Computer Consultant Businesses, 1250 Connecticut Avenue NW, Suite 700, Washington, DC 20036, Tel: 202-637-6483, Fax: 202-637-9195 (provides technical support services in programming, systems analysis, and software/hardware engineering).

- Information Systems Consultants Association, PO Box 467190, Atlanta, GA 30346, Tel: 404-458-3080 (consulting services related to business information systems).

- Franchise Consultants International Association, 5147 S. Angela Road, Memphis, TN 38117, Tel: 901-761-3084.

- American Association of Cost Engineers, 209 Prairie Avenue, Morgantown, WV 26507-1557, Tel: 304-296-8444, Fax: 304-291-5728.

- American Consulting Engineers Council, 1015 15th Street, NW, Suite 802, Washington, DC 20005, Tel: 202-347-7474, Fax: 202-898-0068 (Independent private practice engineering companies).

- The Expert Marketplace©, Internet address—http://expertmarket .com/em. Bills itself as the marketplace for consultants—"The" manufacturing resource for identifying and selecting consultants.

(continued)

THE THREE RS *(continued)*

- Association of Professional Material Handling Consultants, 8720 Red Oak Boulevard, Charlotte, NC 28217, Tel: 704-558-4749.
- Institute of Certified Business Counselors, PO Box 70326, Eugene, OR 97401, 541-345-8064. Describes itself as a professional organization dedicated to the continuing successful operation of privately held businesses, either through change of procedure or ownership.
- Professional and Technical Consultants Association, PO Box 4142, Mountain View, CA 94040, Tel: 800-747-2822. Members must adhere to ethical standards and provide references and be examined before joining. It offers a no-fee referral service and produces the *Directory of Consultants* ($15.00), which lists its over 300 members. It also produces an annual *Survey of Consulting Rates and Business Practices* ($25.00), which is very useful.

REFERENCES

- *Choosing a Consultant (Information Technology Consultants).*
- *Choosing and Using a Consultant.**
- *Encyclopedia of Associations*   Most libraries will have this set of books from which you can locate names and addresses of trade groups and rep organizations. Sometimes you can call a trade association and obtain the rep association's address and telephone number.
- *Hiring Independent Contractors*****   A good resource for learning about the legal aspects of hiring consultants, it includes sample contracts.
- *How to Select and Use Consultants*   Although it may be difficult to obtain, this is a worthwhile text.
- *How to Select and Manage Consultants.*
- *Making the Most of Management Consulting Services.*
- *The Secrets of Successfully Finding, Negotiating with and Retaining an Expert Consultant*   This is a good basic discussion of all the issues relating to retaining consultants.
- *Utilizing Consultants Successfully.*

6

CREATIVE SERVICES

This chapter covers a broad spectrum of creative services providers: advertising agencies, architects, graphic artists, industrial designers, packaging designers, and public relations firms. Although the mix of subjects in this chapter may seem a bit strange, almost everyone would agree that architects and graphic designers fall into the category of "creative professions." Because architects, product designers, and graphic artists offer the same management challenges of balancing their creativity with functionality, I packaged them in the same chapter.

The commonality of dealing with most of the creative people we encounter while running a business is balancing their creativity with our need for practical and functional solutions. I have enjoyed most, if not all, my interactions with product designers and graphic artists. They can be fun people with which to work. But over the years, I discovered that creative types often work without considering the *purpose* of what they have been asked to produce. For them, a catalog sheet is a clean canvas on which they get paid to be creative, while I see the catalog sheet as a marketing and selling tool. How many times have you looked at an advertising piece and been unable to figure out what is being offered? It may be beautiful, even elegant, but what is the product or service? Have you ever seen a building that looks great—but the people who work there hate it? It is as important to understand that many creative people know as little about how to sell your product as your attorney knows about how to manage your finances. You eat, sleep, and drink your business, and you know your customers and your competitors. Therefore you must maintain strong control over these creative people. If not, they will create something that simply won't work for you.

Earlier, I discussed the importance of learning the vernacular and the language of the profession being sought. Nowhere is this advice more important than with this general grouping of professions. The References at the end of this chapter even include several dictionaries of graphic art terms.

ADVERTISING AGENCIES

Retail businesses, consumer products companies, and industrial products companies with a broad market base all use advertising agencies to develop and carry out advertising campaigns. Some advertising agencies get involved with corporate identity work, or assist in new product launches and new market penetrations. Most agencies generate the bulk of their revenue from commissions for the placement of the advertising. "Advertising agencies can brainstorm your ads, produce ads for all print and broadcast media, buy space in magazines and newspapers, and buy air time on radio and TV. They can create direct-mail campaigns and rent the appropriate mailing lists. They can design your signs and stationery. They can produce your brochure, sales video, or annual report. They can place your billboards across the country. Agencies serve their clients with every conceivable advertising and design service and, in many cases, also offer public relations services."[1]

The *function* of an ad agency includes these tasks:

- Help you sell more product or service.
- Develop concepts and advertising programs to promote your company and aid in the sales of your product(s).
- Coordinate all the creative personnel necessary to implement an advertising campaign.
- Assist in the selection and then place the advertising in the appropriate media.

"Are You Ready for at Least Three Months of Exquisite Agony?" That is a chapter title in *Conducting an Agency Search* by Allan Gardner, published by the American Association of Advertising Agencies (AAAA). The AAAA has produced a number of other useful brochures, all available from their Publications Department (see Resources and References at the end of this section). Gardner goes on, "You think this is going to be fun, huh? The smell of the hunt. The thrust and parry of competition. The thrill of victory. The agony of defeat. Well, yes, there is all of that. There's also the drudgery. And the tedium. . . . And the time.

The time. The time." After Gardner puts the fear of the process into the reader, he goes on to provide valuable guidelines for managing that process, including an outline and approximate schedule for selecting an agency. He also discusses the pros and cons of hiring a consultant to help you find the agency.

Dennison recommends, "A good small business agency will be able to handle the following:

a) Strategy development.
b) Copywriting.
c) Design/art direction.
d) Production of print ads, including illustration and photography.
e) Production of TV and radio spots.
f) Media buying.
g) Overall coordination, planning and budgeting.
h) (Perhaps) Public relations."

Developing a list of candidates may be another daunting task for you as a first-time exercise. The usual sources, such as business acquaintances or the Yellow Pages, may not be very helpful. Asking salespeople from the local radio and TV stations and newspapers may be asking for problems. They are likely to recommend agencies with whom they have a good relationship and not necessarily agencies appropriate for your needs. One method of developing a list of candidates is to make a list of advertisers whose ads you find particularly appealing, calling the companies, and asking who created the ad. At the same time, you can perform a preliminary interview to find out how satisfied the advertiser was with the agency.

> Two essential points must be kept in mind as the selection program proceeds. The first is that the interviewing of possible agencies must be handled as if it were new employees who were being hired. The same standards and the same criteria (such as talent, competence, reliability, dependability, integrity, and financial responsibility) must be applied not only to the candidate agencies themselves but, also, to those within the agencies who would be handling the account—those with whom company personnel would be working.
>
> Second, after the choice is made, both the integration of the agency into the company's marketing function and operations and the overall company-agency *relationship* must be managed, in a way not dissimilar to that in which departments within the company are managed. The fact that the agency is external cannot allow abdication of the management responsibility, nor denial of the point that the agency is fulfilling a charge which, were it not for the highly specialized and yet diverse creativity required, would belong inherently on the company marketing department's

organization chart. Unless that responsibility is exercised, the agency will not be able to assume its role as an integral part of the company's marketing apparatus.[2]

War Story. We developed a new product with packaging, specifically the graphics, that presented serious problems. The item was a snap-together rigid plastic grid system that enabled the consumer to create shelving in a closet. To highlight the product on both the package and in the advertising material, the in-use photograph illustrated the white product in an all-red closet with all the accessories and clothing in various shades of red. The effect was dramatic—the product jumped out of the photograph. Nevertheless, the photograph was produced by four-color process. I attended the "press proofing," which involved standing on the bridge of a $2.5 million four-color printing press and checking the output. No matter what the printer did, he was unable to get the color right. Finally, we determined that the problem was in the color separations. They had to shut down the press, redo the color separations, remake the plates, and schedule another press proofing. I have no idea what it cost the printer to have such an expensive piece of machinery tied up for such a long time without generating revenue, but I learned a valuable lesson. If you don't take an active part in the process, you will not be satisfied with the results and will have no one to blame but yourself.

One expert suggested preparing a job description just as you would for an executive or the way you define departmental responsibility.[3] For an entrepreneur hiring for the first time, this may seem to be a difficult, if not impossible, task. But it involves simply establishing criteria or preparing a list of tasks you want the agency to accomplish. This will help immeasurably in the process of evaluating agencies. Your list should also include your corporate objectives and specific limitations, such as finances, human resources, geographic area, and media. Defining your company's *requirements* from an advertising agency and your company's *limitations* will automatically narrow the field of contenders. Some agencies, to support their overhead, require minimum annual billings for any one client to be in the six-digit-plus range. If your advertising needs are limited to print media in specific industrial markets, your agency should be compatible with that reality. If your business is a local retailer, you shouldn't be spending money for a national firm. Try to gather information from up to a dozen agencies, interviewing six, and then narrowing the group to three finalists.

"Prepare a rough outline of your marketing and advertising objectives. Have these guidelines handy when you start your inquiries into ad agencies."[4]

The interview process itself will generate additional guidelines for the final selection phase. Each interview will reveal ideas you can apply to the next interview. You can go back to candidates interviewed earlier and pose some of the issues revealed during the later interviews.

"Because many of those who choose advertising agencies and make decisions about advertising don't know how to judge whether or not an advertisement will be effective . . . There are advertising agency people who educate their clients. There are advertising consultants who create effective advertising. There are media salespeople whose recommendations have made the difference between a campaign's success or lack of success."[5] You can decide beforehand what you want to achieve with your advertising, or together with the candidates. Additionally, you should agree on the milestones and measures of success of an advertising campaign.

Common Mistake 1: "Putting in charge of advertising a person whose responsibilities do not coincide with the purpose of the advertising." Absent a clear understanding of who that ought to be, the CEO should undertake the responsibility. Even if the consensus in the organization is that the purpose of advertising is to increase sales, we shouldn't designate the human resources person (only available person with extra time) to manage the process. That HR person may have had experience in advertising or managing advertising for another company, but the HR person will naturally tend to view advertising from his or her perspective and role within the company. More importantly, it is paramount to have a clear understanding within your business before you begin the process of what you want your advertising to accomplish.[6]

Common Mistake 2: "Choosing an advertising agency with the wrong expertise." There are dozens of specialities within the practice of law. There are also large firms and small firms. So too with advertising agencies. Specialization runs the range of media—print, radio, TV, direct mail or direct response, trade and institutional, consumer, and so on. Because my sense is that most readers of this book, and especially this chapter, are not about to launch a search for a major New York advertising firm for a several-million-dollar advertising campaign, the discussion will focus on issues relating to small advertising budgets.[7]

First you have to define what you want the advertising program to accomplish: greater sales (which is ultimately what is desired anyway), greater traffic (in a store or at a trade show), introduction to the market of a new product, general interest in the company, etc. Then you have to decide how much you want to spend, either as a percentage or as a real number. You may also insert into the evaluation

Exhibit 6–1   Interview Questions for Creative Services

1. Which of your clients market their products or services the way we do?

   _____

2. How successful has your advertising (graphics, copy, photos) been for them? _____

   _____

3. Were criteria established beforehand to measure success? _____

   _____

4. Whom can I call at those clients for more information? _____

   _____

5. Is our account likely to be profitable enough for you to put forth your best efforts? _____

   _____

6. Who will actually work on our account? _____

   _____

7. What are the qualifications of these people? _____

   _____

8. How do you suggest measuring the effectiveness of your work? _____

   _____

9. Please describe the process you will go through to develop our project.

   _____

10. What are your fee structures and billing arrangements? _____

    _____

11. What do you understand about our business? _____

    _____

Exhibit 6–1 *(continued)*

For graphic artists, and so on.

a. What projects were performed directly with the client? Advertising agency?

_____

b. How much of the project was defined beforehand?

_____

c. What was the client's background relating to advertising?

_____

process consideration of where you anticipate taking your business. This has been mentioned in earlier chapters. If this is the first of what may be many advertising campaigns, growing progressively in size, scope and cost, you will probably want to talk with agencies large enough to accommodate your anticipated business. Remember, you don't want to be moving your account every few years; the selection process is time consuming and invariably causes upheaval.[8]

Exhibit 6–1 lists questions to ask candidates before you hire an ad agency.

Ask yourself:

- Does the agency discuss its fee structure willingly and openly?
- Does the style of their printed and broadcast work fit my style?
- Does their personal style fit mine? Am I comfortable with them as people?
- Are they willing to explain the reasoning behind their advertising decisions?
- Will they welcome my participation in brainstorming or creative strategy sessions?
- Have they handled accounts similar to mine?
- Does the agency handle advertising for my direct competitors?[9]

THE THREE RS: ADVERTISING AGENCIES

RECAP

- Define your needs—before your search, identify what you expect from the advertising campaign.
- Interview agencies as though they were potential employees—perform the same type of due diligence as if they were working for you.
- Choose an agency with the correct expertise for your needs—knowledge of and experience with other firms in your industry is of critical importance.
- After selection, you have to manage the relationship—you may not assume that careful selection absolves you of the obligation to manage the ongoing relationship.
- Choose the appropriate person to manage the relationship—the person overseeing the agency's work should be the individual with responsibility for the goals of the campaign (e.g., the sales manager if the goal is an increase in sales volume).

RESOURCES

- American Association of Advertising Agencies, 666 Third Avenue, New York, NY 10017-4056, Tel: 212-682-2500. Offers a wide range of useful literature and information.
- American Advertising Federation, 1101 Vermont Avenue, Suite 500, Washington, DC 20005, Tel: 202-898-0090.
- Cable TV Advertising Bureau, 757 Third Avenue, New York, NY 10017, Tel: 212-751-7770.
- League of Advertising Agencies, Two South End Avenue, Suite 4C, New York, NY 10280, Tel: 212-945-4990.
- Newspaper Association of America, 711 Third Avenue, New York, NY 10017, Tel: 212-856-6300.

THE THREE RS *(continued)*

- Point-of-Purchase Advertising Institute, 66 North Van Brunt Street, Englewood, NJ 07631, Tel: 201-894-8899.
- Radio Advertising Bureau, 304 Park Avenue South, New York, NY 10010, Tel: 212-254-4800.

REFERENCES

- *The Advertising Handbook for Small Businesses***** Not only advertising agencies, but all aspects of advertising and public relations, are covered in this excellent basic book.
- *Conducting an Agency Search* This is a superb monograph, under 50 pages but full of information; there are chapters on all the stages of a search.
- *Marketing Handbook, Volume 1: Marketing Practices, Chapter 37** It has a textbook format, with good information.
- *The 27 Most Common Mistakes in Advertising* A thin, very easy-to-read, and informative book, it discusses the pitfalls and mistakes companies and people make.
- The AAAA Publications Directory includes some interesting titles such as *Reasons for Choosing an AAAA Agency, Guide to Buying Advertising Art and Photography* (useful in selecting graphic artists and commercial photographers), *Glossary of Advertising Art-Buying Terms*, and *A Client's Guide to Working with Your AAAA Agency*.

PUBLIC RELATIONS FIRMS

Publicity can be a stand-alone device for marketing your company, or its products and services; or it can be used together with an advertising campaign. Public relations (PR) firms and freelancers can assist you in getting media exposure that you would be unable to develop on your own. Publicity can offset a negative image or generate a positive image of your company, its products, and its employees and management. "The objective with publicity is to increase the number of times you deliver your message to your target audiences, to make new impressions on them, and develop in more detail the message communicated."[10] Public relations is everything you do, outside of paid advertising, to garner media attention or shape broad public perception of your business.[11]

The *function* of a publicist includes these tasks:

- Improve or change the image of your company or its management within the local, regional, or national community at large, or your industry.
- Establish or introduce your company to the business community or community at large.
- Introduce a new product or process.
- Manage an event, positive or negative, which has or will occur.

"The key to any agency-client relationship is picking the right one at the beginning, and supervising it properly. Personnel departments write job descriptions before screening applicants. Go thou and do likewise. Know where you want to go before you hire someone to help you get there."[12] How many times have you read similar advice in this book? My hope is that restating the message in different ways will help you understand its importance.

We are again discussing a profession that requires you to look within your organization and your business before you begin searching for the right agency with which to work. Before beginning the search, develop an internal document that defines your expectations for the engagement.

One of the best and most concise descriptions of hiring and managing PR professionals appears in an article in *O'Dwyer's Directory of Public Relations Firms.* This advice alone is probably worth the $110 price tag for the directory, even if you don't use the listings. Additional information is also available from the Public Relations Society of America (PRSA) and its inner circle, The Counselors Academy. There is no shortage of books on PR; the PRSA's *Bibliography for Public Relations Professionals* is 62 pages long.

Exhibit 6–2 lists Jack O'Dwyer's Ten Rules for Shopping for a PR firm from *How to Hire and Get the Most from Outside PR Counsel*.

Barhydt gives some more advice on selecting a publicist: "Check with members of your trade association, or its executive director. Ask the public relations person handling press arrangements at your industry's trade show."[13]

Exhibit 6–3 lists questions to ask publicists before retaining one.

"When you have selected your agency, phone the others and give them the bad news in as positive a manner as possible." Follow up with a letter thanking them for their time and effort.[14]

Be certain that you have either a confidentiality clause in your agency agreement or have a confidentiality agreement inserted as an addendum to the engagement letter or contract. In addition to addressing confidentiality, your agreement should include:

- A clear statement of purpose.
- A description of the services to be provided.
- A defined explanation of compensation.
- Clarification of your right to use the work.
- Stated term of the agreement and conditions for cancellation.

Exhibit 6–2 Ten Rules for Shopping for a PR Firm

---

1. Obtain complete current account lists of prospective firms with names and phones of client contacts.
2. Check with the media in your city and industry on what PR firms and counselors are highly regarded.
3. Ask for people who will be on your account to attend presentation.
4. Keep client review committee small.
5. Beware overpromising by PR firm. You will be biggest factor in success of PR effort.
6. Insist on fast start to account; test media contacts of firm right away.
7. PR is supposed to be efficient. Beware of high-cost communications materials like booklets, advertising, sales promotion devices. Advertising is often pitched as PR.
8. Third-party endorsement is key element of PR. Press, analysts, government reps must fully understand your story including negative elements.
9. Don't hire a PR firm to reach the accounts it handles.
10. Beware of the firm that brags about its famous clients and can "squeeze you in." It may have little time for you.

Exhibit 6–3   Interview Questions for Public Relations Firms

1. Please provide a complete list of current accounts with the names and telephone numbers of contacts. _____

   _____

2. Will my company fit in with your current client list? _____

   _____

3. Please describe your understanding of my company's markets. My company's industry. _____

   _____

4. Please share with me some creative programs you have developed and explain the measurable results. _____

   _____

5. What is your turnover rate and why did the last four clients leave? _____

   _____

6. What would it cost to have a written proposal prepared? _____

   _____

7. What would you anticipate would be the initial engagement term, the cost, and the measurable results? _____

   _____

8. Please explain your billing policy including management, account service executives, and so on. _____

   _____

9. Will you provide some examples of your agency's writing skills? _____

   _____

10. What is your firm's policy regarding briefings, how is information transmitted from the client to the firm's staff? _____

    _____

Exhibit 6–3   *(continued)*

11. What kinds of mailing lists do you use and how do you keep them up to date? _____

_____

12. What can we do to get the relationship off to a fast start? _____

_____

13. What is the role of our CEO? _____

_____

14. What does the PR account team need from us? _____

_____

15. Who will be the people working on our account? _____

_____

16. What other accounts will our account executive be working on? _____

_____

_____

THE THREE RS: PR FIRMS

RECAP

- Be sure you understand what you want accomplished—define your goals, have measurable, quantifiable targets.
- Be certain you are prepared to be available for the PR process—PR doesn't happen in a vacuum; you must actively participate in the process itself, as well as supervising, by being available for interviews, public speaking, and so on.
- Ask for names from editors in the media where you want exposure—they can tell you about PR firms they have worked with.

(continued)

THE THREE RS *(continued)*

- Obtain from candidates a complete list of their clients—as opposed to a partial list that only includes their satisfied customers.

RESOURCES

- Public Relations Society of America, 33 Irving Place, New York, NY 10003-2376, Tel: 212-460-1462, Fax: 995-0757. Offers a *Bibliography for Public Relations Professionals, Counselors Academy Directory.*

REFERENCES

- *The Advertising Handbook for Small Businesses*****   This is an excellent basic book for all aspects of advertising and PR, not only advertising agencies.
- *The Complete Book of Product Publicity**   If you can locate a copy in a public or university library, this is an interesting book, even if it is a bit out of date.
- *O'Dwyer's Directory of Public Relations Firms*****   In addition to providing profiles on most PR firms, the directory includes interesting articles on selection and use of such firms.

GRAPHIC ARTISTS, COMMERCIAL PHOTOGRAPHERS, COPYWRITERS, PRODUCT DESIGNERS, PACKAGE DESIGNERS

Since there is a great deal of crossover between this section of the book and the section later in this chapter on freelancers, I urge you to read both sections. You may avoid direct contact with freelance graphic artists, copywriters, and commercial photographers if all your advertising efforts are managed by an advertising agency. However, most start-up businesses do not have the luxury of assigning the oversight of these functions to an agency. Graphic artists create the graphics and then produce the final mechanicals of advertisements, catalog sheets, packaging, and so on. Copywriters write the descriptive copy incorporated into the artwork provided by graphic artists. Commercial photographers create and produce the photographs sometimes used by graphic artists. You will probably never find one of these professionals who has ever actually sold a product or a service (other than their own services) although you may find professionals who have worked on projects for similar products or services, or clients in the same industry.

A copywriter can restate your description of a product in grammatically correct English, but in all likelihood will not know the conventions and vernacular of your trade or industry. Copywriters are also not perfect—I have corrected "final copy" received from copywriters.

Since graphic artists, commercial photographers, and copywriters may be key contributors to your effort to develop your company, understanding how to select and manage them is essential.

The *function* of graphic artists and copywriters includes these tasks:

- Create sales and point of purchase materials.
- Translate your ideas into graphic representations and/or written presentations.
- Incorporate creative concepts and informational data into company's sales and communications materials.
- Assist in communicating company's message to target markets, investors, employees, and vendors.

I have had some of the most enjoyable and most frustrating interactions in my business career working with graphic artists, commercial photographers, copywriters, and product designers. One of the problems with these professionals is that they tend, of necessity, to be generalists. You are unlikely to find a graphic artist who has specialized in your industry, or any industry for that matter. You may be able to find a copywriter who has focused on writing for company employee communications, but it is doubtful you will find a copywriter who has concentrated on writing retail consumer product ads or catalog sheets for electronic components. As a result, you must educate the professional about your business, your product or service, and your industry. You either pay for this learning process up front or indirectly through the trial-and-error process that will occur if they aren't provided with proper orientation to the business.

The process of preparing a Request for Proposal (RFP), which was detailed in Chapter 5, will assist you in defining the firms or individuals you want to retain for this phase of your business. The RFP itself will define out some of the unqualified candidates who may waste your time if you don't have an RFP. The RFP will provide the candidates with a method of developing a proposal and will give you a way of comparing the proposals. Lastly, the RFP will serve as a benchmark against which you can measure performance once you hire someone.

Even if you have retained an advertising agency to manage your advertising efforts, that doesn't absolve you of your management responsibilities over the graphic artist and copywriter who will be hired by the agency. Allowing the agency to be intermediary is like "whispering down the lane," and you can be almost certain you won't get what you asked for.

Maintain a file of resumes and brochures of commercial artists, copywriters, commercial photographers, product designers, and packaging designers. Each time you receive unsolicited literature and each time you request literature, add it to this file. Even if you are satisfied with your current vendor, collect information on others to build up your resource file.

Every time you observe an advertisement or some other sales vehicle that intrigues you, attempt to find out who created it and place this information in the resource file. Then when the time comes for a change in vendors, you will have accumulated a list of candidates.

If you don't already have a list and need to make a change, contact the usual sources—friends, business associates, allied professions. A good printer should be able to recommend some graphic artists, copywriters, and commercial photographers. A model maker or a patent attorney may be able to recommend a promising product designer. Your packaging vendor ought to be able to offer some suggestions about packaging designers.

Look for professionals who not only have talent, but who also appear to be compatible to your style of working. Take note of candidates' attitude and ask references about the ease of working with the candidates. You want to avoid having to do battle over design elements of every project.

A note of caution. Creative people like to trot out their awards. Graphic design awards are issued by graphics trade magazines and professional organizations. They have little to do with the commercial success of the package or sales material receiving the award. I have been involved in developing packaging that received two very prestigious design awards—the Package Designers Council Award of Excellence and a Desi Award from Graphics Design: USA (see Exhibit 6–4). And I can assure you those awards didn't sell one more product, nor did the judges make their decisions on the basis of commercial success. Winning awards is important to designers and may give them a warm feeling but they don't translate into more sales. Choose the designer who can show you his design increased sales by 50 percent over the designer with a wall full of awards.

Exhibit 6-4   Design Awards

Package Designers Council

Recognition for Excellence in Design

CLOSET ACCESSORIES PACKAGING
Independent Products Co., Inc.
Design: Peter Bressler Design Associates, Philadelphia PA
          Peter Byar, Allyson Smith, Peter Bressler

This certificate is awarded to Finalists in the
Annual PDC Gold Awards Package Design Competition.
Jurors of the Competition represented professionals
from Corporate Design Services, independent design
consultants, marketing executives, and editorial directors.

PRESIDENT

COMPETITION COMMITTEE CHAIRPERSON   DATE

Award

Graphics Design: USA

and the judges for the 1981 Desi Awards cite		
Allyson Smith Peter Byar/Peter Bressler ADs Peter Bressler Design Associates		
for excellence in the creation of a graphic design and its execution for the following medium		
Direct Mail "Hook Clip"		
for the client named		
Date 1981	Independent Products Co., Inc.	Graphics Design: USA

Graphic Artists and Commercial Photographers

It is important to keep in mind the title "graphic artist" consists of the noun "artist" and the adjective "graphic." So, first and foremost you are dealing with an artist. Some artists focus on commercial graphics because they find they can't make a living creating fine art. Others have studied commercial art or photography because the subject represents an interesting approach to venting an artistic leaning with a potentially lucrative career. Whatever the motivation, few if any graphic artists, photographers, or copywriters have actually studied marketing and sales. And fewer have had hands-on experience selling anything but their own services—certainly not your product or service. Finally, few if any have been compensated based on the commercial success of the material they created.

The other side of this picture is that many clients come to these creative people without having a clear idea of what they want and then give the artists too much leeway.

> *War Story.*   One of my earliest encounters with the creative process was working with a commercial photographer on a "shoot" for graphics for new packaging of a plastic shoe tree (our company's key product) my Dad invented. At the time, women's shoe fashions included klunky high heels. The photograph we finally chose to use on the package incorporated several of these outrageous shoes that went out of style within two months. We were left with outdated packaging almost as soon as the product hit the shelves. I take the blame for this blunder on several levels:
>
> - I did not identify our customer. The product was a plastic shoe tree purchased by either older women or women who worked on their feet, such as nurses and waitresses; primarily a market with conservative tastes.
> - I did not understand the fickleness of fashion. I should have realized that I was creating packaging that would outlive the fashion and sought more timeless styles.
> - I did not exercise enough control over the photographer. I was influenced by his desire to shoot fashion photography and not by the requirements of the market.
> - I did not put the photographer on a budget. What should have been a half-day shoot at maximum took over a day and we were paying by the hour. I didn't have a firm quote for the project.

It is fundamental that you have a clearly defined statement of your company's mission and a well defined goal from the proposed engagement. If you do not perform this exercise beforehand, you will be vulnerable to reacting to the creative person rather than being proactive and directing the creative person to achieve your desired goals. It also puts the creative person on notice that he or she has to work within prescribed parameters.

> *War Story.*   I was a partner in a start-up company in Israel. The first time I met my partner Eric was during a visit to Russia to meet with Jewish "Refuseniks" in the days before Perestroika. Later, when Eric emigrated to Israel, I helped him start a company based on a technology he had developed for producing submicron precious metal powders which are used in, among other things, conductive coatings by the electronics industry. The project reached a stage in its development when we were ready to begin marketing the process and we wanted to develop some sales aids. The company had a very small budget for advertising and the target market was the technical staff of 200+ customers worldwide. These people were primarily interested in benefits, characteristics, and performance rather than fancy graphics. The review of material produced by major players in the market indicated that we could produce a simple black and white sheet, front and back, with several SEM (scanning electron microscope) photographs and a particle distribution graph, details of the properties, and some other technical information, and that would be sufficient. There was no need to stretch our limited budget to produce a high-quality slick presentation. I often see start-ups invest disproportionate sums on fancy graphic sales literature that is not needed.

The search and selection process for graphic artists and commercial photographers is made easier because these candidates all have portfolios of their work. However, you should review these portfolios with a critical eye and probing questions. You should determine whether the individual projects in the portfolio were produced by the candidate in direct contact with the client or whether the client had an advertising agency, an in-house art director or some other creative person overseeing the project. You should also determine the client's background either from the candidate or by talking with the reference. Is the client firm owned or managed by someone with a strong foundation in advertising, who gave substantial direction to the project? How much of the end result was a by-product of the candidate's input and how much was generated by the client? Also, ask references about problems that may have occurred during the process and whether the problems were attributable to the candidate or external issues.

Try to determine how much research the candidate engaged in before actually doing the creative elements of the project.

In addition to reviewing the candidate's portfolio, ask for references from projects not illustrated in the portfolio.

Copywriting and Copywriters

The focus of this section has been on commercial artists and photographers, but I don't want to overlook some issues regarding copy and the search for copywriters. I place a great deal of importance on good grammar and correct spelling (see Exhibit 11–2, paragraph 4B). Your catalog sheets and advertising material are as much a reflection of your company and you as your product or service and your business card. How do you feel when someone sends you a letter that is full of errors? Perhaps nine out of ten people who read your material won't notice the mistakes. However, the tenth reader could be an important potential customer. What does it say about a company or individual when a cover letter or advertising material is full of errors? Does it suggest that perhaps the same lack of detail is reflected in the product or service being offered? In an already very imperfect world, given the choice between two otherwise similar products, wouldn't you prefer the one produced by the firm with the attention to detail?

> *War Story.* When my father received the final draft of his first patent application from his patent attorney for review and approval, he took several days off and retired to a small hotel in the mountains. He read and reread the application over and over again. On his return, he advised the attorney of several typographic, spelling, and grammar errors. The patent attorney shared this story with me in later years and added that Max was the only client who ever corrected one of his applications. It was also the only patent written in his office that was issued six months after it was filed! This from a man who did not go to school beyond the sixth grade but attended to detail. I have seen patent applications come back from a first rejection with notes from the examiner highlighting spelling errors, as well as questions about technical elements.

There is a presumption, when hiring a copywriter, that you are purchasing not only a service to effectively describe your product or service, but also to describe it in good English. Copywriters are human and spelling-checker software is not infallible. Don't assume that the copywriter hasn't made simple spelling or grammar errors; check everything twice. Also, read all copy to be sure it is in the vernacular of your profession, industry, or market.

When talking to references provided by copywriter candidates, ask how many revisions were made before the final copy was approved. Ask candidates to provide you with sample copy they have written for clients, and when talking with the references, be sure to ask them to comment on the quality of the workmanship, attention to detail, and ability to translate the client's requirements into workable copy.

Product Designers and Packaging Designers

Entrepreneurs may or may not be technically competent to take a product concept from the initial idea through prototype to final working model and/or detailed mechanical drawings. Also, a functionally creative idea may require the input of someone with an aesthetic perspective. Large companies sometimes use product designers to create new products. In a sense, a product designer is similar to an architect. The *product* designer will fashion the "building" that houses or incorporates the functions of the product you want to produce. Similarly, a *package* designer will assist in designing a creative solution to packaging a product or service you wish to sell. Packaging *engineers* specialize in resolving technical problems regarding packaging issues, such as breakage, cost, disposability, safety.

Often, product designers and packaging designers are one and the same. They may also be involved in the design of point-of-purchase displays and trade show booths.

After you have established a working relationship with one creative person or group on a project, it is useful to have a second and even a third group submit proposals on all future projects. This will provide, among other things, an ongoing "audit" of the process.

When talking with references provided by designers, be certain to ask:

- What are the weaknesses of the individual or group?
- How close did the final design come to the original concept drawings?
- How practical was the proposed design to actually produce?
- How successful was the product or package?
- What was the reference's contribution to the process?

THE THREE RS: OTHER CREATIVE SERVICES

RECAP

- Recognize that these creative people do not know your business or industry—you are hiring them because of their knowledge of the graphic process, language skills, and design capability.

(continued)

THE THREE RS *(continued)*

- Know whom you are targeting—who is your customer? Sales literature should be targeted to your customer, not the end user or the graphics magazine editor.
- Exercise strong control—follow your instincts, not the creative person's instincts.

RESOURCES

- Yellow Pages.
- Local business press.
- North Light Books, 1507 Dana Avenue, Cincinnati, OH 45207, Tel: 800-289-0963. In addition to being the publisher of one of the books I have recommended, they also publish a wide range of books on subjects such as logo development, package design, and letterhead design.
- International Association of Graphics Arts Consultants, PO Box 290249, Nashville, TN 37229, Tel: 615-366-1799.
- Graphics Arts Technical Foundation, 4615 Forbes Avenue, Pittsburgh, PA 15213-3796, Tel: 412-621-6941. Publishes a product catalog intended primarily for professionals in the graphics arts business. However, it contains several titles of interest to beginners.
- American Institute of Graphics Arts (AIGA), 164 5th Avenue, New York, NY 10010, Tel: 212-807-1990. Publishes the *Membership and Resource Directory.*
- Industrial Designers Society of America (IDSA), 1142 Walker Road, Great Falls, VA 22066, Tel: 703-759-0100. Produces an annual *Directory of Industrial Designers.*
- Institute of Packaging Professionals (IoPP), 481 Carlisle Drive, Herndon, VA 22070, Tel: 800-432-4085. http://www.packinfo-world.org. Publishes the *Who's Who and What's What in Packaging,* a directory of members, detailed information on packaging and packaging trade associations. Touted as an important source of information ($130). Has a certification program (CPP). Operates the IoPP Packaging Bookstore with titles such as *Packaging User's Handbook.*

THE THREE RS *(continued)*

- Printing Industries of America, Inc. (PIA), 100 Daingerfield Road, Alexandria, VA 22314, Tel: 703-519-8100. Publishes the *Printers' Resource Catalog*, an excellent list of books on printing and graphics.

REFERENCES

- *Getting It Printed*****   This is an important general information and reference text for anyone engaged in purchasing printing services.
- *Graphic Arts and Desktop Publishing, Pocket Dictionary* and *Graphic Arts and Desktop Publishing Terminology, Complete Dictionary*   These are good "learn the vernacular" resources.
- *Hiring Independent Contractors*****   With more information than the average person will require, the package includes a diskette that has standard forms and contracts, making it easy to customize agreements. It is especially useful for work with freelancers.
- *Printing Impressions Magazine*, 401 North Broad Street, Philadelphia, PA 19108, Tel: 215-238-5300. Publishes an annual "Industry 500" and "Who's Who in Printing."
- *Publishing and Production Executive Magazine*, 401 North Broad Street, Philadelphia, PA 19108, Tel: 215-238-5300. Publishes annual Buyer's Resource Issue including Who's who of suppliers and services and associations to call as well as an index to articles.

ARCHITECTS

Design and construction are inherently exciting. There are few things more satisfying than a successful project. The secret to success lies in the professional, business and personal relationships between owner and architect. (The AIA's *You and Your Architect*)

The *function* of an architect includes these tasks:

- Prepare drawings, specifications, and budget for construction of a new office, store, factory, and/or warehouse.

- Prepare drawings, specifications, and budget for remodeling of a property you own, are buying, or have purchased.
- Program the functional requirements of your business with you, within a prescribed budget.

Unless you are in the real estate development business or have a business that is expanding so rapidly that you are constantly building new facilities and have an in-house real estate department, you may only work with an architect once or twice in your life. The question then arises, if only once in my life how much energy do I have to invest in learning the vernacular of the profession? I will respond with a war story of a very close friend which will illustrate the price one can pay for inadequate attention to detail when working with an architect. War stories about building projects gone awry either because of the architect, the builder, the consulting engineer, or the client could easily fill a book. The entrepreneur or manager who undertakes a project that involves an architect and who doesn't invest the requisite effort and time is almost certainly buying himself or herself many long-term problems.

> *War Story.*   At the height of the cigar craze, a friend who is a successful tobacco retailer purchased a building to be renovated for an upscale and swank cigar salon. He hired an architect with a very good reputation for designing retail shops, but did not actually check with the references that were provided with the architect's portfolio. My friend was also very busy managing his wholesale business, mail-order operation, and importing company. These other businesses were operating from a different location, and sometimes days would go by when he was unable to visit the renovation in progress. In addition, he relied heavily on the architect's project manager to perform oversight of the renovation. The end result—the project came in at 50 percent over budget. A major design flaw in the heating, ventilation, and air conditioning resulted in inadequate venting of the cigar smoke from the smoking lounge precluding further expansion. Due to the failure to complete all the work by the deadline (a highly advertised grand opening), a nonpermanent floor finish had to be applied and must be reapplied every six months. The architect "disappeared" and my friend has little, if any, recourse.

My limited experience with architects, which includes working for one many years ago, has given me the impression that many do not emphasize functional considerations. An architect friend expressed his belief that architects are trained to listen to the client and to incorporate the client's needs into any design project. He went on to say that he didn't necessarily agree with the tendency to hire someone who has had experience in designing like structures. My problem with his position is based on my observations of botched jobs, which suggest to me that failures should be shared by the owner and the architect. Often, owners don't really know what they want or what the consequences will be of using a particular design. Presumably, an architect who has had experience doing similar jobs will already have learned the usual mistakes at someone else's expense.

> *War Story.* Early in my business career, after working with the kitchen design department of a major food service company, I worked for an architect who had developed a reputation for designing hotel and restaurant dining rooms and kitchens. My one and only project working with this professional was in the design of the kitchens of the Hotel Inter Continental in the Ivory Coast. I prepared a layout for the bakery according to what I knew was the natural flow of the production process, which was also the way just about every bakery I had ever seen was planned. The architect stood behind me at the drafting table and insisted that all the equipment of one height be placed together. I would argue workflow and he would argue aesthetics. This experience actually contradicts an earlier observation—the architect did have extensive experience designing kitchens but he still did not understand how people work in a bakery.

The pamphlet, *You and Your Architect* published by the American Institute of Architects (AIA), is as excellent a starting point as I have found to date for someone who wants to retain an architect. The pamphlet discusses:

- Getting started—assessment of your own skills and knowledge.
- Selecting the architect—questions to ask.
- Identifying the services you need.
- Negotiating the agreement.
- Compensating your architect.
- Keeping the project on track.

To develop a list of potential candidates, you can tap several sources:

- Every time you pass a building that appeals to you, make a note of the owner or occupant and call to find out the name of the architect. You can also ask about any problems that were encountered.

- Call the AIA, either the national office or the local chapter, and request names of architects who have done similar work; then take a look at their work before you call.
- Ask local real estate brokers or developers to recommend an architect with whom they have worked; also ask about strengths and weaknesses of candidates.
- Call your trade association to find out whether the staff knows of any other members who have worked with architects.
- Review the trade journals of your industry or even call the editor to ask whether he or she knows anyone who has recently worked with an architect in your industry.

Finally, do your homework. Read! Read! Read! Since I have not personally read or even perused the following books, they do not appear in the reference section of this chapter or the Bibliography at the back of the book. Based on the descriptions in the AIA Bookstore catalog, however, they appear to be good background resources while you search for an architect and may serve you well once you begin working with one:

Cramer, James P., *Design + Enterprise,* AIA Press, 1994.

Cruikshank, Jeffrey L., and Clark, Malcolm, *Herman Miller Inc.: Buildings and Beliefs,* AIA Press, 1994.

Spectorcorp: Partnerships in Corporate Architecture, Rockport Publishing, 1994.

Stitt, Fred, *Construction Administration and Inspection Checklists: A Complete Guide for Exterior and Interior Projects.* Florence, KY: Van Nostrand Reinhold, 1992.

Stitt, Fred, *Project Management Checklist.* Florence, KY: Van Nostrand Reinhold, 1992.

In addition, the AIA Bookstore catalog offers a number of titles dealing with specific subjects including offices, restaurants, retirement facilities, medical and dental space.

Exhibit 6–5 lists questions to ask when interviewing and evaluating architects.

Marvin Verman, a friend and a practicing architect for many years, offers the following valuable advice:

- Select an architect with whom you are compatible from a personal, business, and financial point of view. Do not rush the process. *Be sure.*

Exhibit 6–5   Interview Questions for Architects

1. What projects have you either been lead architect or part of the team, that were similar to ours? _____

2. What are the primary considerations in your mind regarding this project?

3. What do you understand are the needs of my business? _____

4. How will you gather information, establish priorities, and make decisions?

5. After the initial design phase, what ongoing role will you play in the construction? _____

6. Whom may I call for references? Clients? Contractors? _____

7. What do you expect from this project? _____

8. Who in the firm will work on the design phase? The construction phase?

9. How will engineering or other design services be provided? _____

10. What are the quality control mechanisms in place in the firm? _____

11. What is the firm's construction-cost experience? _____

(continued)

Exhibit 6–5   *(continued)*

12. How will you be compensated?_____

_____

13. What documentation will be provided?_____

_____

14. Why do you want this commission?_____

_____

_____

- Define the scope of the work and be sure both the architect and you understand the decisions.
- Architects work in stages. Understand these stages. Decisions made early in the working relationship are crucial. For example, if programmatic decisions are turned into design drawings and then the program is changed, this will result in loss of time and money. If the process continues based on bad decisions, the problems will multiply and rectification will be more and more difficult. The cost will not only be time and money but also the loss of the required respect in the architect-client relationship.

THE THREE Rs: ARCHITECTS

RECAP

- Prepare for the project carefully—learn as much as you can beforehand about what you want built or remodeled and about the process of design and construction.
- Invest time and effort in the selection process and ongoing management of the project—you cannot delegate either the selection process or the management without expecting problems.
- Have trust and confidence in the architect—if you have any doubts, look further.

THE THREE RS *(continued)*

RESOURCES

- American Institute of Architects, 1735 New York Avenue, NW, Washington, DC 20006-5292, Tel: 800-AIA-9930. The AIA also has many local chapters that offer referral services. In larger cities, the chapters operate their own bookstores. The Washington office will provide a mail-order catalog of books they carry, Tel: 800-365-2724.

REFERENCES

- *You and Your Architect***** This really useful monograph put out by the AIA is worth reading if you are contemplating hiring an architect.
- *Raising the Rafters* Although the book is basically a consumer text, targeted at home owners, it offers some good insights on managing a construction project.

FREELANCERS

I have successfully used freelancers over the years for a variety of work—photography, graphic arts (mechanicals, price lists, "down and dirty" ads used for recruiting employees or selling used equipment), repairs and maintenance, and so on.

It might be an interesting exercise to try to build an entire business using only, or primarily, freelancers. It is important to define what I refer to as freelancers. I do not include a sole practitioner accountant, lawyer, or consultant. Nor do I include an incorporated business consisting of more than one or two employees. A freelancer could be your former personnel director who still functions as your personnel director but receives a monthly retainer rather than a salary. A freelancer could be an independent copywriter who works for you once a month or whenever you have a project.

Freelancer engagements tend to be less formalized; neither party is really interested in entering into involved or complex negotiations, unless the engagement is significant. If you plan to use a freelancer on a regular and consistent basis, you should establish the nature of the relationship to avoid possible legal problems later on. You do not want

Exhibit 6–6 Checklist for an Agreement with an Independent Contractor[15]

_____ **Preamble:** Should include: your company's name (and address), hereinafter_____
Contractor's name (and address), hereinafter Contractor
Date of agreement
Term of agreement

_____ **Services to Be Performed:** Clear definition of work to be performed (may reference the RFP or the proposal which should then be included as addenda).

_____ **Payment:** Should specify whether payment is single or multiple payments, by the hour, day, week. The total sum due should be indicated with the amount that has been agreed on or a notation that the amount will not exceed a predetermined sum.

_____ **Terms of Payment:** Should indicate frequency of payments. Or if payment is to be made against certain performance requirements (i.e., upon delivery of final report), upon submission of an invoice.

_____ **Expenses:** If you have agreed to reimburse for out-of-pocket expenses, it should be noted. If contractor must obtain prior approval above certain sums, it should be noted. If all expenses are the responsibility of contractor, it should also be noted.

_____ **Independent Contractor Status:** Any agreement or engagement letter should include language such as: Contractor is an independent contractor. Contractor's employees or contract personnel are not employees. Contractor is entitled to the following rights consistent with an independent contractor relationship. Contractor has the right to perform services for others during the term of this Agreement. Contractor has the right to perform the services required by this Agreement at any place, location, or time except as noted in RFP or Proposal.

_____ **Intellectual Property Rights:** Ownership of designs, improvements, art, and so on, should be defined with language such as: Contractor assigns all rights in all designs, creations, improvements, original works of authorship, formulas, processes, know-how, techniques, inventions, and all other information or items created by Contractor. The rights assigned include title and interest in all patent, copyright, trade secret, trademark, and other proprietary rights.

_____ **Confidentiality:** Even though this is implied, it can't hurt to state it in an agreement:

Contractor will not disclose or use, either during or after the term of this engagement, any proprietary or confidential information of without prior written permission except to the extent necessary to perform services.

Exhibit 6–6 *(continued)*

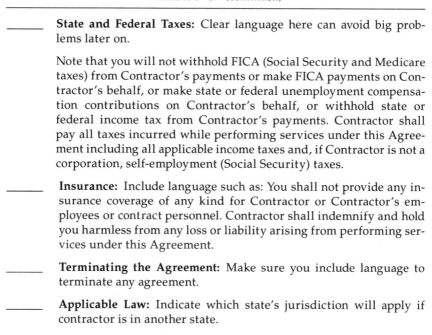

_____ **State and Federal Taxes:** Clear language here can avoid big problems later on.

Note that you will not withhold FICA (Social Security and Medicare taxes) from Contractor's payments or make FICA payments on Contractor's behalf, or make state or federal unemployment compensation contributions on Contractor's behalf, or withhold state or federal income tax from Contractor's payments. Contractor shall pay all taxes incurred while performing services under this Agreement including all applicable income taxes and, if Contractor is not a corporation, self-employment (Social Security) taxes.

_____ **Insurance:** Include language such as: You shall not provide any insurance coverage of any kind for Contractor or Contractor's employees or contract personnel. Contractor shall indemnify and hold you harmless from any loss or liability arising from performing services under this Agreement.

_____ **Terminating the Agreement:** Make sure you include language to terminate any agreement.

_____ **Applicable Law:** Indicate which state's jurisdiction will apply if contractor is in another state.

to find yourself liable for payroll taxes, disability, or workers' compensation. Exhibit 6–6 provides an overview of the elements you should consider in a long-term engagement with a freelancer.

Using freelancers can be economical; however, it places an additional burden on your organization and you. You must assume a stronger management position than you would with a more structured engagement. A freelancer can be less expensive for a project than a public relations firm or an advertising agency, sometimes by as much as 25 percent.

Here are some places to look for freelancers:

- The Yellow Pages.
- Local newspaper editors, who may supply names of retired journalists or periodic contributors.
- Local organizations such as chambers of commerce and other nonprofit organizations.

THE THREE RS: FREELANCERS

RECAP

- Identify your requirements—define and specify requirements with clear and measurable results.
- Evaluate sources carefully—make your selection on the basis of value contribution and total cost.
- Establish terms of the relationship—negotiate price and performance based on reasonable achievable measures.

RESOURCES

- The Outsourcing Institute, 45 Rockefeller Plaza, Suite 2000, New York, NY 10111, Tel: 800-421-6767, http://www.outsourcing.com. Publishes an annual Buyer's Guide, and a wide range of material including the Year-end Trends & Issues Survey, an Online Bibliography, a quarterly publication, *The Source.* The OI also runs a Referral Help Desk.

REFERENCES

- *Hiring Independent Contractors*****   You will find good information on the legal consequences of retaining freelancers as well as a sample contract.

7

INSURANCE AGENTS, REAL ESTATE BROKERS, COLLECTION AGENCIES, AND OUTSOURCING

Entrepreneurs and managers frequently deal with numerous professions that you may not have thought of as problematic and as such not requiring guidance in their selection and management. There are other professions many entrepreneurs utilize infrequently or not at all. Examples of the former are real estate brokers and insurance agents; examples of the latter are collection agencies and business brokers. If your business does not involve consumer credit or large numbers of accounts receivables, you may never need a collection agency. If your business operates as a one- or two-person operation out of your house, you may never need a real estate broker. Should your future requirements include any of these service providers, however, this chapter will provide the information you need for successful selection and management.

INSURANCE AGENTS, BROKERS, CONSULTANTS

It is virtually impossible to operate a business without some forms of insurance. Health insurance, life insurance, and key person insurance, workers' compensation, fire insurance, commercial liability, product liability, and business interruption are some kinds of insurance even a start-up business may require. If you rent an office or building, the landlord may require you to have certain minimum coverage. If you sell a product, many potential customers won't even talk to you without evidence of product liability. If you borrow money from a bank or any other lending institution, you may be required to have key person insurance as well as adequate liability coverage. The bottom line is you need insurance; ergo, you will need to work with an insurance agent or broker.

The *function* of your *insurance company* includes these tasks:

- Provide protection of physical and financial assets.
- Reduce the likelihood of a loss.
- Reduce the amount of a potential loss.
- Assume the risk of a loss.
- Transfer the risk of a loss.

The *function* of your *insurance agent* includes these tasks:

- Place your account with a reliable insurance company.
- Assure that you have adequate coverage, but not too much.
- Facilitate your firm's relationship with the insurance company.
- Assist in making claims.
- Be your advocate to the insurance company.

War Story.   One of the most frightening periods in my business career occurred during the early 1980s when the insurance industry was going through a major upheaval. The media was full of horror stories of insurance underwriters canceling policies, refusing to renew policies for certain businesses and/or risks and doubling, tripling, and even increasing premiums by 10 times the prior year. We produced a line of plastic consumer products, the hangers and clips mentioned in earlier chapters. Our customers were retailers who required all their vendors to provide evidence of insurance and certificates naming the customer as additional insured. Many major accounts would not even consider a product line from the perspective of marketability or compatibility unless and until the insurance issue was confirmed. Our ability to evidence product liability coverage became a matter of life and death for our business.

For three months prior to the expiration date of our policy, I called our broker weekly to determine whether the insurance underwriter was going to renew the policy and what the premium would be. I was assured that the policy would be renewed. The brokerage was a firm we had been using for many years, and I relied on its integrity and their historically strong relationships with insurance companies.

A week before the anniversary date, I was advised that the insurance company intended to cancel our policy. We obtained a 30-day rider with threats and cajoling and then went through an anxious period of trying to find another broker who could place our coverage. In the end, a new broker placed our coverage, but with a premium that was 50 percent higher than the previous year's premium.

There are a couple of lessons I garnered from this experience: (1) Always try to maintain a relationship with more than one broker, and (2) *insurance companies have no loyalty so there is no benefit in being loyal to them.* After seven years of paying significant premiums and making no claims whatsoever, we were canceled for no reason by a major and highly respected insurance company; claim history appears to have little value in their decision process.

Selecting an Insurance Agent or Broker

Insurance agents or brokers are first and foremost salespeople. And what they have to sell is primarily themselves. An *independent agency* can place your insurance with most if not all insurance carriers that do not use *exclusive agents* or *direct writers.* Personality and likability aside, an important element of broker selection is the insurance underwriters the broker has worked with the most, and both the broker and underwriter's experience with your type of business.

Trade associations may be a good resource for names of brokers. Perhaps a sharp broker has recognized that parlaying experience with a few businesses in the same industry provides entrée and legitimacy with other businesses in that industry. Also, the broker may have developed a stable of insurance companies that are interested in underwriting certain industries.

Other businesses in your industry can be a reliable resource for names of brokers. Anytime you can find a broker who already has some understanding of the idiosyncrasies of your business, you will save time and maybe also money. The time saving comes from not having to educate the broker about your business and the money saving can occur when discussing extent of coverage, deductibles, and exposure to risk. You may not need certain types of coverage, and an educated broker can advise you properly.

For example, the major physical assets of my business were plastic injection molds and molding machines which produced plastic hangers and clips which were sold to retailers. Molds (or dies) are enormous blocks of tempered steel encasing the tempered steel cavities that produce the parts. The risks of such assets being destroyed in a fire are remote to nonexistent. The risk of serious damage occurring by vandals is also small. Therefore, I felt there was no point in insuring the molds for their replacement value. Also, when considering the extent of coverage for business interruption insurance, we could factor in that the molds could be moved out of our building and given to any one of hundreds of custom molders to get us back in business temporarily even if our molding operation was inoperable. Understanding these realities enabled us to save significant sums in premiums while not putting our business at unnecessary risk.

It is also important to realize that agents and brokers represent you, but receive their compensation from the insurance company. The larger the premium, the larger their commission. If your business is large enough, it may make sense to hire a risk management consultant before discussing coverage with an insurance agent or broker.

An unscrupulous broker may take payment from you and not place the insurance, leaving you exposed in the event of a claim. An easy way to protect yourself is to require a letter or a binder from the insurance underwriter until you actually receive the policy (which may take several weeks). Not all agents are authorized by the underwriters with which they work to issue binders on behalf of the company, therefore it is important to ask for evidence of authorization before accepting a binder issued by a broker.[1]

When evaluating broker candidates, it is important to visit the broker's office and see what kind of facility and staff the broker has for claim processing. You should also ask for references of clients for whom the broker has managed major claims. The real test of the broker is not obtaining insurance nor even getting a good premium; the test is helping you to collect in the event you have a claim. And there can be a big difference in claim management from one broker to another.

How Insurance Agents Differ from Insurance Brokers

Although I use the terms "agent" and "broker" interchangeably throughout this section, strictly speaking this is not correct. There are important differences between the two that you must understand to determine which one will best serve your needs.

A simplistic explanation of the difference is that *agents* represent the insurance company and *brokers* represent the client. Some agents are exclusive agents; they represent one insurance company and can only sell the policies of that company. Most agents are "independent agents," which means they have been appointed by several insurance underwriters to represent those companies and are authorized to sell the policies issued by those companies. Brokers do not represent any particular insurance company and therefore can attempt to place your business with any underwriter they feel will best serve your needs or provide the most competitive rates.

There are other differences: Brokers can charge fees since they may assist clients in setting up self-insurance programs; brokers can place insurance with any underwriter (market); whereas independent agents are limited to underwriters with which they have a prior arrangement; brokers tend to be larger and handle more commercial coverage and service many of the major companies.

There are similarities, too: Both agents and brokers have to be licensed by the state in which they are doing business. Licensing requirements are different for brokers and agents. Both receive their compensation from the insurance companies in the form of a commission, which is a percentage of the premium charged.

An independent agent will likely meet your needs if you are operating a small retail operation, a business out of your house, and so on. If your plans for your business provide for substantial growth, you may want to work at the outset with a larger broker so you won't face outgrowing your agent's capabilities.

Do You Need a Consultant?

If your business is large or, more importantly, is complex or unusual, or does something or produces a product that might be construed as dangerous or complex; you may want to consider talking to a "risk management consultant" or a "loss control specialist." Most of the large insurers and many larger brokers retain one or more of these specialists and may even make their services available free of charge to clients. Their services may range from fire safety inspections and advice on sprinkler systems to product design, factory efficiency, and preventive measures against stock theft. Risk management consultants assist in minimizing the chance of loss and in doing so reduce the likelihood of the insurer having to pay you for losses. This sort of exercise should aid in reducing premiums.

Evaluating Insurance Agents

Exhibit 7–1 lists questions to ask when considering a new agent; in the following paragraphs, Patricia Borowski, of the Council of Insurance Agents, explains why some of these questions are so critical:

Is the agent properly licensed? To sell insurance in the United States, agents must be licensed. Every state has a licensing authority and slightly different requirements. In general, an agent must have at least

Exhibit 7–1　Interview Questions for Insurance Agents, Brokers, and Insurers

Agents/Brokers

1. What is your license status? May I see your license? _____

2. What kind of companies do you deal with? Have you had experience with companies whose needs are similar to ours? _____

3. What, if any, authority do you have to represent the underwriter? _____

4. What insurers have you placed insurance with over the past 90 days? ___

5. What is the procedure and length of time to have certificates of insurance issued? _____

6. What are your in-house capabilities to monitor the underwriter's billings? _____

7. Who will perform risk assessment and management? _____

8. What methods of communication do you use to report trends and news from the industry and the underwriters? _____

9. Whom may I call to obtain references on your firm? _____

10. Have you had any complaints filed against your firm in the insurance commissioner's office in the past 12 months? _____

Exhibit 7–1   *(continued)*

11. What other certification, if any, do you have besides the license? _____

_____

Insurers

12. What is the insurer's rating? Are any complaints lodged at the commissioner's office? _____

_____

13. Does the insurer have knowledge of my industry? _____

_____

14. Does it offer all the coverages I require? _____

_____

15. What kind of service is provided? _____

_____

16. How much will my package cost? _____

_____

a high school diploma, have completed a prelicensing course and passed a state licensing exam. In addition, the agent must have been sponsored by someone. The licensing authority normally performs a background criminal check and a cross-check with the other licensing authorities. More and more states are requiring fingerprinting as an added precaution. It is a good idea to request the agent's license number and call your state insurance department to confirm the agent's license is up to date and there is no pattern of complaints on record. There are continuing education requirements in every state, in order to maintain the license.

What kinds of companies does the agent deal with? Here, give the agent some parameters, describe your business and its needs, and try to determine whether the agent works with underwriters who issue insurance for your trade or industry.

What is the extent of the agent's authority to represent the underwriter? Most agents do not have the authority to bind a customer without the preapproval of the underwriter. However, some agents have contractual arrangements with underwriters to temporarily bind policies. If the agent answers in the affirmative, you can and should call the company for verification.

How long does it take to obtain certificates of insurance? Depending on the business you are in, such as consumer products and electrical equipment, you may require these certificates. There are two types, one simply confirms you have adequate coverage and the other is a "notice of an additional insured," which is used when you buy or lease equipment and the lessor or loan grantor wants to protect its interest. It also is used with vendors to retail chains. Additional insured certificates may have a cost associated with them and may not be issued by the broker. You should know this in advance.

Ask about accounting issues. Insurers usually issue the invoices for premiums and send them directly to the insured as opposed to having their agents perform the billing function. The agent's copy may arrive after the insured's bill. If your accounting department works as it should, someone should confirm that the invoice price matches the quote, especially on renewals. But it would be nice to know that the agent's accounting capabilities includes auditing their copies of the bills for accuracy.[2]

Get several quotes. Have your broker/agent obtain between three and five quotes for your required coverage.[3]

Get references. Here are questions to ask references provided by candidates:

- Have you had any claims experience with the agent?
- How did the agent perform?
- Do you get your policies on time?
- Have you ever had a problem with the insurer?
- How did the agent manage the problem?

Discuss travel coverage. Discuss with candidates issues such as your overseas exposure, including you or members of your staff traveling and the need for additional if temporary coverage.[4]

Who does the risk assessment and management? Identify the responsibilities of the company and the broker.

Make sure communication is adequate. What kind of communications and updating is maintained by the agent? How does the agent apprise you of news and trends in the industry, news from the underwriters, and matters such as expectation of renewals?

INSURANCE COMPANIES

Your universe of insurance companies will normally be limited to those from which the broker you select obtains quotations. If you have identified an insurance company with which you would like coverage, you might call the company's regional office and ask for the name of one or two local brokers with whom the company works on a regular basis.

Not all insurance companies work with independent agents. Some have dedicated direct sales staffs. The process for evaluating the agent or salesperson and the insurance company should not be any different, if you have determined that you want to work with that underwriter.

You may also find that you are unable to have a package underwritten by one company. Product liability, property insurance, boiler and machinery, automobile liability, and some other types of insurance are usually underwritten in packages. Umbrella liability, workers' compensation, health insurance, and life insurance may or may not be underwritten by the same carrier. If you have already chosen your broker, you should be able to rely on the broker to assemble the missing pieces of the package for you.

Some insurance companies will rely on the survey performed by the broker, others will send out their own inspectors. I always preferred the insurance company to send out loss control personnel (people responsible for limiting potential losses or claims by inspecting business to be insured before issuing a policy). We ran a clean, neat, and safe plastic injection molding plant—it was important to me that the loss control department in the insurance company not put me in the same category as many other molders who ran dirty, sloppy and unsafe shops.

Conventional wisdom says to take the financial strength of the insurance company into account. When evaluating quotes from two insurance companies that are otherwise identical, I might take that advice. If I trust my broker, however, and he or she has had good experience with a firm that has a lower rating, I am inclined to follow the broker's recommendation. If I have no experience with or confidence in my broker, I head off to the library to review *A.M. Best's Insurance Reports* or one of the other insurance rating services.

Depending on the nature of your business, you may want to factor into your selection, an insurance company that has a proactive loss control department. I always felt more secure when an OSHA inspection was due, if the insurance company's loss control people had been through the plant.

War Story.   We had developed a plastic clip used on clothing hangers that had a plastic spring with a breakage problem. We asked our insurance company's loss control department for guidance on resolving the problem and on managing the potential risk. While they were not particularly helpful in resolving the problem, the communication with loss control reduced the possibility of the underwriting department raising our premium or even canceling the policy. Between the risk management personnel, our broker, and our attorney we were able to develop a procedure for settling all the complaints before they became litigation and impacted on our premiums. Complaints involved the springs breaking and hitting customers in the eye. When our company received a complaint we acknowledged there was a problem and offered to compensate the consumer for medical bills, lost time, and so on.

Again, Exhibit 7–1 lists questions you should ask when evaluating insurance underwriters; the following discussion explains why these questions can be helpful:

Does the insurer have knowledge about my industry? This is an important issue for unique franchise businesses. However, many businesses such as retailing, distribution, and many manufacturing businesses are so numerous and have so much in common that any reasonable-size underwriter should be knowledgeable about the business. If your business has a unique production process or product and you can identify underwriters who have targeted your industry, you will benefit from working with an underwriter with experience in your industry. It may be easier to find a broker or agent who has developed expertise in a given industry or class of trade. Some will even forge relationships with that industry's trade association or advertise in the trade press.

Do they offer all the coverage I need? One of the businesses I owned produced product for the consumer market. Frequently, before a major retailer would talk to a potential new vendor, the retailer would require us to provide evidence of insurance or even an additional insured certificate. This fact of life required a quick response capability (24 hour period) from the carrier and/or the broker (if the broker was authorized to issue the certificates). Over the years, it was one of the elements that we had to consider when evaluating new underwriters.

What kind of service will they provide? This is a critical question. My earlier war story about the insurance company that abruptly canceled our policy shows the issue of service can change overnight. You should obtain references describing good service experiences. Even though the underwriter is ultimately responsible for service, your broker is an integral part of the process. A good broker with a good working relationship with the underwriter is the most important element aside from the underwriter's financial strength.

Are they priced competitively? Do they participate in premium reducing programs? Depending on the insurance market, as my war story illustrates, you may be glad that they price at all, never mind competitively. But yes, all other things being equal between under-writers, you should be satisfied that the pricing is competitive.

What is the financial stability or solvency of the underwriter? The agency? Most underwriters provide, as part of their promotional material, rating information and general financial information. It would be prudent to ask some questions and get some confirmation about the agency as well. I have heard stories about agencies in financial difficulty not transferring funds on behalf of clients and the clients finding out too late that their policies lapsed.[5]

THE THREE Rs: INSURANCE

RECAP

- Confirm agent or broker is licensed—every state has a licensing authority; check, with the state licensing authority, whether the agencies you are considering have complaints registered against them.
- Determine experience with your business—agencies with prior experience with businesses in your industry are more desirable.
- Check status with companies and how many companies—even independent brokers tend to work with a few key underwriters on a regular basis, try to confirm the relationship.
- Confirm performance with references—focus on how claims were handled.
- Check out underwriter's rating—use published rating information.
- Question underwriter's experience with your industry—the underwriter should have a broad base of insured companies in businesses similar to yours.
- Ask about claims process and renewal lead times.

RESOURCES

- American Association of Insurance Services, 1035 South York Road, Bensenville, IL 60106, Tel: 708-595-3225.
- American Insurance Association, 1130 Connecticut Avenue, NW, Suite 1000, Washington, DC 20036, Tel: 202-828-7100.

(continued)

THE THREE RS *(continued)*

- Council of Insurance Agents and Brokers, 316 Pennsylvania Avenue SE, Suite 400, Washington, DC 20003-1146, Tel: 202-547-6616, Fax: 202-546-0597. Has 300 members, generally the larger brokers and agents. Will provide a directory of members with breakdown by specialty areas serviced.
- Insurance Information Institute, 110 William Street, New York, NY 10038, 1-800-331-9146. Offers several brochures and books at a nominal cost.
- National Insurance Association, PO Box 158544, Chicago, IL 60615, Tel: 313-924-3308.
- Professional Insurance Agents, 400 North Washington Street, Alexandria, VA 22314, Tel: 703-836-9340, Fax: 703-836-1279. Represents 18,000 independent agents. Will provide a list of members in your geographic area.
- Society of Risk Management Consultants, 58 Diablo View Drive, Orinda, CA 94563-1507, Tel: 510-254-9472. Will supply list of members, doesn't have any certification process but does have a code of ethics.

REFERENCES

- *Business Insurance Magazine*   It advertises itself as reporting weekly on corporate risk, employee benefit and managed health care. Subscription Department, Tel: 800-678-9595, $85.00 per year.
- *Best's Insurance Reports*   This is available in most public libraries, and rates insurance underwriters.
- *The Guide to Buying Insurance*   Although intended only as a consumer's guide, it simplifies elements of the insurance business.
- *Insuring Your Business*   Put out by the Insurance Institute, this is a basic explanation of various forms of insurance available and what typical businesses require in coverage.

REAL ESTATE BROKERS

I suppose it is possible that someone is reading this book who inherited a large farmhouse from his or her parents and in addition to living there has built a business without ever having to move to larger quarters. That reader can pass over this section. Otherwise, as an entrepreneur or manager, at some point in your career you will have to rent or buy space—office, commercial, or industrial. Of necessity, you will then require the services of a real estate broker.

The *function* of your real estate broker includes these tasks:

- Facilitate the sale, purchase, or lease of a property you own, wish to own, want to lease out or wish to rent.
- Be your advocate to various agencies such as zoning commission, business occupancy and licensing departments.
- Assist in determining fair market value.
- Recommend tradespeople or contractors to price out and/or perform needed work.

Agent's Responsibilities to Principal are these: *Care, Obedience, Accounting, Loyalty, Disclosure.*[6] When selecting a real estate agent to represent your interests, you would be well served to use those five characteristics as measures of any candidate. I would add a sixth—*Persistence.* "In the long run, persistence always make the best brokers."[7]

In many ways, residential real estate is much more regulated than commercial or industrial real estate. By law, many more protections are available for the private individual than exist for business consumers. So, the choice of an appropriate real estate broker requires a different mind-set than it would if you were selling your house.

The *tasks* an industrial real estate broker can provide:

- *Financing.* Brokers are actively involved in structuring deals with banks, industrial development authorities, and other sources of real estate finance.
- *Valuation.* Typically, the commercial broker, or his or her firm, will be more actively engaged in valuing a property whether it is a sale or a purchase.
- *Development.* Often, brokers work with developers or may even be developers. You may consider a piece of real estate that is too large for your current needs but will meet future needs, and the ability to lease out a portion may be the clincher in doing a deal.

- *Brokerage and Related Services.* This speaks to the traditional role of the broker as we normally view him or her.[8]

> A good broker is first and foremost, experienced in doing the kind of business the entrepreneur needs. It is important that the entrepreneur pick a broker who specializes in his requirements. If he wants an industrial property he should pick an industrial broker. If he wants an office property he should pick an office broker and if he wants a retail property he should pick a retail broker. . . . A good broker is one who is seasoned in his field. . . . A good broker maintains his competency by continually attending classes and conventions that improve his skills and enable him to keep abreast of trends in commercial real estate that are not only happening in his market, but happening throughout the country.[9]

In a small market, there may not be a large selection of commercial real estate brokers. In fact, there may not even be a firm that deals only in commercial real estate. In a large metropolitan market, commercial brokers specialize between commercial and industrial, and between office and retail. In large metropolitan areas, some firms are even neighborhood specific, and there are some regional and national firms today.

Multiple listing services make the inventory of properties available to every agent, but that doesn't mean that any real estate agent is competent to represent you in a commercial transaction.

Real estate is another profession where buyers are basically not paying for the service being provided creating, to some degree, a dual loyalty. A further complication in real estate is that the listing broker may split the commission with the broker bringing in the buyer. That is all the more reason to look even more deeply into the candidate's *professional integrity* and *professional competence.*

One of the enjoyable aspects of researching the professions for this book was the opportunity to meet knowledgeable representatives of these fields through my telephone interviews. My research on real estate brokers brought me to the Society of Industrial and Office Realtors and their PR person, Lottie Gatewood, of Vanguard Communications. The SIOR and its members appear to be an incredibly useful resource. The SIOR's members are certified specialists in Industrial and Office Real Estate. To qualify for the SIOR designation, the SIOR's more than 1,700 members must:

- Have at least seven years' experience in the industry.
- Have achieved a minimum dollar volume and number of transactions in each of the seven years.

- Take courses and passed an examination administered by the SIOR.
- Be recommended by two people in the industry who verify the candidate's professional ethics.
- Participate in continuing education programs to maintain their status.

All this is in addition to having their state licensing in real estate brokerage. Lottie pointed out that you can identify another SIOR member in a different geographic area through a local SIOR member should you be seeking space outside your region.

Lottie recommends performing a *Needs Assessment*. "Assessment of your needs before selecting a commercial real estate broker forces the establishment of parameters, priorities and expectations for your lease or acquisition. Be as specific as possible. . . ." Ask yourself:

1. Are you buying or leasing?
2. Determine your growth requirements.
3. What is the desired square footage/acreage?
4. Is it a short-term or long-term investment?
5. What is your budget?
6. Determine what your lease term will be.
7. What type of property?
8. Location?
9. Will financing be required?
10. What are the geographic parameters of the area I want to be in?
11. Define your parking requirements.
12. Determine what kind of finish level you need.
13. As you go in, plan an exit strategy.[10]

For the disposition of property, you should determine:

- What are recent comparables for similar property?
- What is the market activity?
- How quickly can you expect to sell?

Develop a list of candidates, tapping resources such as business associates, developers, bankers, real estate lawyers, and SIOR's membership list. Once you have developed the list, begin your analysis by evaluating:

- The company history and reputation (check with the real estate licensing authority to see if there are any complaints).
- Scope of services, market knowledge, cash flow and lease analysis capabilities, knowledge and depth of sales personnel.
- Review marketing plans they have produced and when your list is narrowed, have them produce a marketing plan for you and compare.

Exhibit 7–2 lists questions to ask when interviewing and evaluating real estate brokers.

Finally, here are some suggestions on what to do once you have chosen a broker.

- Establish the parameters of the relationship. The best way to accomplish this condition is to have a written engagement letter, in addition to any standard contract you may sign.
- Determine the frequency of reporting and whether it is to be verbal or written. Some brokers may want to contact you daily, others won't communicate at all unless they have either a property for you or a potential buyer. Depending on the size of your business and your presence at the location under contract, you may have delegated the responsibility of taking people through the property to someone in your organization and may not even be aware of how many prospects are being shown the building. The engagement letter should include a brief written report weekly or monthly listing prospects and status.
- Agree on deadlines. This includes developing the marketing campaign (if the transaction calls for one), when a deal can be expected to reach the stage of an offer and an acceptance, and when the deal should close.
- Resolve the financial issues—compensation. Commission rates are not as standard as most brokers would like you to believe. The range, depending on the size of the property and the difficulty in marketing it, can be significant. General business conditions can have a tremendous impact on the ability to find a buyer or tenant. Availability of similar properties will also affect the marketability. Also clarify who is responsible for the marketing costs and be sure this issue provides for costs incurred by the broker when a deal is not consummated.[11]
- Be firm with your broker.
- View the broker as part of your team.
- If you have selected carefully, trust his or her judgment.

Exhibit 7–2 Interview Questions for Real Estate Brokers

1. Have you participated in any transactions of properties similar to our needs? When? What? How many in the past year? _____

   _____

2. May I examine the marketing plans you prepared for the last three transactions in which you were involved? _____

   _____

3. What is your experience in business, outside the real estate business? __

   _____

4. Are you a member of SIOR? If not, how long have you been engaged in commercial real estate? _____

   _____

5. May I see your license? Have any complaints been registered against you in the past year? _____

   _____

6. What are your cash flow and lease analysis capabilities? _____

   _____

7. What type of marketing program do you propose (if sale or lease)? _____

   _____

8. Please discuss your view of the current market as it relates to my needs.

   _____

9. What is the time frame you anticipate for bringing the transaction to closure?_____

   _____

10. What compensation arrangements have you worked with over the past year? _____

    _____

11. How can I reach you on short notice? _____

    _____

THE THREE RS: REAL ESTATE

RECAP

- Perform a needs assessment—determine the requirements of the space you are seeking: size, location, parking, appearance, and so on.
- Develop a list of candidates.
- These are the broker's responsibilities—care, obedience, accounting, loyalty, disclosure.
- Evaluate each candidate's capabilities—look for professional integrity and competence.
- Once you choose a broker, establish the parameters of the relationship—agree in advance about your responsibilities and the broker's responsibilities for achieving a successful closing.

RESOURCES

- National Association of Realtors, 430 North Michigan Avenue, Chicago, IL 60611-4087, Tel: 312-329-8200.
- Society of Industrial and Office Realtors (SIOR), 700 11th Street NW, Suite 510, Washington, DC 20001-4511, Tel: 202-737-1150, http//:www.sior.com. Offers a variety of literature at nominal cost and will provide either its membership directory or a list of members in your geographic area.
- National Association of Master Appraisers (NAMA), 303 West Cypress Street, PO Box 12617, San Antonio, TX 78212, Tel: 800-229-6262. Affiliated with the National Society of Environmental Consultants and the Real Estate Law Institute, National Association of Counselors (same address). Publishes an annual Registry of Real Estate Specialists.

THE THREE RS *(continued)*

REFERENCES

- *Comparative Statistics of Industrial and Office Real Estate Markets* It presents fairly dry statistical analysis, market by market.
- *Guide to Industrial Site Selection*   If you are planning to build a manufacturing facility, this ought to be reviewed.
- *Industrial Real Estate*****   This is more like a textbook, but is loaded with useful information.
- *The Office Building* If you are thinking about buying or building an office building, this is a worthwhile reference.
- *Real Estate Fundamentals* Although probably too advanced for someone just trying to get an overview of the business, it is an excellent reference book.
- *Real Estate Investing**   The focus is on investment with some advice about dealing with agents.

COLLECTION AGENCIES

Some businesses require the ongoing use of collection agencies. Usually these businesses have a large consumer component such as retail, tradesmen, and so on. Other businesses, while not consumer oriented, may have a large number of accounts with relatively small balances, such as industrial supply or commercial office products. However, even businesses with a limited number of accounts receivable and with a blue chip customer base will very likely require the services of a collection agency at some point during the life of the business. Entrepreneurs are sometimes reluctant to use collection services, perhaps because of the historical reputation of the industry. Today however, the profession is much more regulated than in the past. Also, the industry has embraced a lot of technology and has become a sophisticated professional service provider.

The *function* of a collection agency includes these tasks:

- Improve cash flow and accounts receivable turnover.
- Relieve your bookkeeper, controller, and you from the collection function.

- Recover lost revenues from delinquent accounts.
- Assure that your credit collection policies are in compliance with the state and federal credit laws.

Some practitioners in the debt collection industry have tarnished the reputation of the professionals, therefore you must *be very selective* in identifying candidates to perform the collection function for your business. A good starting point is the American Collectors Association. The ACA's 3,700 members subscribe to a Code of Ethics and are bonded either as required by their state regulating body or by the ACA, absent state requirement. The ACA also offers a certification program.

Not every state has licensing programs for collectors. Those that do may operate through the state banking department or the state attorney general. Therefore, when initiating a search, determine whether your state has a licensing authority. The easiest way to find out is to ask the candidates themselves. Some other questions and issues are:

- Is the agency a member of a national trade association? Membership is an indication of professional integrity.
- What is the agency's reputation in the community? Check with the state licensing authority and with the local Better Business Bureau. Talk to other credit grantors.
- Ask for a list of references. When talking with the references ask:
  —How has the agency performed?
  —What is the agency's "net back"? (Net back is the actual dollars collected as a percentage of the total receivables turned over for collection. Exhibit 7–3 is an example of how net back is calculated.)
  —Do you get complaints from customers about the agency's methods?
- If necessary, is the agency able to place accounts with other collectors in other areas in the country (known in the trade as "forwarding")?
- Visit the agency's office. Observe the practices, the people, general atmosphere, state of the technology.
- Ask the agency for a proposal.
- Ask the agency about its training program for collectors.
- What is the agency's turnover of collectors? (Rule of thumb—collectors should have a 3–5 year longevity and turnover annually should not exceed 25%–30%.)
- Ask for a copy of the firm's Collection Policy and Procedure. (The agency may decline to provide this, but you can ask for an outline of the policy and procedure.) Exhibit 7–4 is an example.

Exhibit 7–3 Calculation of "Net Back"

Net back was explained to me as follows: some agencies may propose to take a 10 percent collection fee, while others may propose a 30 percent collection fee. For a 10 percent fee, the agency will generate perhaps two dunning letters and a phone call. For 30 percent, the agency will perform a skip trace, litigate, and expend considerably more effort. Likewise, the effort on the 10 percent fee may yield a 15 percent collection rate, and the effort on the 30 percent rate may yield a 25 percent collection rate. Your interest should be the net back—or how much you actually get back and not how much you have to share with the agency.

Example 1		Example 2	
$1,000.00	placed for collection	$1,000.00	placed for collection
× 15%	collection rate	× 25%	collection rate
$ 150.00	recovered	$ 250.00	recovered
× 10%	fee	× 30%	fee
$ 135.00	net back to creditor	$ 175.00	net back to creditor

Exhibit 7–4 Professional Finance Company Collection Policies

- All accounts received for collection are inputted (manually, by tape, diskette or modem) into the computer within 24 hours of receipt.
- Initial demand notices are created and mailed the same day the account is activated in the computer.
- All new accounts are automatically assigned to the unit of a specific collection specialist, usually determined by account balance, industry, and so on.
- Collection specialists begin attempting telephonic contact within 7 days of assignment. The objective of all initial contact is to receive payment in full.
- Collection specialists perform skip tracing, negotiating of payment agreements, asset and employment determination, legal recommendation, and all related follow-up.
- All accounts assigned for collection are reviewed every 7 days unless a date for payment has been reached or legal action has been taken.
- If a payment arrangement has been made, the file is reviewed the day following the promise of payment. If the payment was not received, immediate contact is attempted.
- Legal action is recommended only on accounts with verifiable employment and assets.

Note: Courtesy of Mike Shoop, President, Professional Finance Company, Greeley, Colorado.

As with any long-term business relationship, you have to work with the agency. A well-managed agency should be able and willing to supply you with quarterly reports.

A professional agency should be willing to assist you in developing internal collection procedures and assist with credit bureau selection, and may or may not charge for these additional services.

"Since professional collectors' services are personal in nature—with the debtor as well as with you—see that your collector is fully acquainted with the nature of the goods or services involved. This helps the collector handle intelligently the many complex situations that normally arise during collection activity. In addition, the collection service should be given a fair understanding of your accounting system so that the collectors can maintain mutually acceptable records and keep books in balance with yours."[12]

THE THREE Rs: COLLECTION AGENCIES

RECAP

- Develop a list of candidates from the national trade associations or from local references.
- Check the list against the complaint list of the state licensing authority to be certain you don't have any problem collection agents on your list.
- Visit the candidates' offices to see how professional they are and to observe working atmosphere.

RESOURCES

- American Collectors Association, 4040 West 70th Street, Minneapolis, MN 55435, Tel: 612-926-6547, Fax: 926-1624. Offers free brochures entitled "Selecting a Professional Collection Service" and "A Collection Guide for Creditors."
- International Credit Association (ICA), 243 North Lindbergh Boulevard, St. Louis, MO 63141-1757, Tel: 314-991-3030. Publishes a bimonthly magazine, *Credit World,* and a monthly newsletter, *Consumer Trends.* Also publishes credit management books and will provide a list of members in your geographic area. Membership includes in-house credit collection professionals as well as credit collection agencies.

THE THREE RS *(continued)*

REFERENCES

- *Collector Magazine*   This is published by the ACA, same address and telephone number as given in Resources; subscription $25.00 per year.
- *Credit World Magazine*   This also published by the ICA (same address and telephone number as given in Resources); subscription $50.00 per year.
- *Comprehensive Credit Manual*   Because the book covers a broad range of credit collection and management topics, as well as information about collection agents, it may be helpful in developing a comprehensive credit collection policy.

OUTSOURCING

Outsourcing is one of the buzz words of the 1990s. Companies providing outsourcing services have been around for over a hundred years. The Outsourcing Institute defines outsourcing as "the utilization of outside resources which frequently include the transfer of assets. Growth through other people's resources not through the acquisition of resources." OPR (other people's resources) replace OPM (other people's money).

You should *consider* outsourcing if:

- You have a function that is difficult to manage or out of control.
- Resources are not available internally—if you do not have in-house computer skills for example hiring an outside supplier of computer services may make sense.
- Cash infusion—selling a cafeteria operation in a factory to an outside company will provide immediate cash.
- Capital funds available—rather than buying equipment, having subcontractors supply services.
- You want to reduce operating costs—costs get moved from operating expenses to cost of goods sold.
- Free resources for other purposes—selling equipment and contracting out that function may enable you to acquire other equipment.

- Share risks—someone else bears the risk such as warehousing being performed by a public warehousing company.
- Accelerate re-engineering benefits—companies may be limited in employing new technology for lack of cash flow.
- Gain access to world-class capabilities—a sub-contractor who only does one thing should be more state of the art than a fully integrated facility.
- Improve business focus[13]—speaks to the definition of your business. Are you a marketing company or a manufacturing company? Instead of "feeding" machinery (keeping the machines running) you focus on your core skills of selling or developing new products.

These are some of the services that an outsource vendor may perform:

- Human resources—payroll, staffing, hiring, benefits.
- Transportation—shipping, warehousing, logistics.
- Technology—manufacturing, packaging, information systems.
- Administration—accounts payable, maintenance, clerical.
- Marketing and Sales—telemarketing, customer service, field service.

Companies are finding more and more functions that make sense to outsource rather than try to perform in-house. However, the same rules apply in deciding whether to outsource as with hiring an accountant, consultant or PR firm. And if you decide to outsource, the selection and management of the vendor is not any different from that of any other profession or vendor.

The following disciplines must be applied:

- The definition and specification of requirements in terms of clear and measurable results. Examples are a 30 percent reduction in clerical and administrative staffing, a reduction in order entry to order fill cycle from 5 days to 36 hours, an increase in process yields from 87 percent to 99.2 percent.
- Evaluation and selection of sources on the basis of value contribution and total cost. Focus on their experience in your business and business processes, assess qualifications of their staff, and weigh adequacy of their facilities and financial strength.
- Negotiation of price and performance considerations that are reasonable for the responsibilities and risks involved.[14]

As you begin the process of outsourcing, keep in mind that you are picking a roommate, not a one-time acquaintance. Therefore, you should ask some basic questions of your vendor and yourself as you work through the selection process:

- Is the vendor truly in the outsourcing business?
- Is the vendor able to adjust to your inability to forecast future sales or volume of work?
- You need to identify issues and clean up your mess before you turn it over to someone else.
- You should talk to people in your industry who have out-sources to find out why they did and what the results were.
- You need to develop a clear and concise RFP (Request for Proposal).
- You should also identify an attorney experienced in outsourcing contracts.[15]

After you have identified candidates, you will want to talk to their references; ask specific questions:

- What originally led them to outsource?
- What were the criteria they used to select the vendor? Location, size, expertise?
- Why did they pick the vendor?
- How is it going in relation to expectations?
- What has been their experience with the flexibility of the vendor?

My main experience with outsourcing to date has been in two areas: custom molders and payroll services. Payroll services are reasonably cut-and-dry affairs, unless you have some sort of hybrid compensation system for your employees. We made a fairly intense study of the costs associated with doing payroll ourselves and having it prepared by a payroll service and found the outsourcing was not only cheaper but vastly more efficient. Things don't always go smoothly but compared with the problems we had in-house, the glitches are nominal with the outside vendor.

My experience with custom molders is another story. A custom molder is a contractor who will put your plastic injection molds into his machines and produce parts or components for you. The price you pay is a function of the hourly rate for the machine and the cost of the material used. A molder may provide other services, such as assembly and packaging, for which you will pay extra. Billions of components are produced every year by custom molders who perform work for Fortune 500 firms and for small mom-and-pop businesses alike. The quality of the work performed is generally in direct correlation to the effort you invest in selecting and managing these outside vendors. With hindsight, I must attribute some of my nightmare experiences with custom molders to my own poor management.

THE TWO RS: OUTSOURCING

RECAP

- Define and specify requirements with clear and measurable results.
- Evaluate and select sources on the basis of value contribution and total cost.
- Negotiate price and performance based on reasonable achievable measures.

RESOURCES

- The Outsourcing Institute, 45 Rockefeller Plaza, Suite 2000, New York, NY 10111, Tel: 800-421-6767, http://www .outsourcing.com. Publishes an annual Buyer's Guide, and a wide range of material including the Year-end Trends & Issues Survey, an Online Bibliography, a quarterly publication, *The Source,* and the OI also runs a Referral Help Desk.

8

SALES
REPRESENTATIVES
AND BROKERS

Many businesses do not need independent sales representatives such as retail shops. Businesses that depend on independent agents to develop sales and maintain customer contact, however, may find that the selection and management of sales reps is a daunting task. Turnover and changes in marketplace, as well as the need for more than one rep by most businesses, mean that the selection process and management effort often require much more attention than other professions discussed in this book.

The *function* of a sales rep includes these tasks:

- Market and generate sales of your products or services.
- Initiate contact with prospective customers.
- Open new accounts.
- Maintain regular contact with existing accounts.
- Introduce new products or programs to customers.
- Act as liaison between various departments within customer and vendor organizations.

- Advise of developments and trends in their market.
- Provide cost-effective alternative to in-house sales staff.

DETERMINING WHETHER YOU NEED SALES REPS

Since excellent references are available on the selection and management of independent sales representatives (sales reps), I will not attempt to provide a detailed explanation of the process here. If your firm is dependent on this profession, I urge you to acquire at least one of the references listed at the end of the chapter.

Successful marketing through reps involves the following factors:

- *Understanding the partnering philosophy.* All too often the rep is viewed as an outsider, not as a partner. There is a normal tension between principals and reps whether the rep is working with a hired sales manager or an entrepreneurial owner. Reps may have to divide their time between multiple lines but principals are only concerned about their own line. Reps don't get paid if they don't sell, whereas sales managers normally enjoy base salaries regardless of sales.
- *Understanding what each partner should expect from the other.* This is one of those Catch-22 situations: Does the rep understand that you don't want sales for the sake of sales and do you realize that the rep sees a smaller commission as being better than no commission?
- *Being sensitive to the reps' motivation.* Reps live with the fear that if they do too good a job, the manufacturer may take the account away, or reduce the territory, or cut commissions. Being fair to reps will pay dividends.
- *Communication.* This is another two-way component. Does the rep fulfill the obligation to inform the principal about trends in the market and about customers who are having problems paying other vendors on time? And is the principal being fair and effective in advising the rep of problems shipping orders or special offers made to customers in other territories?
- *Field visits and other contacts.* Reps know how to sell and how to maintain a good working relationship with customers, but they need visits from the factory managers to learn how to sell your products and overcome objections to your line.
- *Additional support.* How generous are you in supplying samples, sales literature, leads, news of other success stories?
- *Understanding the future.* What are the principals and reps doing to remain at the cutting edge of the ever-changing marketplace?

Manufacturers should expect agencies (reps) to uphold the following standards:

- Guarantee of 100 percent loyalty (won't sell conflicting and/or competing lines).
- Knowledge of the customer's industry, the market, and the territory.
- Knowledge of the manufacturer's products.
- An equitable share of the agency's time and effort in presenting the manufacturers' products to customers.[1]

The phenomenon of independent sales reps is no longer the bailiwick of companies who cannot afford or justify in-house sales organizations; even large companies utilize independent sales reps. Businesses using reps must rely on people over whom they maintain little control to represent their firms and reflect their image in the marketplace.

These are the advantages of working with sales reps:

- They can give you immediate entry into a territory.
- They can make regular calls on customers and prospects.
- They can provide sales expertise.
- Their cost is a predetermined selling expense—a percentage of sales as their commission.

These are the disadvantages of working with sales reps:

- Your control over their selling techniques is more limited than when you train and use your own employees.
- If, and when, you cancel a contract, the agent may take many of your customers.
- On a large volume of sales, the selling expense may be greater than it would be with your own employees.
- Agents' allegiance to your company and its products is not total because they serve other clients also. They have to have extra financial incentives to push your products (although reps also are motivated by other factors such as the product, the market, the personality of the principal, and the support they receive from you).[2]

The following list suggests points to consider in matching an agent to your company's character and image:

1. What sort of selling skills are necessary for selling my products? Does the agent need technical knowledge and experience in addition to personal selling ability? Does he or she

have the clout that will open the door for my company's products or services? If reps *do* need training, is my company equipped to handle it?

2. What marketing functions, if any, do I need in addition to selling?

3. Must the agent service my product as well as sell it?

4. Do I need a one-person agency or an organization? If the latter, how large an organization?

5. Is the agent's record of success in products and territories similar to mine?

6. How long has the agent been in business? What is the agent's reputation? How well can we trade on it?

7. Are the other lines carried by the agent compatible with mine? Will the agent's contacts for existing lines help gain entry for my line?

8. Is the trade the agent specializes in the one I want to reach?

9. Does the agent cover the geographic area, market segment, or customers I need covered, and in what depth?

10. Do the character, personality, values, and integrity of our two organizations correspond?

11. Can the reps who are employees of the sales agency manage their own territories, or will they need sales management and guidance from the agents, or from me?

12. Is the agent the type that merely follows instructions? Or does the agent have a reputation for offering constructive suggestions? What type do I need?

13. Is the "chemistry" right? Will we enjoy working together?[3]

If you are reading this chapter in anticipation of your first search for a sales rep, the following is a general description of what you can expect:

The average sales rep may be a sole practitioner or may work in a three- or four-person partnership. The rep's territory may be defined by a geographic area (New York City), by a specific trade (drug chains), or by a combination. There are even reps who specialize in specific accounts (Kmart, Wal-Mart). Most reps have 5 to 15 vendor accounts, of which three or four will generate the bulk of their income. In some classes of trade or territories, however, a rep may handle only a single vendor—or 50 vendors. Some reps operate showrooms, based on the tradition of a given trade (e.g., toys and gifts). Some reps may exhibit at national or regional trade shows, again depending on the practice of the trade. Typically, vendors supply reps with all the sales materials and samples at no cost. Reps work on anywhere from 2 percent to 20 percent of net invoice value as a commission.

"It is not off base to say that most bad experiences with sales reps could have been avoided if the company had hired the right rep in the first place."[4] You should use a search methodology consisting of six elements: commitment, planning, responsibility, search, screening, and selection.[5]

A business that requires sales reps usually needs more than one. Sometimes, a business must develop a network of reps in a relatively short period. For a small business with limited resources, such an undertaking can be overwhelming. If possible, it is preferable to target a given market and to fill one position at a time. However, whether you are seeking one rep, or several, the methodology is the same.

FINDING CANDIDATES FOR EVALUATION AND GETTING RECOMMENDATIONS

As has been noted with other professions, you need to develop a list of candidates. The sources for that list will diverge to some degree from the methodology discussed in other sections of the book for list development. The following sources are listed in order of preference:

1. *Customers.* Many of the best reps I ever hired were recommended to me by buyers. Even if you are not already doing business with a firm, you can either telephone or ask the potential customer face to face to recommend one or two good sales rep organizations. This approach offers the added advantage of developing rapport with buyers, especially if you end up hiring the recommended rep.

2. *Peers.* It is unwise to try to hire agents who represent your direct competitors. However, think about this idea: We produced plastic shoe trees and one of our principal target markets was the U.S. military—PXs, base exchanges, and so on. Kiwi Shoe Polish had a network of military distributors and did not sell shoe trees as part of their stock assortment. So we approached all the Kiwi distributors, and ended up selling everyone.

I also wouldn't rule out establishing contact with a competitor's rep. The rep may be willing to drop the other line to carry your line or may be on the verge of being dropped because of some conflict. If you can identify peers in your industry who do not have conflicting products but do have parallel distribution and can obtain their rep list, you may have a prequalified set of reps. Some trade show directories will include the names of the reps in the exhibitor information and some companies list the names of their reps in their literature.

3. *Other reps.* If you have a good rep in one territory, he or she often can provide the names of reps in other areas. However, don't think that you have performed your due diligence by obtaining the name from a reliable rep. He or she may not know how good or bad the other rep is, only that the rep has some of the same lines.

4. *Trade shows.* Whether exhibiting at trade shows or just walking around as a visitor, you can meet many sales reps. Trade shows are not the ideal time to evaluate sales reps but they can be effective in establishing first contact on a face-to-face basis. You can also perform some preliminary screening by visiting other exhibitors represented by a candidate.

5. *Trade magazine advertising.* Whether through an ad you placed or the rep placed, trade magazines do represent a resource. However, I cannot recall ever having hired a rep from a trade magazine ad.

6. *Trade associations and/or trade association rep organizations.* Many trade associations provide matchmaking services and larger trades or industries have associations of sales representatives who also provide matchmaking services.

7. *Manufacturers' Representatives Educational Research Foundation (MRERF).* In addition to offering a Bibliography that includes the names and addresses of trade-oriented rep associations and books and articles, MRERF has produced a thorough and useful manual for managing your rep relations. The book, *Thriving with Reps,* is well worth its price tag of $289, as it includes sections on evaluating and selecting your sales channels, preparing to recruit reps, recruiting, selecting and start-up. I wish I had the manual when I ran my business.

8. *Manufacturers' Agents National Association (MANA).* In addition to its membership directory, MANA publishes a monthly magazine—*Agency Sales*—with a four-page section entitled "RepLetter," which may be worth the subscription price. "RepLetter" is targeted toward manufacturers and apparently was once a separate publication. MANA's *How to Work Successfully with Manufacturers' Agencies* cannot compare with the MRERF package, but for 10 dollars it will provide you with some basic information.

According to Henry Lavin, "Manufacturers list the following approaches as most productive to them in recruiting representatives:

- Recommendations from customers—36 percent.
- Recommendations from other principals—35 percent.
- Recommendations from representatives—22 percent.
- Representatives' association listings or directories—9 percent.
- Trade publication ads—6 percent.

- Solicitation of competitors' representatives—5 percent.
- Other methods—3 percent.

(The total is greater than 100 percent, since more than one approach is used.)"[6]

EVALUATING SALES REPS

Most established rep organizations have prepared material describing the people in the organization, perhaps abbreviated resumes, lines carried, markets serviced, and other basic information. Part of your list-building exercise will be to accumulate this promotional material.

At some point, preferably prior to the interview, you will qualify the candidates by checking out their references. No rep is going to give you a reference who will paint a negative picture. However, a reference may reveal the rep is exaggerating his accomplishments. Have your questions ready, be professional and efficient, and above all listen to the responses you receive when talking with references (in Appendix IV, I have included three forms from *Thriving with Reps*, "Representative Recruiting and Start-Up Status Log," "Representative Data Sheet," and "Representative Survey Report" a Telephone Reference Check).

When you have narrowed the list, you need to make a trip to the territory and visit each rep agency. Ideally, you should arrange to spend at least part of a day visiting customers with at least one member of the agency. Your visit to their offices will reveal how professional the rep's organization is. Your visits to their customers with them will reveal how well they have prepared for these sales calls and how effectively they have established rapport with the buyers, receptionists, secretaries, and merchandise managers. Also, you should visit the rep's office and discuss what he or she does to keep up on developments.

Exhibit 8–1 lists questions to ask when interviewing prospective sales reps. In addition, the MANA monograph offers an interesting perspective to the interview stage of the selection process. It discusses the kinds of questions *you* should be prepared to answer when meeting with candidates; Exhibit 8–2 lists some of these. Preparing yourself for the questions reps may ask will help you in defining the features and benefits of your product and how to sell your company to a prospective rep.

If you get to ask the rep all the questions you want and he or she asks even half of the questions in Exhibit 8–2, you are going to have a very good picture of the capability and motivation of the candidate.

Exhibit 8–1   Interview Questions for Sales Representatives

1. Describe your agency's business—lines, territory, customers. _____

2. What are the things that principals do that turn you off as a rep? _____

3. What have some of the companies you represent done that you thought were good business practices? _____

4. Are there any specific problems in your territory? _____

5. What other lines do you represent that are compatible with mine? (i.e., require calling on same buyer, have same seasonality, etc.) _____

6. What do you think your other principals would say about your strengths and weaknesses, if I were to ask them? _____

7. What would the buyers say in response to number 6? _____

8. From what you have seen of our line and literature, how would you position our line and present it to the buyers? _____

9. If you had the opportunity, what would you do to our packaging and/or literature to improve it? _____

10. What do you know about our competitors? _____

Exhibit 8–1   *(continued)*

11. What did you do for the five years prior to forming your agency? _____

_____

12. Why did you decide to go into business for yourself? _____

_____

13. What are your plans for your agency for the next five years? _____

_____

14. Would you be willing to expand your agency to accommodate a new account? If so, how would you go about expansion? _____

_____

15. Would you be willing to expand your territory? How would you go about that expansion? _____

_____

16. How many lines do you represent? _____

_____

17. What would you consider the minimum sales volume necessary to handle our line? _____

_____

18. Would you be willing to assist us in compiling market research for use in establishing sales goals? _____

_____

Note: Lavin recommends obtaining answers to some of these questions in advance of a meeting with the rep. This will also act as a prequalification of the agency.

Exhibit 8–2   Questions Sales Reps May Ask *You* about Your Business[8]

---

1. What are the advantages and disadvantages of your product compared with those of your competitor?
2. How do you establish your prices? What are the policies on discounts, returns, and special products? How do your prices compare with those of your competitors?
3. What is your share of the national market? What is your share of market in the territory we will cover? What do you plan to do to increase this share of market?
4. How many actual customers do you estimate there are for your product in the territory? How do they buy? Is there regular repeat business once a sale is made? Who are the buying influences?
5. Describe the competitive situation in terms of number and strength of competitors, location, policies, strength in territory, growth, and estimated profitability.
6. How good are the competitive salespeople? Are they company paid, or agents? Is there a high or low turnover rate?
7. Describe your present sales organization in terms of internal and external support services? How do you communicate with your agencies, and do you do it on a regular basis? What are your sales objectives for the next year? The next five years?
8. How quickly can your production department deliver? Do you stock in sufficient depth to keep customers happy?
9. Describe your trade advertising program. Is it geared to producing inquiries? Are the inquiries prescreened and sent to the field immediately? What are your policies on cooperative advertising?
10. What are the boundaries of the territory?
11. If you have house accounts, how are commissions to agencies handled?
12. Describe your field backup policies.
13. What are your procedures for termination?
14. Are you prepared to invest in plant expansion?
15. Are commissions paid 30 days after shipment?
16. What are your provisions for paying commissions on business that exists in the territory?
17. Does your controller have a problem writing a big commission check? Do we both agree that the more I earn, the more you earn?
18. Are we getting together for the long pull?
19. How many representatives do you have, how long have they been with you, and may I talk with some of them?

PREPARING YOUR ORGANIZATION AND YOURSELF FOR HIRING AND MANAGING INDEPENDENT SALES REPS

Before you engage in the time-consuming and often frustrating process of shopping for sales reps, you should do a lot of homework. The references suggested in this chapter have done a much more thorough job than I could here in the space allocated for this profession. Nevertheless, I would be remiss if I didn't at least provide you with some guidelines. Imagine for a moment that you decided to build a house after having lived in apartments all your life. Logically, you would develop a profile of your family's requirements for space. You would spend hours, even days and weeks, looking at existing homes, layouts, locations, and so on trying to determine your needs and desires. You then would evaluate your current financial situation, your potential future situation; and consider market conditions. The recruiting process requires the same depth of input. You need to:

- Review the product offering.
- Understand markets.
- Assess the internal organization.
- Evaluate sales channels.
- Select sales channels.
- Develop a recruiting process and action plan.
- Create a representative agreement.
- Set up a rep marketing policy and program.
- Allow time and money to build an effective rep organization.
- Construct recruiting and selection tools.[7]

All this should be done before you begin the recruiting process for sales representatives.

Henry Lavin has graciously permitted me to use Exhibit 8–3, Sales Tools of Personal Marketing, and Twenty Ways to Motivate the Representative to illustrate the importance of managing the sales rep relationship.

Exhibit 8–4 is a sample Representative's Sales Agreement provided as the type of document you ought to have as part of your effort to be professional in hiring reps and present that appearance to the reps.

Exhibit 8–3   The Sales Tools of Personal Marketing by Independent
Sales Representatives[10]

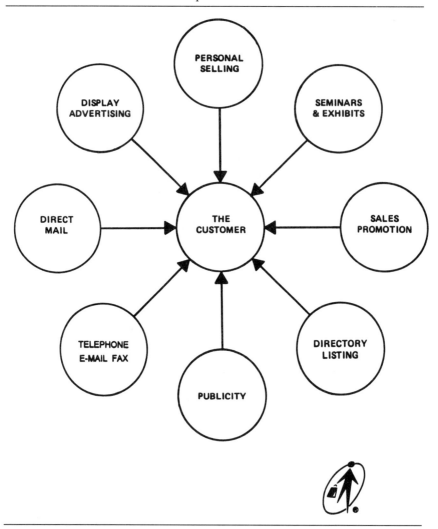

Twenty Ways to Motivate the Representative[9]

1. Do not keep house accounts. Pay the representative something on special accounts.
2. Pay more for more sales. Pay an extra bonus over a quota arrangement.
3. Pay the representative's commissions on time and on invoice.
4. Have an exclusive sales contract with the stated performance guidelines spelled out.
5. Praise the representative's good sales work by letter, with a plaque, or with free or discounted company stock. (Avoid gift giving!)
6. Do not cut commissions. If the representative does not earn them, get another representative.
7. Ask the representative for advice. Representatives are independent businesspeople and can be very helpful in business planning. Many manufacturers use "rep councils"—periodic key representative meetings—to help plan company marketing strategies.
8. Confirm all communications with a letter or memo.
9. Explain new literature and products in detail. News of successful product sales application is of prime importance to the representative.
10. Check your office bureaucracy. It may be causing communication problems.
11. Communicate with the customer through the representative. Treat your representatives like royalty in their territories.
12. Advise representatives at once if something goes wrong. It is their problem too.
13. Pay close attention to the representative's reports of customer reactions. They can be harbingers of good or bad sales situations.
14. Promptly pass on inquiries and sales leads to the representatives.
15. Cooperate with the representative in trade shows, ads, and direct mail.
16. Provide periodic stocking reports on your products.
17. Prepare realistic market potential, sales forecasts, and quotas; and discuss quotas with reps before assigning them.
18. Provide catalogs, samples, data sheets, and other sales aids that will help them sell the product. Condensed catalogs for representative mailings are especially helpful.
19. Ship orders promptly. Always give the rep advanced notice of shipping delays.
20. Select your rep with great care. Taking time in hiring cuts the cost and headaches of firing.

Exhibit 8–4   Sample—Representative's Sales Agreement

_____

_____
    (Principal)

                                    AND

                            _____
                                              (Representative)

hereby agree as follows:

1. APPOINTMENT. Principal appoints Representative as its exclusive sales representative for the territory described in Appendix A to solicit orders for those products and services listed in Appendix B together with any modifications thereof and those products or services which the Principal shall request the Representative to sell in the future. Representative accepts this appointment and agrees to promote the sale of Principal's products and services.

2. ORDERS AND COLLECTIONS. Orders for products obtained by Representative shall be forwarded to Principal and are subject to Principal's acceptance. Principal agrees to refer all inquiries relating to the territory to Representative and promptly to furnish Representative with copies of all correspondence and documentation between Principal and Customer relating to matters in the territory. All invoices, in connection with orders obtained by Representative, shall be rendered by Principal directly to the Customer. The Representative shall assist in collecting past-due accounts. However, full responsibility for all collections and bad debts rests with the Principal.

3. COMMISSIONS.

(a) Principal shall pay the Representative commissions at the rate specified in Appendix C attached hereto. When more than one Representative is involved with a particular order, the commissions specified in Appendix C shall be split among the following parties according to the percentages specified below:

_____% of the commission to the Representative in whose territory the order originated.

_____% of the commission to the Representative to whose territory the order is shipped.

_____% of the commission to the Representative who substantially facilitated the placement of the order, securing engineering and other specifications.

Commissions are payable on the net invoice price of all orders obtained from Customers in the territory, exclusive of sales taxes, insurance and freight charges.

(b) Commissions are earned by Representatives upon Principal issuing an invoice to Customer and are payable not later than the 15th day of the month following the date of invoice. Principal shall provide Representative with a monthly commission statement which shall include Customer's name,

Exhibit 8–4 *(continued)*

address, invoice number, invoice amount, date of invoice and the amount of commission earned.

(c) In the event the Customer fails to pay the invoice, after Principal has taken all reasonable and necessary steps to effectuate collection, Principal shall advise Representative in writing of its intent to charge back commissions on the unpaid balance of such invoice. Principal may then deduct the amount of commissions earned on the unpaid invoice amount from Representative's next commission check. However, in that event, Principal shall assign the debt to Representative who may at its option take such steps as Representative may elect to collect the entire amount of the debt or any portion thereof and upon collection, retain the amount of commissions and all costs of collection, including attorney's fees, and remit to Principal the balance of the amount collected, if any.

4. SALES POLICY. All prices and terms of sale shall be established by Principal, who has the right to change them upon thirty (30) days written notice to Representative.

5. USE OF REPRESENTATIVES. Representatives shall have the right to appoint sub-representatives to sell Principal's products in portions of the territory. Sub-representatives may, however, only be appointed with the Principal's approval in writing, which approval will not be unreasonably withheld. In the event sub-representatives are appointed, they shall be bound by all of the applicable terms and conditions of This Agreement.

6. GOVERNMENT REQUIREMENTS. Each party hereto shall comply with all statutes, ordinances, government regulations and governmental requirements in the conduct of its business. Failure to do so will be a material breach of This Agreement.

7. RELATIONSHIP OF PRINCIPAL AND REPRESENTATIVE.

(a) Representative shall maintain a sales office within the territory and shall use its best efforts, and devote such time as may be reasonably necessary to sell and promote the sale of Principal's products and services.

(b) Representative will conduct all of its business in its own name and in such manner as it may see fit. Representative will pay all the expenses of its office and activities and will be responsible for the acts and expenses of its employees.

(c) Nothing in This Agreement shall be construed to constitute Representative as the partner, employee or agent of the Principal; nor shall either party have any authority to bind the other in any respect, it being intended that each shall remain an independent contractor responsible only for its own actions.

(d) Representative shall not, without Principal's prior written approval, alter, enlarge or limit orders; accept the return of or make any allowance for products sold.

(continued)

Exhibit 8–4   *(continued)*

(e) Representative shall furnish to Principal's Credit Department any information which it may have, from time to time, relative to the credit standing of any of its customers.

(f) Principal shall be solely responsible for the design, development, supply, production and performance of its products and the protection of its tradenames and patents. Principal agrees to indemnify, hold Representative harmless against and to pay all losses, costs, damages or expenses whatsoever, including counsel fees, which Representative may sustain or incur on account of infringement or alleged infringements of patents, trademarks or tradenames resulting from the sale of the Principal's products, or arising on account of warranty claims or product liability claims. Representative will promptly deliver to Principal any notices or papers served upon it in any proceeding covered by this Indemnification Agreement, and Principal will defend such litigation at its expense. Representative shall, however, have the right to participate in the defense at its own expense unless there is a conflict of interest in which case the Principal will indemnify Representative for the expenses of such defense including counsel fees. Principal shall provide Representative with a certificate of insurance evidencing Representative as an additional insured on Principal's product liability insurance policy.

(g) Principal shall furnish to Representative, at no expense to Representative, samples, catalogs, literature and any other material necessary for the proper promotion and sale of its products in the territory. Any literature which is not used, samples or other equipment belonging to Principal shall be returned to the Principal at its request.

(h) Whenever Representative, at Principal's request, takes possession of Principal's products for the purpose of delivering such products to customers or for any other purpose, the risk of loss or damage to or destruction of such products shall be borne by Principal; and Principal shall indemnify and hold Representative harmless against any claims, debts, liabilities or causes of action resulting from any such loss, damage or destruction.

(i) Principal shall provide Representative and Representative's employees with reasonable training and instruction in connection with Principal's products.

(j) Representative agrees that it will attend, at Principal's request, a reasonable number of trade shows necessary for the promotion of Principal's products and will perform necessary work at such trade shows. Principal will pay reasonable room costs and Representative will pay other costs and expenses incident to the attendance at such trade shows.

(k) Principal shall furnish to Representative a copy of all correspondence with customers in the territory or relating to the territory including but not limited to drawings, acknowledgments, letters, quotations, inquiries, invoices and past due notices. In addition, Principal shall advise Representative in a timely fashion of all phone and other communications from Customers in the territory.

(l) Principal shall promptly furnish to Representative a copy of all sales leads from Customers or prospective Customers located in or related to

Exhibit 8–4 *(continued)*

Representative's territory. Representative will promptly follow up on such leads unless he has a valid reason for not doing so.

8. WARRANTIES AND REPRESENTATIONS.

(a) Representative agrees to make no false or misleading representations with respect to Principal or Principal's products. Representative shall make no express or implied warranties to Customers or prospective Customers or their representatives or to any other person on behalf of Principal with respect to any of Principal's products without Principal's express written consent. Representative agrees to hold Principal harmless from all damages resulting from Representative's breach of obligations of this paragraph (a).

(b) Principal shall repair or replace (within the limitations of such applicable express written warranty as may be issued by it) any products or parts thereof which prove to be defective in workmanship or material at Principal's expense.

(c) If Principal requests Representative to perform warranty work or repairs, the parties shall enter into a separate agreement relating to the Representative's performance and compensation for such work.

9. WAREHOUSING. In the event that Principal requests Representative to warehouse Principal's products, Representative will perform warehousing services at its own expense but will receive an additional commission of _____ percent on all sales within the territory.

10. PROCEDURE ON TERMINATION. In the event of termination or non-renewal of This Agreement, Representative shall promptly return to Principal all samples, literature and product, if any, warehoused by Representative, the cost of shipping to be borne by Principal.

11. HIRING EMPLOYEES. Representative and Principal agree that during the term of This Agreement and any renewal thereof and for six months thereafter, neither will hire or engage or attempt to hire or engage an employee of the other or an independent representative under contract to the other without first obtaining prior written approval from the other.

12. TERM. This agreement is effective the date written below and shall continue for three (3) years. Thereafter, it shall automatically renew, for successive three (3) year periods, unless either party terminates it upon ninety (90) days written notice to the other before the end of the initial term of This Agreement or any renewal term. Upon termination or non-renewal, Representative is entitled to the commissions specified in paragraph 3 on all orders placed prior to the effective date of termination or non-renewal, regardless of when Principal accepts, invoices or ships such orders. In the event that, prior to termination or non-renewal of This Agreement, Representative has secured an order for a prototype or model which order Principal accepts at any time, Representative shall receive commissions from all orders subsequently placed with Principal based on acceptance of such prototype or model. No

(continued)

Exhibit 8–4   *(continued)*

termination or non-renewal shall be effective unless the terminating or non-renewing party is current in its financial obligations to the other. Anything in This Agreement notwithstanding, This Agreement may be terminated for the following reasons only:

(a) In the event that either party hereto shall commit an act of bankruptcy or file a voluntary petition for bankruptcy, or be declared bankrupt in an involuntary proceeding, or file for a plan under any Bankruptcy Act, or place its affairs in the hands of a receiver, or enter into a composition for the benefit of creditors, or perform any other act based upon or due to its inadequate credit position, then the other party to This Agreement may terminate This Agreement immediately by written notice of termination to the other party.

(b) Should either party be in material breach of its obligations and responsibilities under This Agreement, then the other party may terminate This Agreement by giving sixty (60) days advance written notice of termination to the other party. However, after receiving such notice, the party receiving same shall have thirty (30) days to cure the alleged breach.

13. QUOTA. Principal shall set an annual quota as provided in Appendix D for sales by the Representative. If Principal fails to set a quota for any year, the last quota set shall continue in force. Sales quotas shall be reasonable. In establishing sales quotas, Principal shall consider such factors as prior sales in the territory by the Principal and by this or prior Representative(s), extent of recognition of Principal's name, trademark or reputation and general economic conditions or trends in the industry. Failure by the Representative to meet quota shall not be a basis for termination if such failure is caused by matters beyond the Representative's control. If Representative fails to meet quota in any year but its sales in that year, as compared to sales in the territory during the prior year, are at least equal to Principal's national sales of products listed in Appendix B in the quota year as compared to Principal's sales of such products the prior year, Representative's failure to meet quota shall not be a basis for termination of This Agreement.

14. ARBITRATION. Any controversies or claims relating to any aspect of This Agreement, or to its breach, or to the relationship created shall be settled by Arbitration under the rules of the American Arbitration Association in the state where Representative has its principal place of business. The laws of that state shall be deemed controlling as to all matters arising under This Agreement or relationship. The parties agree to abide by the Arbitrator's award and also agree that a judgment may be entered upon the award as a final judgment of a court of record. The Arbitrators shall have the power to grant injunctions and mandatory injunctions as well as other types of award. Notwithstanding any rule to the contrary, the prevailing party shall be entitled to recover attorney's fees and costs of Arbitration. If any provision of This Agreement is held contrary to law, the remaining provisions shall remain valid. The award of Arbitrators shall be binding and non-appealable.

Exhibit 8–4   *(continued)*

15. ENTIRE AGREEMENT. This Agreement contains the parties entire understanding, shall supersede any other oral or written agreements, and may not be modified except in a writing signed by both.

16. NOTICES. All notices between the parties shall be in writing and effective when sent by certified mail to the addresses above stated.

IN WITNESS WHEREOF, Representative and Principal have caused This Agreement to be signed on the date set forth below and be effective on the last date specified below.

Principal: _____

By: _____

Title: _____

Date: _____

Representative: _____

By: _____

Title: _____

Date: _____

APPENDIX A
REPRESENTATIVE'S TERRITORY

APPENDIX B
REPRESENTATIVE'S PRODUCTS

APPENDIX C
REPRESENTATIVE'S COMMISSION SCHEDULE

APPENDIX D
REPRESENTATIVE'S SALES QUOTA

Note: Courtesy of the Manufacturer's Representatives Educational Research Foundation.

THE THREE RS: SALES REPS

RECAP

- Do additional reading before jumping into the process— learn about marketing and selling in general and then specifically about your business and only then study about selling through independent sales reps.

- Determine what you need first from your sales reps—specify feedback from buyers, introduction of your company and its products or services, sales to certain classes of trade, program selling, and so on.

- Develop a list of candidates.

- Screen candidates carefully including field visits—do not hire reps with whom you have not actually spent time in the field. Confirm what buyers and principals say about candidates.

RESOURCES

- Manufacturers' Representatives Educational Research Foundation (MRERF), PO Box 247, Geneva, IL 60134, Tel: 708-208-1466, Fax: 708-208-1475. This is an umbrella organization for about 70 associations of sales reps. They will guide you through the process including directing you to the appropriate association for your class of trade. They also offer a wide range of material from sample contracts to guides on managing your relationship with sales reps.

- Manufacturers' Agents National Association (MANA), PO Box 3467, Laguna Hills, CA 92654-3467, Tel: 714-859-4040, Fax: 714-855-2973. An association of primarily industrial sales representatives. Claims a membership of 7,500 agencies and offers a membership directory—the *Directory of Manufacturers' Agents.*

- Lavin Associates, 12 Promontory Drive, Cheshire, CT 06410-1497, Tel: 203-272-9121, Fax: 203-250-1461. Provides consulting services to manufacturers on hiring and use of sales reps, publishes a number of texts on managing independent sales reps. Lavin also offers a range of forms—"Rep Selection and Evaluation Tools."

REFERENCES

- *Agency Sales Magazine*   This marketing magazine for manufacturers' agencies and their principals has a section entitled "Rep Letter," which is directed at principals. Subscription Department, Tel: 714-859-4040, $49.00 per year.
- *Sales & Marketing Management Magazine*   Articles on management of sales reps appear periodically in this general sales management monthly. Subscription Department, Tel: 800-821-6897, $48.00 per year.
- *Selling through Independent Reps*****   Probably the seminal text on the subject, this book is worth having if you are serious about developing and maintaining an independent sales force.
- *Thriving with Reps*****   Although slightly slanted toward sales reps, it is, nevertheless, an excellent reference.

The following references have not been reviewed by me and therefore do not appear in the Bibliography. Many may be out of print; however, if you are able to locate them, I am sure they will add to your knowledge base. I have selected titles from a bibliography supplied to me by Ed Bobrow and from Harold Novick's Resource Guide in his book:

- *How to Build Sales with Manufacturers' Agencies,* James Gibbons, Englewood Cliffs, NJ: Prentice Hall, 1989.
- *How to Get—and Keep!—Good Industrial Representatives,* Dr. Henry Lavin, Cheshire, CT: Lavin Associates, Tel: 203-272-9121 ($90.00). Hank is a well-known author and consultant in the field of utilization of reps. It should be a useful reference.
- *How to Get—And Keep!—A Profitable Rep Agency by Effective Marketing,* Dr. Henry Lavin, Cheshire, CT: Lavin Associates ($41.00).
- *How to Hire and Motivate Manufacturers' Representatives,* William Krause, New York: AMACOM.
- *Is the Independent Sales Agent for You?* Edwin Bobrow, Small Business Administration (#200).
- *Understanding and Motivating the Manufacturers' Agent,* Dick Berry, Florence, KY: CBI Publishing.
- *Will Using Independent Sales Agents Meet Your (Clients') Sales Goals,* Edwin Bobrow, MANA, Tel: 714-859-4040 ($10.00).

Part II

MANAGING THE RELATIONSHIP WITH CONSULTANTS, PROFESSIONALS, AND FREELANCERS

9

COMPENSATION

Most of us love our consultants, lawyers, and advisers until they send us the bill. We see the detail of the 20-minute telephone conversation that cost us $100 and we know that we were just "shooting the breeze" for 10 of those minutes, and then we begin a "slow burn."

What you must consider in all your dealings with all professional advisers is *all they have to sell is their time.* Even an insurance agent or a real estate broker, both of whom are compensated primarily through commissions, evaluate their risk/reward ratio as a function of their return of money on investment of time. Understanding this fundamental reality and constantly reminding ourselves of it can, over the life of our relationships with advisers, save us a great deal of anger and angst.

The second and equally important element to incorporate into our thought process is *what is this service worth to me?* Worry less about how much it is *costing* and more about the economic *benefit* to your business.

In this chapter, I will discuss negotiating the method of compensation, determining or measuring value, controlling costs, and managing the process.

War Story. My first patent infringement litigation cost me upward of $100,000 and ended in what I have often described as a Pyrrhic victory—the verdict held that my patent was valid but not infringed. The development of this product came about from a visit to the factory of a vendor, a Swedish company, after I had been doing business with the company for several years. During the visit, I came across a component they were producing that I hadn't seen before. It was an improvement on the wire components used in jaw-type pant and skirt hangers. The improvement consisted of a nylon locking element that replaced the metal-to-metal locking element, which had a tendency to fatigue and deposit the garment on the floor. I decided to incorporate this element into a new hanger with plastic jaws. We were granted a design patent in short order.

Having limited distribution and feeling the product had a lot of potential, I took it to a major manufacturer and offered to supply the product under the manufacturer's label. At first the manufacturer turned me down and I started to market the product on my own. As we gained some success and exposure, the manufacturer came back to me and asked to market the product. Unbeknownst to me, the manufacturer was having a "knock-off" made in Taiwan. As soon as the knock-off was ready, the manufacturer dropped our product and substituted the Taiwanese import.

For a long time I was angry about the decision and what I felt was the less-than-effective management of the litigation on the part of my counsel. The trial took place with a jury. It began on a Wednesday afternoon with a stern warning from the judge that it would be over by Friday afternoon or else! The judge was an older man as was the defense counsel. My attorney was young and dressed in a rather loud suit. I felt I had not taken an active enough role in the preparation for trial and relied too heavily on counsel. I had no experience in litigation and was not fully prepared for the events in the courtroom. I was devastated when I lost; counsel had never prepared me for that outcome.

Much later, I realized I had achieved some real, serious, and meaningful long-term economic benefit from the outcome. I established the reputation within our industry as being litigious. As a result, my competitors were much more careful and took longer lead times to introduce knock-offs of my products. The lead time we had the market to ourselves on new products went from the typical six months to two years. In our industry, an extra year and a half without competition represented the potential of several million dollars in additional revenue.

In another patent infringement case years later (for another hanger I had developed), I negotiated a contingency fee with counsel. Ultimately, we won the case, and the proceeds were in excess of two million dollars. Since I had sold the business, the primary beneficiary was a company that seemed to be extremely bothered because the contingency fee was 50 percent and the attorneys were getting over one million dollars. They overlooked that their purchase of the company was not contingent on the successful prosecution of the patent litigation and that the attorneys had invested time over a seven-year period without compensation. Instead, they were busy "putting their hands in someone else's pocket." The compensation the company received in part funded their acquisition of the company. They should have been thrilled with the windfall and worked with the attorneys to go after other infringers.

METHODS OF COMPENSATION

The attorney's compensation in a contingency fee arrangement should be viewed in much the same way as the net back with collection agencies (illustrated in Exhibit 7–3 in Chapter 7). Don't worry about what the attorney earns; be concerned with the benefits your business and you accrue.

Cost questions arise more often when an engagement is nonspecific. For example, if I am sued and I have to engage a litigator to defend me, it may be difficult for the attorney to estimate the cost associated with my defense. Many variables (e.g., appeals, changes of venue, special motions) may need to be dealt with, but they cannot be anticipated when the engagement is initiated.

> *War Story.* I was involved in a lawsuit in Chicago and filed a separate unrelated suit against the same party in Philadelphia. The other party tried to obtain a change of venue (moving our suit to Chicago to be heard by the same judge) for the Philadelphia suit, and we spent considerable sums arguing the venue issue. When the judge ruled in our favor in the venue issue, the other party agreed to pay me what he owed me under the contract in dispute. However, I would have had to pursue the litigation to recover my earlier legal expenses with no assurance of prevailing on the recovery of those expenses. The bottom line: I was out of pocket one third of the money due me because I had to pay counsel from my own pocket. When it costs you part of the money you are owed to collect that money, the experience can be extremely frustrating. Trying to recover legal costs can backfire, however, and end up costing even more.

Exhibit 9–1 charts traditional methods of compensation for each type of professional and consultant discussed in this book. It also identifies which professions work with specific compensation forms. You can see that many of the professions, including the law specialties, will work with a variety of compensation methods and will work with combinations.

In the war story noted earlier in this chapter, I mentioned that the patent attorney worked on a contingency fee. This case, we ultimately won, had been in the works for about two years and we had already paid counsel in excess of $30,000. The new owners of the company I had

Exhibit 9–1   Compensation by the Hour, Job, Retainer, Contingency, Equity, Commission, Combinations, and Discounts

Profession	Hour	Job	Retainer	Contin-gency	Equity	Com-mission	Discounts	Combi-nations
General counsel	X	X	X		X		X	X
Patent attorney	X	X		X			X	X
Litigators	X	X	X	X			X	X
Real estate	X	X	X				X	X
Estate planning	X	X	X				X	X
Mergers and acquisitions	X	X	X	X	X		X	X
Taxation	X	X	X				X	X
Bankruptcy	X		X					
Labor	X	X	X				X	X
Accountant	X	X	X				X	
Bankers						X	X	
Consultant	X	X	X	X	X	X	X	X
Graphic artists	X	X	X				X	X
Advertising agencies		X	X			X		
Architects	X	X	X			X	X	X
Sales representatives						X		
Insurance agents						X	X	
Real Estate agents						X	X	
Collections						X		

sold advised me that they were not interested in funding the ongoing litigation and were willing to assign the rights to me. I met with counsel and advised them that I was willing to invest some of my own money but much less than would be necessary to prosecute the matter to its natural conclusion. In retrospect, I believe that patent counsel had worked long enough on the case and had learned enough from the discovery process to see the potential monetary benefit to be willing to propose working on contingency.

It was an eye opener for me on several levels. First of all, I had never heard of a patent attorney taking a case on contingency. As noted in the section on patent attorneys in Chapter 2, they are so busy all the time anyway on work with guaranteed income, there is no need to assume any risk with contingency fee based work.

Second, this experience persuaded me that no fee structure or condition of payment is preset; *everything can be negotiated*.

Another good example of everything being open for negotiation is my experience with sales reps. Our contracts with sales reps provided a sliding scale for commissions to a low of 5 percent. On more than one occasion, to avoid losing a very large promotional order, reps offered to go as low as 2.5 percent. The rep understood that 2.5 percent of something was better than 5 percent of nothing.

The third reason this experience was an eye opener was that I learned *you can renegotiate* terms of compensation midway through a project or litigation. I hope that you will see from this example that you shouldn't assume anything is fixed when negotiating compensation issues with any outside service provider.

When eliminating candidates, you should consider economic issues to some degree. If you are a start-up with limited resources, you probably have eliminated the corporate counsel candidates that charge twice the going rate, even if they come highly recommended. I am also presuming that you have not reached a stage where you have two excellent candidates but one is twice as expensive as the other. Both these observations should include the following caveat: Simply because a firm has a published rate does not mean you have to pay that rate. Assume for a moment that you have in fact two firms vying for your business and one is substantially more expensive than the other. The circumstances are not any different than for two vendors of products. You simply tell the more expensive supplier that, as much as you would like to buy their product, you cannot justify the price when you can acquire something less expensive of comparable value. More than likely, even if the more expensive firm doesn't *need* your business, they will want it, rather than lose to a competitor. A partner may not be able to offer you a lower rate per hours because of firm policy, but he or she can develop a package with a net cost that does not exceed the competitive bid.

EVALUATING COSTS VERSUS BENEFITS

This brings me to another observation: *What is it worth?*

> *War Story.* I was partner of a start-up in Israel with a patented process to produce ultrafine precious metal powders based on technology developed by a Russian immigrant and we were negotiating with a private investor. The investor offered us a three-stage package where his maximum exposure would be $150,000.

> His attorney was so demanding regarding the agreements and doc-
> umentation that the investor ended up paying in excess of $25,000
> in legal fees to his counsel. Many of the investor's attorney's de-
> mands were unnecessary and burdensome, considering the size of
> our business and the risk he was assuming as a venture capitalist.
> The investor did not get his money's worth. He did not control his
> legal counsel and the exercise evoked a great deal of ill will.

If the maximum you can win in a litigation is $100,000 and it will cost
you $150,000 to prosecute the case, it probably isn't worth it. Using the
same example, if your attorney will agree to limiting your exposure to
$50,000, it may be worth it for you to proceed. When evaluating costs
versus benefits, you need to evaluate all the costs, including your time
away from your business, the risk of losing and having to pay the other
party, and so on. An example of considering benefits beyond the direct
monetary benefits is part of my earlier way story: My reputation for
being litigious made my competitors wary of copying my innovations
and gave me longer periods of reduced competition to my new products.
So you can see that indirect benefits can be difficult to quantify but
should be reviewed.

You can apply the "what is it worth" question to any project,
case, or consulting engagement. An advertising agency, information
technology consultant, or anyone else should be prepared to discuss
with you a measurable yield or benefit from using their services and
that number should make economic sense. In the collection agency
business, the important criterion is *net back,* defined as how much
money you will collect from overdue receivables and not how much
money the agency makes.

DRAFTING A FEE AGREEMENT

You should have a written fee agreement with your lawyer, accountant,
consultant, or adviser. Some states require lawyers to have fee agreements with their clients. A fee agreement like an engagement letter
should be signed by both parties. The following elements should be included (some of these elements may not apply to specific law specialties or other professions):

- Identification of the client.
- Responsibility for payment.
- Legal matters to be included (can substitute "accounting mat-
  ters" or "consulting matters," etc.).
- Legal matters not to be included—again you can substitute
  pertinent information for other professions.

- Insurance for legal fees—obviously fairly specific to personal injury.
- Minimum and maximum fees.
- Schedule of payment.
- Out-of-pocket fees.
- Rates for determining fees.
- Provisions if the case is lost (substitute "project" or "consultation is not completed").
- Probable and possible results.
- Nonbinding arbitration—for a fee dispute.
- Definition of retainer.
- Identification of who will work on case (project).
- Provisions for handling future problems.
- Provision for changing law firms.[1]

NEGOTIATING COMPENSATION

It will certainly help in any discussion of compensation if you have determined in advance what the added value or benefit the professional's input will generate for your business or you. If you want to sell a property because it is causing a financial drain on your business, you shouldn't get bogged down on the broker's commission. Look at the following example:

> I have a lease on a 20,000-square-foot industrial space that I moved from into larger space. I want to find either a sublet tenant or a new tenant suitable to my landlord to take over my lease because the property is costing me $8,000 per month every month it isn't rented. My broker candidate wants 6 percent of the monthly rental for the balance of the lease term. The commission would be $480 per month, but I try to negotiate a lower commission, say down to 3.5 percent or $280 per month. That lower commission may very well also represent a disincentive for the broker to find a tenant. I have tried to chisel on the commission when my real economic interest is in getting the space rented as soon as possible and lifting the $8,000 per month burden.

The same exercise can be applied to retaining counsel to prepare a contract or handle a piece of litigation. You must analyze the economic benefit to the company and you and put a value on the service to be provided. The next step is to present your interpretation of the potential economic benefit to the service provider and obtain confirmation. Once you have performed this exercise, you and the professional can have an intelligent, meaningful discussion about what the professional would like to be paid and what you can afford. At this stage, the negotiations should consist of reaching consensus. You can offer incentives for achieving better results, and you can discuss penalties for below-target performance. Using the example noted earlier, I might offer a bonus of an additional 6 percent on the first two months' rent if a tenant is obtained within the next 30 days, or reduce the percentage if the property is vacant more than 60 days. In a litigation matter, I could offer the attorney a contingency fee for any settlement in excess of a targeted sum on condition that the hourly rate be lowered. Incentives or disincentives must be material to represent the proper motivation.

REVIEWING AND QUESTIONING A BILL, MONITORING THE CHARGES

As will be seen in this section, my research revealed substantial material about controlling legal costs. Although I found very little information about controlling other professional costs, many, if not all, of the suggestions for controlling legal costs can be applied to all professional services. For most entrepreneurs and managers, it is really a mind-set issue. We simply have to discipline ourselves to audit every bill, either every month or every quarter, with a skeptical and critical eye.

There are firms that will audit and control legal expenses for you for a fee. Most start-up businesses cannot afford, nor do they need, the services of these auditors. However, we can learn a lot from their techniques. "Lawyers are under tremendous pressure to bill. They've usually got quotas set for billable hours and their compensation is tied to how much they bill clients. The pressure to pad time—and bills—is omnipresent, even for honest lawyers. The more information you get, the less likely it is that extra charges will just slip in without noticing. Also, if you ever decide to perform a legal audit, billing summaries such as Exhibit 9–2, and bills such as Exhibit 9–3 make it simple for an expert to detect a pattern of overcharging and win you financial relief."[2]

It is a practical and worthwhile idea to ask for a schedule of charges (see the foreign patent attorneys' fee for services "menus" shown in Exhibits 2–5 and 2–6). Also request a projection of legal work—with hours and cost estimates—for approval before work is performed.

The following key elements can provide effective cost control:

- Obtain preliminary estimates—cost estimates for basic discovery, filing fees, motions, and so on.

Exhibit 9–2   Billing Summary

```
DATE: 30/APR/96                    Canterbury Law Firm
BILL NO: _____      BILLING INFORMATION SUMMARY TO 30/APR/96 REQUESTED BY FQC
                    ************************************************************

CLIENT:                                      FILE:
LENBR   Bruce Lennie                         98768   Acme Corp. purchase
        345 Bloor Street West                        30 St. Patrick Street (120)
        Suite 3400                           LAWYER-IN-CHARGE Michael King
        Toronto, Ontario                     ASSIGNED LAWYER Fred Q. Canterbury
        CLIENT LAWYER Michael King


UNBILLED TIME SUMMARY
                                             **********************************************
  LAWYER              HOURS    VALUE  LAST ENTRY LAST DOCKET  *         BILLING INSTRUCTIONS        *

  1 Fred Q. Canterbury  1.0   200.00  20/APR/96   20/APR/96   * FILE#  98768   BILL LAWYER  1 FQC   *
  2 Gwenneth R. Read     .4   120.00  19/APR/96   19/APR/96   *                                     *
  5 Michael King        1.1   440.00  01/APR/96   01/APR/96   * BILL DATE _____  BILL NO: _____ *
    TOTAL UNBILLED TIME  2.5   760.00*                        *                                     *
    G.S.T. ON   760.00         53.20                          * BILL UP TO 30/APR/96 _____   *
UNBILLED DISBURSEMENTS                                        *                                     *
CD DESCRIPTION                      AMOUNT                    * FINAL  PERIODIC  INTERIM  WRITE-OFF  *
                                                             *  []       []       []       []     *
 48 Register Mortgage               50.00                    *-------------------------------------*
  1 Photocopies                      5.75                    * BILL AMOUNT          $_____    *
  2 Telephone Charges               23.42                    *                                     *
  4 Fax                             18.63                    * DISBURSEMENTS BILLED  $_____   *
    TOTAL UNBILLED DISBURSEMENTS    97.80                    *   INCLUDING UNPOSTED $_ _ _ _ _      *
                                                             *   PHOTOCOPIES        $_ _ _ _ _      *
G.S.T.Calculated on:   47.80                                 *   TELEPHONE          $_ _ _ _ _      *
Goods & Service Tax                  3.35                    *   OTHER _____  $_ _ _ _ _      *
                                                             *                                     *
                                                             * FEE BILLED           $_____   *
                                                             * G.S.T.AMT            $_____   *
                                                             *-------------------------------------*
 TRUST ACCOUNT   BANK ACCOUNT     BALANCE                    * LAWYER _____ FEE CREDIT $_____  *
                                                             * LAWYER _____ FEE CREDIT $_____  *
                    NO: 0         5,000.00CR                 * LAWYER _____ FEE CREDIT $_____  *
                                                             * LAWYER _____ FEE CREDIT $_____  *
                                                             * PARTNERSHIP FEE CREDIT    $_____  *
                                                             *-------------------------------------*
                                                             * TRANSFER FROM TRUST TO              *
                                                             *      PAY ACCOUNT      $_____   *
                                                             *                                     *
                                                             *-------------------------------------*
                                                             * WRITE-OFF                           *
                                                             *   UNBILLED DISBURSEMENTS $_____  *
                                                             *   UNBILLED TIME        $_____   *
                                                             *   ACCOUNTS RECEIVABLE  $_____   *
                                                             *-------------------------------------*
                                                             *   ACCOUNT APPROVAL _____   *
                                                             **********************************************

              Transaction Levy Surcharge Posted:     0.00
              LAST BILL:           FEES TO DATE:       .00TIME BILLED:     .00SURPLUS:     .00+
                      END
```

Note: This sample provided courtesy of Canterbury Systems. Used with permission.

(continued)

- Establish the conditions on which you will pay for work—no work unless submitted in writing with an itemization of hours required and estimated costs. Exhibit 9–4 provides guidelines in Section 3, Billing Policy, particularly 3a–c.
- Be certain who is working on your case and the appropriate fee schedule for that professional. Exhibit 9–4 provides suggestions, especially in Section 3d–h.
- Be assertive in negotiating fees. I have saved up to 25 percent on billed legal fees by negotiating payment terms (and try to

Exhibit 9–2   *(continued)*

```
DATE: 30/APR/96                      Canterbury Law Firm
BILL NO: _____         BILLING STATEMENT TO 30/APR/96 REQUESTED BY FQC
                       =================================================

CLIENT                               FILE
LENBR   Bruce Lennie                   98768   Acme Corp. purchase
        345 Bloor Street West                  30 St. Patrick Street (120)
        Suite 3400                   FILE LAWYER    Michael King
        Toronto, Ontario             ASSIGNED LAWYER Fred Q. Canterbury
        CLIENT LAWYER Michael King
```

```
******                  UNBILLED TIME                    ******

DATE      DESCRIPTION OF ACTIVITY            LAWYER  HOURS   VALUE   AUDIT
01/APR/96 Telephone call to Acme. Corporation;  5 MDK   .3   120.00   7001
01/APR/96 Conversation with Patricia Brown regarding  5 MDK   .3   120.00   7002
          closing;
01/APR/96 Meeting with Bank Officials and the Board of  5 MDK   .5   200.00   7003
          Directors to discuss financial arrangements;
17/APR/96 Preparation of purchase agreement;    2 GRR   .2    60.00   7004
19/APR/96 Prepare for signing of closing documents with  2 GRR   .2    60.00   7005
          Board of Directors of Acme Corporation and the
          vendor;
20/APR/96 Attend on closing;                    1 FQC  1.0   200.00   7006
                                                       2.5   760.00   TOTAL UNBILLED TIME
```

```
******              UNBILLED DISBURSEMENTS               ******

DATE      CD DESCRIPTION/PAYEE      REFER#   AMOUNT   LAWYER   AUDIT

15/APR/96  1 Photocopies            4001      2.50       S    4001
15/APR/96  2 Telephone Charges      4003     23.42       S    4003
16/APR/96 48 Register Mortgage       437     50.00       D    3001
             Treasurer of Ontario
17/APR/96  1 Photocopies            4002      3.25       S    4002
20/APR/96  4 Fax                    4005     18.63       S    4005

           TOTAL UNBILLED DISBURSEMENTS      97.80DR
```

```
******                  TRUST ACCOUNT                    ******

DATE      CD DESCRIPTION/PAYEE      REFER#   AMOUNT   LAWYER   AUDIT

16/APR/96 80 Trust Receipt Acme Corp.  2001  5,000.00-     R  2001
             BANK 0 BALANCE                  5,000.00CR

           TOTAL TRUST BALANCES             5,000.00CR
```

negotiate out items such as photocopy charges, fax charges—a
fax is cheaper to send than a letter today).

- Track the budget (and monitor what is reflected on the bill
  against your own record of how much time was spent on the
  phone or in a meeting).

- Determine the billing period convenient to you (insist that all
  monthly statements be broken out by case or project).

- The paper trail should parallel the billing (see Chapter 10).

- Don't allow your attorney to fight for the sake of fighting (see
  the discussion in Chapter 2, on selection of a litigator). You can
  end up wasting a lot of money on extraneous motions that only
  serve to pump up the bill and the attorney's ego.

Exhibit 9–3   Sample Attorney's Bill

Canterbury Law Firm
30 St. Patrick Street
Toronto, Ontario M5T 2Z5

Bruce Lennie
345 Bloor Street
Toronto, Ontario M6H 7H7

30/APR/96
Our file no. 98768
Re: Acme Corp. purchase

FOR PROFESSIONAL SERVICES RENDERED—from 01/APR/96 to 30/APR/96

01/APR/96	Telephone call to Acme Corp.	MDK	.3
	Conversation with Patricia Brown re closing	MDK	.3
	Meeting with Bank officer and Board re financial arrangements	MDK	.5
17/APR/96	Preparation of purchase agreement	GRR	.2
19/APR/96	Prepare documents for closing	GRR	.2
20/APR/96	Attend closing	FQC	1.0
	Fee for services		$760.00

Disbursements

Photocopies	5.75
Telephone	23.42
Fax	18.63
Total	47.80
Total Fees and Disbursements	$807.80

Note: This sample provided courtesy of Canterbury Systems and used with permission.

- Weigh alternate dispute resolution (this is probably good advice; however, my experience with arbitration hasn't reinforced this recommendation).

War Story.   I fired a sales manager when I discovered he had been running up phony charges on his expense account. He also had the company car impounded by the Canadian tax authorities for trying to import goods illegally across the border and had committed numerous other violations of the company's personnel manual. He sued me for a year's salary because we had just renewed his contract prior to my discovering his misdeeds. On advice of counsel, we went to arbitration. Under oath and in front of the arbitrator, he admitted to his deeds, but the arbitrator found against us. There is no appeal option in arbitration if you are not satisfied with the verdict. I subsequently removed the arbitration clause from every agreement to which I was a party. At least when you use the court system, you have the option of appealing a decision you believe to be unfair. This option for appeal often leads to settlements.

I have restated here many of the same points I have made in other parts of the book. They are so important and so basic that they cannot be repeated too many times.

I have not found any book or magazine article on controlling costs with the warning that *both attorneys and consultants will try to charge you for the time you spend negotiating the bill,* or that your attorney may charge you for the dunning letter he sent to you last month. This actually happened to me at the end of a fairly long-term relationship with one firm and I only discovered this fact when I disputed their bill, stopped using them, and passed a billing cycle where the only communication was a collection letter. They may even try to charge you for the time they spend itemizing the bill at the end of the billing cycle.

Not only are attorneys' bills a problem for small businesses and entrepreneurs, the lack of a uniform billing system has also frustrated many large users of legal services such as insurance companies and banks. As a result, the Litigation Department of the American Bar Association(ABA), together with the American Corporate Counsel Association and a consortium of major corporate clients and law firms developed the Uniform Task-Based Management System (UTBMS). The UTBMS is intended "to enable the providers and recipients of legal services to track, by time and task, cost information on legal services and to implement budgeting and billing systems utilizing this information." You can download the UTBMS from the ABA's Web site—http://www.abanet.org.

Here is an idea I find intriguing! Attorneys, accountants, and consultants use *time management and billing software,* such as Timeslips.® The software is not expensive. Using your own time management software, monitor each of your service providers. Track your telephone conversations and enter the time spent at meetings. The only items you won't be able to monitor will be the time they spend generating correspondence, preparing briefs or studies, and holding conferences when you aren't present. But at least you will be able to compare what they bill you for meetings and telephone calls with your own records.

Exhibit 9–4   Guidelines for Attorneys Providing Legal Services

(I am not suggesting that you use these guidelines for an occasional relationship with an attorney. I have included this sample so you can see the efforts made by large users of legal services to control costs.)

1. CONFLICTS OF INTEREST—We expect counsel to be free of conflicting interests and the appearance of conflict. It is counsel's obligation to confirm this without charge to client.

2. COMMUNICATION AND PLANNING—Counsel should prepare a litigation plan. Counsel should keep client informed of emerging facts.
   a. ACKNOWLEDGMENT—Counsel should acknowledge acceptance of case and notify client who will be handling the case.
   b. INITIAL REPORT—Within 30 days of acceptance, a preliminary plan should be offered.
   c. LITIGATION PLAN—At the conclusion of preliminary discovery, counsel must prepare a litigation plan which will include the following:
      • Outline of tactics, discovery, depositions, etc.
      • Recommendations for resolving litigation.
      • Forecast of legal fees and costs by stage.
   d. ONGOING STATUS REPORTS—Shall include summaries of depositions, records, and appearances.
   e. OPINION REPORT—A final pretrial report prepared after final discovery with an opinion of win/lose probability, settlement range, length of trial, strengths and weaknesses of both sides' cases.
   f. POSTTRIAL REPORT—Should include a summary and evaluation with recommendations for handling future cases or future handling of this case.

3. BILLING POLICY
   a. INTERIM BILLING POLICY—In order to monitor legal costs and expenses, client should be billed at least quarterly.
   b. BILL FORMAT—Invoice should include the following:
      1. Date identified function was performed.
      2. Initials of billing attorney or paralegal.
      3. Description of single itemized service provided.
      4. Specified, accurate time in tenths of an hour.
      5. Total charge for the individual line item.
      6. Summary section to include:
         a. Initials of every attorney or paralegal on bill.
         b. Status (partner, associate, etc.).
         c. Total hours billed by individual.
         d. Hourly rate per individual.
         e. Total amount charged by individual.

(continued)

Exhibit 9–4   *(continued)*

7. Description of professional services rendered—should be more detailed than: discovery, meeting, research. Description should be sufficient to properly identify work performed.

c. TIME CHARGES

1. Billing increments—Should be tenths (.10 = 6 minutes) of an hour.

2. Actual time expended—The time entered should be actual time expended on the function being billed.

3. Standardized billing for form work product—Standardized charges are not acceptable. Many documents are form in nature—preprinted and computer generated and minimal time is necessary for their preparation. Charge should be for actual time expended.

d. SECRETARIAL AND CLERICAL FUNCTIONS—Secretarial/clerical functions performed by attorneys, paralegals, etc., will not be reimbursed. Secretarial/clerical functions performed as part of the course of managing an office are not to be billed; they should be considered part of overhead. This includes organizing files, booking or scheduling meetings, indexing files, pick-up and delivery of documents and records, managing telephone calls, transmitting correspondence, collating documents, copying and binding, filing, preparation of forms, enclosure correspondence, subpoenas, etc.

e. INTRAOFFICE CONFERENCING AND MEMOS—Attorneys are discouraged from billing for intraoffice conferences and memoranda which are educational, instructional, supervisory, or administrative in nature. Attorneys should be sensitive to excessive charges for substantive and strategy related conferences and memoranda.

f. MULTIPLE PERSONNEL—Prior approval should be sought when scheduling attendance of more than one attorney, paralegal, etc. at depositions, hearings, arguments, trials, or meetings if not included in the Litigation Plan and preapproved.

Excessive file review in preparation for depositions, hearings, etc. should be avoided, especially when it involves more than one attorney.

g. EXPERT WITNESSES—The Litigation Plan should include all details including costs associated before engaging experts for a given case.

h. LEGAL RESEARCH—The Litigation Plan should include a budget for legal research. Any research not scheduled, in excess of one hour, must receive prior approval. Requests should include purpose of research, who will perform it, if research can be performed by lower level personnel, if the firm has performed research on these or similar issues before, hours to be spent. The firm was retained because of expertise and experience in this field; justification for this research should be provided.

i. FILE REVIEWS—General reviews will only be compensated if the file has been inactive for more than three months. Transfer file reviews will not be paid for because of a decision by the firm to transfer the case between firm personnel.

Exhibit 9–4   *(continued)*

j. DISBURSEMENTS AND EXPENSES
  - PHOTOCOPIES—In-house photocopy is an overhead expense.
  - LOCAL TRAVEL—Also an overhead expense.
  - TELEPHONE—Only actual long distance charges will be permitted.
  - POSTAGE—Only extraordinary postage expenses will be accepted as reimbursable.
  - FACSIMILE CHARGES—Telecopy charges both domestic and overseas are less expensive than postage and are considered part of overhead unless a specific request for transmission of a very long document.
  - MESSENGER, COURIER, EXPRESS MAIL, FED EX—Considered part of normal overhead and not reimbursable unless such services were requested in an emergency.
  - COMPUTER-ASSISTED RESEARCH—Viewed as part of library maintenance and therefore not reimbursable.
  - DATA-ENTRY CHARGES—Not reimbursable except in unusual circumstances such as document-heavy matters.

FINAL BILLING—Should be submitted as soon as resolution is achieved.

REDUCING YOUR LEGAL AND OTHER PROFESSIONAL FEES

> You don't know what you can get away with until you try.
>
> Colin Powell, *My American Journey*

Fees Are Negotiable

It doesn't matter whether we are talking about legal fees or a real estate broker's commission, a bank lending rate, or the percentage of a lawyer's contingency fee. Even when a professional has a published fee structure, you can negotiate a lower fee. On the other hand, you should be careful not to negotiate too hard. If the vendor feels the fee is too low, the work may suffer or the bill will be padded with extra time. "An attorney who charges $75 an hour is more expensive than an experienced attorney who charges $125 an hour but completes the job in half the time."[3] Also, you run the risk of not being considered a priority client or project.

Controlling costs or reducing fees begins with a letter or phone call to the service provider asking for a written estimate of the cost of their services for the next fiscal period, case, audit, project, or whatever it may be. You can advise the provider that you are engaged in budgeting and planning cash flow, and require the information to schedule use and availability of funds. Be sure to request a breakout of the budget. It is important that this proposal include as much detail of charges by category as possible. If you are trying to control a project such as an audit, divide the audit fee by the total number of hours, which will give you the rate per hour you will pay for the audit. You may be surprised, especially if you know the various rates partners and associates get paid. If you are reviewing a repetitive function such as an audit that is performed each year, you should compare this year's proposal to prior years. In Chapter 10, I discuss the importance of maintaining a file for each project, case, and so on. The importance of maintaining good accounting files by provider should be evident by now and will become more evident in this section. Be certain to include copies of any and all correspondence and notes taken during telephone conversations and meetings relating to budget and cost issues.

I have often found it difficult to question a professional's bills. Even though I was the client/customer and responsible for paying the bill, I guess I somehow felt it was a challenge to the provider's professional dignity. On the other hand, I have had very good relationships with other vendors over the years—printers, corrugated manufacturers, mold makers; and for some reason I never had a problem questioning their quotations or bills. So, what I am saying is "do as I say, not as I have done."

You are the client and you have the right and obligation to question any quotation or bill you receive. Accounting firms, law firms, and consultants will often, even if reluctantly, agree to reduced fees rather than lose a client. They will also agree to reduced fees with a new client if they feel the new client has the potential to grow into a significant account paying full rates at some point in the future.

Do Some of the Work Yourself

We use outside service providers for several reasons:

- They provide knowledge and expertise we lack in-house (i.e., filing a patent application, writing a contract, designing an advertising piece).
- There are legal and regulatory reasons for using service providers (i.e., we cannot perform our own audits; the Securities

and Exchange Commission requires underwritings of companies going public to include an attorney's opinion).

- We cannot afford to maintain full-time specialists.
- We don't have time to devote to the project.

So, we have an apparent dichotomy. On the one hand, we seek out professional help, and on the other hand, we seek to perform some of the work ourselves to reduce expenses. Well, perhaps it isn't such a dichotomy after all. If I need an audit because my bank or other lending institution has made it a requirement, I have no choice but to either pay my accounting firm to perform the audit or lose the financing. On the other hand, if I have properly prepared my staff, my accounting records, and my warehouse, I can expedite the time my auditor spends and thereby reduce the cost of the audit. For example, our first audit seemed to go on forever and was very costly. But each subsequent year my staff and I became more experienced and better prepared, so that by the third or fourth audit, my accountant was spending less time testing and confirming our counts, our costs dropped, and the aggravation level also dropped.

There is, however, another element to take into consideration. If your staff and you are already overworked managing the day-to-day functions, when do you propose to fit in these economies of doing some of the work for the service provider? Sure, I can save money by doing the patent search myself rather than pay my patent attorney, but how much is my time worth if I am not focusing my energies on sales and marketing because I am performing a patent search? Another point to keep in mind is that I do not perform patent searches every day; how many hours will I have to invest to achieve the same result my counsel will achieve? These are hard questions with no simple answers, but some food for thought. Perhaps you have a full-time bookkeeper who will agree to work extra hours several evenings a week prior to the audit to prepare. You can either pay the individual for the extra time or offer to give time off at another time of the year. If your attorney requires legal research to be performed, perhaps you can find a third- or fourth-year law student to do some of the research. When the advertising agency or PR firm requires market research, an MBA student or even an undergraduate in a local business school could perform some of the tasks and save you a bundle. Use self-help legal guides and standard form books, which are available in abundance in bookstores and libraries. Most of these books and their incorporated documents are generic and will have to be adapted to your specific needs. They do, however, provide a good foundation and generally have been prepared by competent attorneys. So, unless you are making radical changes to them, these forms and agreements should be legally binding. Another source for standard agreements is your trade association. Keep in mind agreements prepared by consultant or rep organizations will tend to be more weighted on the side of the provider, while agreements supplied by trade associations will tend to be weighted toward the client.

Long-Term Engagements Encourage Discounting

A consultant or lawyer who has assurance that you are not giving him or her a one-time project or case is more likely to make a price concession. If you have been spending, on average, five to six figures per year on patent applications, graphic arts, real estate commissions, and so on, you should be able to get a discount. If the work is not all due "yesterday," but can be fit in to open time slots, you may also have a basis for a discount.

Expenses Are Controllable

Add-ons to a bill such as faxes, courier service fees, and photocopy fees can either be negotiated out of the billing altogether or at least set at the vendor's cost (see Exhibit 9–4 for what large firms think about these expenses). Many lawyers will mark up the cost of these services to amortize their photocopier or fax. A two-page letter is cheaper to send today by fax than by first-class mail, in terms of both actual cost and labor, but I have seen bills where the attorney charged five or ten dollars for a fax. Object when you are charged for a next-day courier delivery that is mailed on a Friday, when you won't be in the office until Monday—second-day economy rate is much cheaper. Protest when regular first-class mail is adequate and the package is sent by courier.

Exhibit 9–5 provides some guidelines for controlling costs.

Travel expenses can get out of hand if you do not monitor them. You have the right and the responsibility to control travel expenses. The service provider will charge you for his or her time to search out the cheaper fare or room rate, which will probably eat up any savings. Therefore you have to take the initiative and locate or negotiate the best rates. I have been on consulting engagements where I was a subcontractor for another consultant; we rented a car to drive from the airport to a hotel and two days later used the car to drive back to the airport. The client could have had us picked up at the airport, or we could have taken a taxi for less money. Your attorney or consultant may not want to sleep at the cheapest motel in town, but neither is it necessary to book the most expensive five-star hotel in town. Also, rates

Exhibit 9–5   Ways to Control Costs

1. DISCUSS FEES. If your lawyer does not bring up the subject of fees, you should. Don't by shy about it. Remember: Lawyers are in business for themselves and are free to set their own fees. It is appropriate for you to negotiate regarding these charges. The best time to discuss fees is at the beginning of each new legal matter.

2. REACH AGREEMENT ABOUT FEE CALCULATION.
   - BY THE HOUR—The rate will depend on where the lawyer practices and on his or her skill and experience. Generally, competent legal services for a small business will range from $100 to $250 an hour.
   - FLAT FEE—X dollars for a simple contract or incorporating a business.
   - CONTINGENT FEE—Typically a percentage in the range of 33% to 50%.

3. NEGOTIATE THE MOST FAVORABLE FEE ARRANGEMENT FOR EACH PROJECT OR CASE.

4. IN CONFLICTS, TRY TO SETTLE CASES RATHER THAN LITIGATE.

5. DEVELOP FORMS WITH YOUR ATTORNEYS THAT YOU CAN USE IN ROUTINE TRANSACTIONS.

6. GUARANTEE A MINIMUM NUMBER OF HOURS OF WORK DURING THE YEAR. This may include a retainer arrangement or a monthly fixed payment (draw) against actual work performed.

7. USE LESS EXPENSIVE PROFESSIONALS FOR SMALL PROJECTS. Use freelancers instead of the advertising agency for small projects, the collection agency instead of a collection attorney.

8. PROVIDE YOUR LAWYER WITH COPIES OF ALL PERTINENT RECORDS IN A NEW CASE. Keep good accurate files, maintaining copies of all correspondence by date, and maintaining notes of telephone conversations and meetings.

9. FIND SOMEONE TO SHARE COSTS WITH YOU. If you are a distributor in one geographic area, identify another distributor from another area who can be a partner in underwriting the costs of advertising, legal expenses (preparation of agreements, policies and procedures, etc.), even consulting services.

10. INSIST ON AN ITEMIZED STATEMENT EACH MONTH.

11. SUGGEST COST-SAVING METHODS TO YOUR SERVICE PROVIDER. Amazingly, I have shown suppliers how to save money on telephone bills, travel expenses, etc.

12. KEEP ABREAST OF DEVELOPMENTS IN YOUR FIELD. Read all the trade journals relevant to your business and become an inveterate article clipper (and filer).

(continued)

Exhibit 9–5   *(continued)*

13. ASK FOR PROGRESS REPORTS DURING PROLONGED PROJECTS AND CASES. This should be a condition of the engagement.

14. CONSIDER ADDING AN IN-HOUSE PROFESSIONAL TO YOUR STAFF, IF YOU FEEL YOU ARE SPENDING TOO MUCH OUTSIDE. Or, hire a freelancer. Offer free work space but allow the person to continue working for other clients.

15. CONSULT YOUR PROFESSIONAL ON SEVERAL MATTERS AT ONE TIME.

16. HANDLE SOME MATTERS YOURSELF.

17. SHOP AROUND, BUT DON'T PROFESSIONAL-HOP.

Note: Adapted from Fred Steingold, "Eighteen Ways to Cut Legal Costs," *Inc.*

vary; sometimes the corporate rate is more expensive than the AAA Club rate. I have called hotels through the toll-free number of the chain, been quoted one rate, and then called the hotel directly and obtained a cheaper rate. You will have to consider issues such as weekend travel versus the per diem that a consultant charges and even check that the cost of the flight has been minimized using discounts such as "back-to-back" tickets.

A back-to-back ticket works as follows: You have to fly to Chicago from Pittsburgh for two days. It is a location you anticipate traveling to several times per year. The round-trip ticket for travel during the week may be as much as $500 but by staying over Saturday, you can get the ticket at $250. You buy two round-trip tickets, one out on Monday and back on Monday the following week, the other originating in Chicago on Wednesday and out on the following Wednesday. You now have two round-trip tickets for $500. You use the first coupon from the first ticket and the first coupon from the second ticket for your initial trip. Your travel agent can then either reissue the second coupons or you can have them stickered with the new dates, which may cost a $50 service fee. This method works and can save you a lot of money. Airlines try to discourage this procedure, but most travel agents will accommodate you.

Don't Pay Twice for Repetitive Tasks

For example, if your business uses confidentiality agreements on a regular basis with vendors and/or customers, have your attorney draw up a standard agreement. Obtain a copy on diskette and modify it yourself each time you want one for a new customer or vendor. This can work for employment contracts, vendor agreements, even financial statements.

THE TWO RS: COMPENSATION

RECAP

- All they have to sell is their time—be reasonable; if the adviser cannot earn a living for his or her time, you aren't going to get any benefit.
- Decide what the service is worth to you—Don't worry about how much the adviser is earning; focus on what your business will gain from the engagement. If you can't be sure that your return on investment is worthwhile, don't start.
- Fees are negotiable—Don't accept the first proposal; you can negotiate lower fees or other methods of compensation, such as contingency.
- Do some of the work yourself—If you have the time and the expertise, you may want to do some of the work.
- Long-term engagements encourage discounting. Advisers use the same calculations as you do when considering overhead absorption for large-scale or long-term projects.
- Expenses are controllable—But you have to control them; don't expect the adviser to do it for you.
- Don't pay twice for repetitive tasks—If you will be using the same basic employment agreement or sales rep contract, don't pay for a new one each time. Get the contract on disk and produce it yourself each time.

REFERENCES

- *The Complete Small Business Legal Guide.*
- *Finding the Right Lawyer*****   This book contains a fairly thorough discussion of issues surrounding billing.
- *The Small Business Legal Advisor.*
- *Taming the Lawyers*****   This book has by far the best discussion of legal fees I have found to date.

10

MANAGING THE UNMANAGEABLE

"You can exercise little control over your vendors and subcontractors" is a myth fueled by poor planning and follow-through.
    Neal Whitten, *Managing Software Development Projects*

There are no simple, hard-and-fast rules for measuring the performance of your attorney, accountant, or architect. There are so many variables, not the least among them being your own life experience. This was probably the most difficult chapter for me to write; after all my years of experience, it is still the most difficult issue for me to deal with in my relationships with professionals. On the other hand, there are situations, projects, and cases where it is relatively simple to evaluate someone's performance.

For example, if I ask my patent attorney to file a patent application, typically, I will receive an oral or written proposal of the approximate cost and time necessary to prepare and file the patent. If the patent is granted within a reasonable time frame (under a year), I have a measure of my attorney's performance. But even this example, which at first glance seems fairly straightforward, is not so simple. I may discover when I have to litigate, that the patent was not carefully prepared and my case is substantially weaker.

218

War Story.   I had a design firm develop a new corporate image for my company. The project included logo development, stationery, packaging graphics, and catalog sheets. The firm selected, and I approved, the use of a specific gray and red to be the theme colors that would tie the whole program together. Too far into the program, we discovered that the two critical colors would not print uniformly in four-color process and caused radical shade variations from project to project. Different weights of paper, different printing processes, and different printers also caused variations. The only solution was to print the red and gray as a fifth and a sixth color in every job that required four-color process. This meant that every job had to have a second pass on a printing press that would normally print a four-color job in one pass. While it didn't double the price, it certainly added an additional burden. Had I been a more sophisticated purchaser of printing services, I might have avoided the problem.

The point is that even when we have a measure of performance in the initial stage, one subjective measure of performance, we may learn later on that what we thought was a satisfactory job was in fact less than satisfactory.

If you expect to be a regular purchaser of a specific service, it makes sense to really learn all you can. How much more difficult is it then, when we don't have easily measurable performance goals to evaluate whether we are getting our money's worth? I suppose the short answer is to refer you back to Chapter 1 of the book and suggest the selection process is a critical component to giving you a comfort level that you are getting your money's worth.

BUDGETING

One management tool you can use with many professionals is a budget. If you and the professional have agreed on a budget, then no matter whether it is a litigation issue, the marketing program for the sale of a building, or a consulting engagement, you have established at least one measure for managing. As with any project within your organization, a project run by an outside service provider should have milestones not only in performance but in budget as well. Chapter 11 deals with record keeping and measurement, so I won't dwell here on evaluating performance against budget. The professional and you should agree on the budget and it should be incorporated into the engagement letter or contract, along with target dates. Budgeting should be a realistic process and incorporate the alternative outcomes of any engagement. I have utilized in my own consulting practice a staged approach to projects and have seen a similar approach used by other consultants and by litigators.

For an example, a consultant may develop a total marketing program for a client. Stage one might be the market research with a price tag and a date for a deliverable (i.e., the market research report). This information could trigger a go-no go decision for the next stage: the development of a marketing plan. Again, the marketing plan stage would have a budget and a target date and at the time of delivery, a go-no go decision for the next stage: the implementation stage of the marketing plan. The first two stages—market research and marketing plan—are finite projects, but implementation is more difficult to monitor. However, if your professional and you agree in advance on the milestones (e.g., sales dollars, new customers, number of orders in stated periods of time), you should be able to manage the consultant. Similarly, you can discuss with a litigator when a case will come to trial, the length of time for discovery, and how long the appeal process will take; then put price tags and target dates on each phase of the case. You can request a Litigation Plan (see Exhibit 9–4).

In the case of a real estate broker, the engagement should be based, in part, on the marketing program submitted to you. The marketing program should include a time line and any out-of-pocket expenses.

In fairness to many professionals, entrepreneurs and managers fail their management obligation during an engagement because they do not take the time to understand or monitor the process.

Public relations agencies are examples of professionals that can be the most difficult to control if you haven't agreed on a budget beforehand. The budget should include an estimate of the number of hours each staff person in the agency is expected to spend on your account. Out-of-pocket costs are often marked up and you should negotiate that markup out of the budget at the outset.

VENDOR CONTRACT PROCESS

There are four elements to the vendor contract process.[1]

- An RFP (Request for Proposal) is created and distributed.
- Vendors create and distribute proposals.
- A vendor is selected.
- A contract is negotiated, signed, and executed.

The RFP describes the work to be performed, when the work is due, and how the work will be measured; it also defines the working relationship between the vendor and your organization. The RFP becomes a major part of the eventual contract. Here are several important lessons:

- There is a direct relationship between the completeness of your RFP and the completeness of the bid proposals received.
- When it comes to quality work from a vendor, you usually get what you ask for. Ask in the RFP!
- Don't blindside your own organization—get your organization's agreement before releasing the RFP to vendors.[2]

You may think, "Here Bisk writes about the problems experienced by professionals in their field and the trouble they have managing vendors. What chance do I have in successfully managing these people when I don't even have a good handle on the services they are supposed to be providing me?" My reply is that the professionals have learned the hard way (if they have learned) by making the mistakes. The information in this book will help you avoid some of these mistakes. *Selecting well does not absolve you of the responsibility of managing well.* And part of selecting well and managing well is the careful definition of what you want achieved—the RFP.

Once the desired organization or professional is selected, the contract is the next order of business. Exhibit 10–1 lists issues to be addressed in any contract.

Exhibit 10–1   Points to Include in Any Contract[3]

I. Contract Items—A clear description of the services and deliverables to be provided:
  A. Expected service levels, performance standards, and performance goals.
  B. Obligations with respect to strategic planning.
  C. Remedies in the event of failure to meet performance standards or to deliver in accordance with expected schedules.

II. Outline of project schedule and expected milestones:
  A. Fee structure and clarification of basis of calculation:
    1. Fixed fee/volume-based fee/expenses.
    2. Payment of fees based on described schedule/milestones.
    3. Basis for adjustment of fees (e.g., based on reduction in services required).
    4. Procedure for resolution of billing disputes.
  B. Terms of agreement, renewal periods, and termination:
    1. Parties' rights on termination.
    2. Cooperation and assistance on termination.
  C. Procedures for change in scope of services and deliverables:
    1. Customer right to change priority or scope of vendor's effect on rights and obligations of parties.

(continued)

Exhibit 10–1   *(continued)*

2. Procedures for requesting changes to vendor's services.

3. Fees and performance standards associated with changes.

   D. Procedures for requesting additional services:

      1. Vendor discretion or obligation to provide additional services and the requisite customer authorization.

   E. Management of project:

      1. Appointment of project managers by vendor and customer to be principal liaisons between parties.

      2. Respective roles of parties.

   F. Management planning:

      1. Status meetings and reports at agreed on intervals.

      2. Use of standard project management methodology.

   G. Personnel and staffing requirements:

      1. Vendor's and customer's rights with respect to change and approval of personnel.

      2. Confidentiality and noncompete.

      3. Succession planning and guaranteed service period for personnel.

   H. Licensing and rights-of-use issues with respect to customer and third-party licensed intellectual property and with respect to vendor intellectual property.

III. Vendor obligations.

IV. Customer responsibilities.

 V. Confidentiality.

VI. Assignment rights of the parties.

VII. Insurance.

VIII. Restrictions of hiring other party's personnel.

IX. Taxes.

 X. Force majeure.

XI. Audits.

ENGAGEMENT BILL OF RIGHTS

As I was writing this book, I found recurring themes in the caveats offered by the professionals with whom I spoke, in the war stories entrepreneurs shared with me, and in my own observations and war stories. I finally concluded that many of the irritants in our relationships with outside service providers could be reduced, or eliminated, if we would establish our mutual responsibilities at the beginning of our relationships.

My assumption hinges on retaining competent individuals at the outset, utilizing the tools provided in this book, and negotiating a compensation program satisfactory to both parties. The *Engagement Bill of Rights* (EBR), if you elect to use it, should be initialed by you and your service provider and appended to any formal agreement or letter that initiates the engagement. I have been using the EBR extensively since I developed it, with wide acceptance by service providers. I generally provide it to a prospective service provider at the same time we discuss contract or engagement conditions. The EBR sample provided in Exhibit 10–2 is just that—a sample. Some clauses may be inappropriate for you in general or for a specific engagement. The professional service provider may object to one or more clauses, or you may want to add clauses as time goes by and you become a more sophisticated consumer. On the other hand, I suggest you be wary of any service provider who objects categorically to the use of the EBR. I say that, not because I created it, but because I have reviewed it with many professionals and almost all agree it is equitable and fair to both parties. Finally, as you will see in the EBR itself, I am recommending that your service provider and you review your engagement agreement and the EBR at least once a year. Modify it, if necessary, and initial it, but don't let it sit in the file after signing, as you will both soon forget what you have agreed to as a modus operandi, and then the problems it was intended to alleviate may start.

The cover letter that you use to introduce the EBR to your service provider should include conciliatory language, as in the following example, because you are introducing the individual to a rather new concept:

> I have already invested a substantial amount of time and effort in identifying your firm and you as the people with whom I want to work. I believe that I have fulfilled step one in building a good working relationship—finding the best person for my company and me. I want to avoid many of the problems that can develop in an engagement such as this one. Therefore, I am enclosing an *Engagement Bill of Rights* that outlines your rights and responsibilities and my rights and responsibilities. Please review this draft and share with me your thoughts about elements that trouble you or issues you think need to be included.

Exhibit 10–2   Sample Engagement Bill of Rights

Preamble: In order to insure that we obtain the maximum benefit from you on the most cost-effective basis, and to avoid as many sources of irritation that can develop between client and service provider, we the parties to this engagement/project/case agree as follows:

Article 1: Time—We both recognize and acknowledge that "time is money." Both parties to this agreement will respect the value of the other's time. Appointments will be kept on a prompt basis and neither party, to the extent possible, will keep the other party waiting. Meetings and telephone conversations will follow preplanned agendas, to the extent possible. Both parties agree to give their undivided attention in meetings and telephone conversations and avoid as many interruptions as possible. Time billed will be properly accounted for with clear explanations of the work performed. Both parties agree to keep social conversation to a minimum during billable working situations.

Article 2: Record keeping—Both parties agree to provide copies of all documents and correspondence generated in relation to the engagement to each other on a timely basis, and each party will be responsible for maintaining their own files. Documents and correspondence include but are not to be limited to any documents filed on behalf of the client in any jurisdiction and any correspondence referencing the client. The parties agree that one party will be designated to generate a summary of any meetings and conversations held and that the other party will initial, as a form of confirmation, said summary before the document becomes a matter of record. Each summary will indicate the starting time and ending time of each meeting or conversation, the date, the parties in attendance, and the subject of the meeting or conversation. The writer will attempt to keep summaries as short as possible.

Article 3: Preparation—The client has the obligation to provide all information and records related to the engagement on a timely basis. Timely basis is defined as the amount of time mutually agreed on by both parties at the time the request is made. If no time is specified, seven to fourteen working days will be considered timely. The client also has the obligation to come to meetings and to participate in telephone conversations properly prepared, which is defined as obtaining the necessary information requested prior to the meeting and/or indicated by the agenda. The client has the right to expect the service provider not only to be prepared as defined above but also to be prepared when representing the client in all appropriate venues, including but not limited to courts, depositions, negotiations, zoning boards, etc. Being prepared in this case includes anticipating all possible reasonable problems, defenses, objections.

Article 4: Finances—To the extent possible, terms of payment will be agreed on in advance. Where a payment schedule has been included in the engagement contract, it will be honored by both parties. In the event compensation is performance based, distributions will be made in a timely fashion and if not indicated within the agreement, timely fashion shall be defined as within

Exhibit 10–2   *(continued)*

fourteen days of one party receiving funds, the other party will receive its share. The billing party agrees not to charge for the time preparing a bill and not to bill for time explaining a bill or resolving a dispute over a bill. In the event that expenses are to be incurred, the parties will either obtain written estimates in advance or agree to a reasonable per diem. In any case, all expenses will be billed at cost and supporting documentation will be provided. Reimbursement for out-of-pocket expenses will be made promptly and shall not be subject to delayed payment for any reason other than a dispute over the charges.

Article 5: Competency—The foundation of this relationship is based on the service provider's knowledge and ability to deliver expertise to the client. However, in the course of performing the work, the service provider may uncover needs outside his or her realm of expertise. In the event the engagement involves skills or knowledge not within the capabilities of the service provider, he or she is under an obligation to advise the client of the fact.

One measure of a successful engagement is the implementation of the project. The client may not have the skills or capability for proper implementation. The service provider is under an obligation to advise the client regarding his or her lack of confidence in the client's competence to implement the project. Likewise, if the client recognizes his or her limitations, the client should advise the service provider.

Article 6: Ownership—Both parties agree that all materials, ideas, and documentation prepared on behalf of the client are the property of the client. To the extent that anything produced for the client is based on material heretofore created and used by the service provider for other clients, the service provider has the right to continue to use the materials, ideas, and documentation for other clients. However, the client should be advised at the outset of this fact. All files, work papers, records, or other material generated on behalf of the client are the client's property and the client has the right to request that the material be turned over to anyone designated by the client in the event of the termination of the engagement. The service provider has the right to be paid for any reasonable expenses incurred in providing this material and to be paid all undisputed amounts due prior to releasing the material. The service provider agrees to release any material that may impact on a legal or administrative issue (i.e., litigation or tax returns), even if there is a dispute about outstanding payments.

Article 7: Ethics—The service provider will divulge any potential conflicts of interest. The service provider will only represent opinions as independent if they are free from subordinated judgment and there is no undisclosed interest in the outcome of the client's decision. Neither party will ask the other party to engage in a violation of the law.

Note: Copyright Leonard Bisk.

Now that I have inserted enough caveats into the process, I will try to give you some basic guidelines for evaluating performance.

I have mentioned a cardinal rule several times before: *If you do not trust the counsel or advice you are receiving, it is time to replace the individual or firm.* When we were kids and we doubted our parents or teachers, there was little we could do to challenge their authority. When we were employees or soldiers, we had to accept the decisions of our superiors. In our capacity as owners or managers, we ought to have confidence in our advisers' counsel. The moment we begin to suspect that we are being overcharged or that we aren't getting good advice, it is time to find someone with whom we can feel comfortable again.

There is a tendency among entrepreneurs, and I have been guilty of this, to mix a combination of inertia and the authority figure syndrome together and suffer in silence with an adviser who isn't performing satisfactorily. If you take nothing else away from this chapter or, in fact, the entire book, remember this: *When you doubt someone, trust your instincts and intuition.*

There are some semiobjective guidelines that can be used to evaluate performance. We can break down work done by advisers into two basic categories—job-specific and ongoing.

Job-Specific Engagements

This category includes items such as a patent application, preparation of a contract, preparation of year-end tax returns, preparing a catalog sheet, putting in an additional room or office, developing a marketing plan for a new product.

Each job-specific engagement should start out with a request for a quotation or a Request for Proposal (RFP), either verbal or written. The quotation itself should never be verbal. If the project is simple and straightforward, the initial phase of the paper trail may end here. If the project is more complicated, you may want a contract that outlines the responsibilities of each party, including status reports, projected completion dates, and costs.

Once you have signed off on the patent application or final mechanical of the catalog sheet, accepted the contract, and taken delivery on the marketing report, you have essentially notified the vendor that you are satisfied. Therefore, it is extremely important to read the draft of the patent application carefully before okaying it, to examine all aspects of the sketches and preliminary layouts before the mechanical is generated, and to review the interim correspondence or reports before the final draft of the marketing report is submitted.

Here is another critical point: *If you aren't 100 percent satisfied with the final version, don't accept it.* It is easy to fall into the trap of seeing some minor error and overlooking it because you feel bad about asking for it to be corrected or because you are in a hurry to get the final version. Time constraints and deadlines may tempt us to accept a project with errors. Thus we often set up the provider for our being unhappy with the results even though we have to bear a major share of responsibility for accepting less than perfect work. We also set a standard that is less than perfect. Many service providers wait until the last minute to file before a deadline and then put us under pressure to react. We have to be sensitive to deadlines and push our service providers to allow for revisions and corrections when scheduling projects. Inevitably the process of managing the unmanageable only works when we accept our responsibility to manage.

Ongoing Engagements

This category includes items such as litigation, acquisitions or sales, relationships on retainer basis, strategic planning, corporate image, and the corporate insurance program.

Evaluating litigation is often a source of frustration for me. Most litigation is not won or lost on a moment of brilliance in the courtroom. It is more a product of discovery, carefully constructed motions, good research, and generally intensive preparation. Very few litigators take cases on contingency, so the litigation appears to be a black hole that swallows up money and time. The litigator also has no control over many elements such as venue issues appeals, and juries. A major construction project can present similar problems. Litigation and construction share some similar attributes: Each phase builds on previous stages, and if the foundation is not laid carefully, the finished product lacks stability.

Changing counsel or contractor midway through a major case or project can seem to be so absurd that even when we have our doubts about the vendor, we are unwilling to make a change. At the same time, if you have lost confidence in the professional, it is, as the cliché points out, foolish "to throw good money after bad."

The easiest way to manage an ongoing project such as litigation or major construction is to have a formal project management document. A litigation plan, formal proposal, bid proposal, and project schedule are all project management components. Support documents such as mechanical drawings and specifications should also be incorporated. The American Institute of Architects can provide a variety of books and software for project management. You should request a copy of your architect's project management plan, your consultant's project management program, and so on. You can ask sales representatives to show you a plan for the development of their market for your product.

You can also request monthly summaries from your consultants, real estate brokers, and sales reps.

Here's another tip: Take a realistic approach to how attorneys normally work. Tucked away in Suzanne Caplan's book entitled *Saving Your Business* is a pearl of wisdom. Caplan's book is subtitled *How to Survive Chapter 11 Bankruptcy and Successfully Reorganize Your Company.* She has written a chapter entitled "Fool for a Client," which is focused on a businessperson's relationship with his or her bankruptcy attorney. However, the advice is appropriate and on target for other law specialties and many, if not all, consultants:

> You should understand that most attorneys juggle cases by operating in a reactive way rather than a proactive one. If the court has given a 30-day deadline to file a motion to the response to one filed by the other side, there will be silence for the first 28 days followed by a flurry of activity on day 29 to meet the deadline. This can create serious hurdles for you because hastily crafted agreements usually require deep concessions that you will have little time to consider. I once had a new agreement with rather serious implications waved under my nose in the hall outside of the courtroom. I refused to agree to any issue I didn't have sufficient time to consider—and you should too.
>
> You will not get any serious commitment from your attorney to change his method of operation. But what you should demand is to be given copies of all pertinent communications sent to your counsel about your case as soon as they are received—not when your lawyer is just getting around to dealing with them. This will give you time to consider the issue before decisions must be made.
>
> If you have chosen the right attorney, you will feel as if you have entered into a partnership with your attorney with a goal that you will decide together and both work to make a reality.

It is true that all the professional service providers discussed in this book are independent contractors that we hire for their expertise. However, when we hire many of our employees, be it a clerk or a COO, we are also hiring them for their expertise, and we assume these employees have a certain work ethic. Yet, we are more willing to direct, supervise, correct, and generally manage our employees than we are our outside service providers. Entrepreneurs and managers alike are guilty of not taking a greater leadership role in these relationships. Time constraints may play a factor: If we don't delegate responsibility, it is impossible to accomplish everything. Lack of confidence in our knowledge may also play a role—after all, we hire these professionals because of our lack of expertise and their accumulated knowledge and experience. However, as I have stated repeatedly in this book, *you know your business better than anyone else.* Your advisers do not wake up in the middle of the night with intense anxiety about making payroll for your employees this week, or about having to fire someone, or about any of the multitude of issues you cope with every day. You cannot abstain from taking an active role in managing both the relationship with an adviser and the work generated.

THE TWO RS: MANAGING THE UNMANAGEABLE

RECAP

- Work within a budget—financial and performance. The proposal or engagement letter should have well-defined financial limits.
- Measure performance—Establish measurable goals and a time line within which to achieve the goals.
- Create a paper trail—Utilize Request for Proposals (RFPs), engagement letters, and contracts to assure both parties understand and agree on the goals.
- Identify mutual responsibilities—Incorporate the Engagement Bill of Rights with all contracts and engagement letters.
- Request periodic updates—weekly, biweekly, or monthly status reports tied to the time line.
- Ask questions when you don't understand—don't assume anything.

REFERENCES

- *Hiring Independent Contractors*****   The focus here is on the legal aspects of managing relationships.
- *Outsourcing Institute, 1995 Buyer's Guide*   It contains some useful articles.
- *Taming the Lawyers*****   Although targeted for use with lawyers, the observations are just as applicable for other professions.

11

MEASURING PERFORMANCE

I should probably have called this chapter "Do as I say, not as I did." So, you have selected the lawyer, accountant, consultant—you identified as the best candidate, successfully negotiated the compensation arrangement, and engaged him or her—what now?

If you had hired a new employee, you would set up a personnel file and you probably even have forms you use to monitor performance. You may perform an initial review of the employee within 90 days of hiring and then conduct either semiannual or annual reviews. Why not apply the same methodology to managing legal counsel or a graphic artist?

If I retain a vendor for a specific job or project, I may not go to the trouble of setting up an evaluation file. For example, if I need to file a trademark registration and my business does not require a patent attorney in the normal course of operations, I probably wouldn't bother including the attorney in my evaluation system. The attorney will give me a standard price for filing, file the application, and our involvement with each other is at an end. On the other hand, if I expect to have a long-term relationship with the attorney, I ought to begin by monitoring his or her work. The sample evaluation form supplied in Exhibit 11–1 is probably sufficient for lawyers, consultants, graphic artists, perhaps even accountants for specific projects. For construction projects and other more complex jobs, you will need a more elaborate

Exhibit 11–1   Sample Adviser Review Form

<hr>

Page _____ of _____

Name: _____

Project: _____   Date initiated: _____

Date for projected completion: _____   Projected cost: _____

Date completed: _____   Actual cost: _____

	Date	Initiator		Length of Call
Contact:		adviser	me	
Comments:				
Contact:		adviser	me	
Comments:				
Contact:		adviser	me	
Comments:				
Contact:		adviser	me	
Comments:				

	Date	Initiator		cc
Correspondence:		adviser	me	
Correspondence:		adviser	me	
Correspondence:		adviser	me	
Correspondence:		adviser	me	

Evaluation: (i.e., delivered on time, in budget, satisfactory work, communicated well, hard to reach).

_____

_____

_____

_____

_____

_____

_____

_____

chart, involving a project schedule. This review form, with some modification will also work for advisers who are on retainer.

RECORD KEEPING

We hear and read about the "paperless office." It may be on the horizon but it hasn't arrived yet. You should get into the habit of generating paper trails. In the modern reality of human resources management, employers have to maintain good records and documentation of all aspects of employee performance. If we utilize the same approach to managing our advisers, we will avoid many of the problems that can arise.

At one point in my life I was a representative of a U.S. venture capital fund engaged in providing seed capital to high-tech start-ups in Israel. In addition to providing the money, the fund also identified and supplied each project with a consultant in the United States, having expertise in the project's field. To properly manage the interaction between the inventors and the consultants and avoid abuse, I developed a guideline for both the investors and the consultants, which has been adopted for general use and is shown in Exhibit 11–2.

Here are the key elements of the guideline for record keeping when managing outside advisers:

- Keep a daily diary of all telephone calls and conversations. Be sure to include the time of the call, length, and a brief note of explanation. If you don't want to keep this diary for all calls, at least keep it for calls with your outside advisers.
- Periodically transcribe the information from the diary to the Adviser Review Form or some other document or file you set up for each adviser or project. You can also photocopy the appropriate pages from the daily diary.
- Note on the form, each piece of correspondence generated (as will be explained, this ties in to monitoring the bills).

A typical bill from a lawyer will itemize all telephone calls, meetings, and correspondence that took place during the billing period. If you have noted in your diary when you spoke to counsel, you will be able to confirm each entry on the bill. Similarly, if you note each correspondence generated on the adviser review form, you can compare the form against the bill. If you don't have time to compare your records against the monthly bills, have someone else in your organization do it: your secretary, bookkeeper, or even your spouse, if he or she is familiar with the business.

Exhibit 11–2   Guide to Effective Communication with Consultants and
Professional Advisers

One of the many aspects of the Fund's involvement in projects is that it provides ongoing professional management, marketing, and technical assistance to the projects. This is in part achieved by assigning a consultant to work with the project manager/entrepreneur. The Fund bears the costs of the consultant's time and while it wants to provide the project manager a degree of freedom in interacting with the consultant; at the same time it must attempt to control costs.

Both the Project Manager and the Consultant are expected to become familiar with the points raised here and to be sensitive to effective utilization of time and limited resources.

1. Paper Trail—Fundamental to effective management is the proper documentation of all aspects of a business. Just as a researcher records every variable of an experiment, a good manager documents all his or her communications. Written communications are relatively easy to document, we need only make a copy; however, verbal communication is frequently relegated to the participant's memory.

   a. Daily Diary—We recommend that project managers maintain a notebook where they record all interpersonal contacts. Noting the date at the top of each page, a brief note explaining each telephone call or interview or meeting with the time and the person with whom you speak will serve as a valuable reference tool.

   b. Meeting or Call Memo—We must insist that each interaction between the project manager and consultant be documented by a follow-up memo. We would prefer that the project manager prepare a summary (but in some cases the consultant may prepare the summary) indicating who participated, the date and the length of the meeting or call, a brief description of the subject(s) discussed, and who is responsible for any follow-up to take place with target dates for answers or further communications. This memo should then be forwarded to the consultant to confirm that the memo in fact summarizes the facts correctly. Thereafter a copy should be supplied to Fund's representative and a copy to the Fund office.

   c. Monthly Reports—Both the Project Manager and Consultant are expected to provide Fund with a monthly report that summarizes, with extreme brevity, the activities in which they were involved on behalf of the project during the previous month. In the case of the Consultant, this document should not be longer than one page but should include a summary of the hours put in on behalf of the project with short explanations for each time segment. Project Managers should focus on performance as measured by the milestones or targets in the project work statement or business plan. Any communications of importance not previously provided to Fund should accompany the monthly report, personnel changes, etc.

(continued)

Exhibit 11–2　*(continued)*

Note: In the event that the Fund determines that a Project Manager is utilizing his or her Consultant in an excessive manner, the Fund reserves the right to limit the number of hours per month without obtaining prior approval.

   d.　Board Minutes—Whether or not the Fund representative is present at a Board meeting, the Project Manager is obligated to arrange to have company board meeting minutes recorded, transcribed, and copies provided not only to all Board members but also to the Fund office.

   e.　Consultant's Correspondence—To the extent a Consultant of his own initiative or at the request of a project manager, communicates with individuals or companies not related to Fund or the project, it is expected that both Fund and the Project Manager will receive copies of letters, faxes, and/or memos of verbal communications.

   f.　Significant Events—The Fund does not expect nor want to receive copies of every correspondence or meeting memo that is generated by or received by the project. However, it does wish to be apprised of significant events as they happen and not only in the monthly summaries. For example, notice of issuance or rejection of a patent, a first purchase order from a customer, a major financial problem, a letter indicating interest from a major potential customer or joint venture partner or any significant breakthrough.

   g.　Financial Documentation—The Fund would like to receive copies of monthly financial reports, quarterly and annual financial statements to the extent they are provided by the project's auditors and/or accountants, the incubator bookkeeper, etc.

   h.　Revisions of Work Statements and/or Business Plans

2. Effective Telephone Communications—Overseas calls are expensive, consultants' time is expensive and time you spend on the telephone is time not being spent on resolving other issues. Everyone benefits from maximizing your telephone communication skills.

   a.　Prepare an Agenda—Each call should be planned: Prepare a small outline, pull together only the pertinent documents to be referred to in the call. Be sure the consultant has a copy of the agenda in advance.

   b.　Schedule the Time in Advance—Be sure that either during the previous telephone conversation or when you send a proposed agenda that you confirm a date and time for the call. Advise your staff that you should not be disturbed when the call is in progress.

   c.　Limit the Call—No agenda should require more than one hour of telephone time. If you are working from an agenda and are committed to no more than one hour you will find that you can be very efficient. Save discussions of family, friends, and weather for social events.

Exhibit 11–2   *(continued)*

3. Files and Records—The paperless office has not yet become a reality, nor am I certain it ever will. Legal requirements and just good business sense suggest that hard copies of your correspondence and correspondence you receive should be permanently recorded and filed.

   a. Daily Diary—This management tool was mentioned in Section 1 and is referred to here because it may be your only hard copy record of a substantial part of your daily communication. As diaries fill up, they should be safely stored for future reference.

   b. Fax Paper—There are two schools of thought: One says that thermal sensitive paper fades and therefore any document received by fax should be photocopied onto plain paper. I myself have faxes that are several years old and haven't faded; if they are not constantly in light they last quite a long time. However, important documents should be copied, and for ease of handling, it is better to photocopy than work with the fax paper.

   c. File Management—I have no intention of giving courses on file management; however, I strongly recommend maintaining customer files alphabetically. Ideally, all files should be maintained alphabetically, but you may wish to divide the files by categories and maintain separate drawers for each category (i.e., sales, financial, accounts payable, general correspondence, personnel).

4. Effective Written Communications—There are some excellent books on writing business letters, and once again it is not my intention to offer a course on this subject. However, I would like to offer some basic rules of good business communications:

   a. KISS—Keep It Simple Stupid (or Short). Whether you are writing a business letter or a monthly report, keep in mind that the person who reads the document will not finish reading it if the document is too long, too complicated, and not clear.

   b. Grammar and Spelling—Imagine that you are responsible for purchasing a valuable and complicated piece of equipment. Your potential supplier sends you a letter full of misspelled words or an error-ridden brochure describing the product. Wouldn't you think, "If his letters are full of errors, I wonder what I'll find in his product?" There are many fine spell-checking programs for English language word processors. Use them! And have someone for whom English is his or her mother tongue double-check your correspondence to be certain that you are using correct forms, tenses, and constructions.

   c. Be Professional—Just because you are a start-up business, have never been in business before, or are a scientist, doesn't mean you cannot approach the written aspects of your business in a professional manner. Remember, your letter or brochure may be the first contact a potential customer has with you and your business; if you want a second contact make sure the first is the best it can be.

Bills from many other service providers are not as specific. You may not require details from a vendor, depending on the method of compensation. However, anyone who is billing you by the hour should provide detailed invoices or billing summaries.

Attorneys and consultants love clients who agree to work on retainer. A retainer may be defined as a fixed fee, usually paid monthly, that provides unlimited access for advice and counsel or for a set number of hours per month. Retainer arrangements are typically reviewed periodically with either a credit adjustment or supplemental payment based on hours actually expended. The problem with retainer arrangements is that while the professionals tend to keep accurate records, clients are less likely to maintain good records and therefore can't audit performance.

Retainers can be useful and beneficial to entrepreneurs and managers as long as they are carefully monitored. A retainer encourages you to call whenever you have a problem, rather than always worrying about the cost of the call.

VIEWING ADVICE IN CONTEXT AND OBTAINING A SECOND OPINION

Often it is difficult, if not impossible, to properly evaluate the advice we are receiving from a professional. Here we are trying to run our business day-to-day, dealing with myriad problems and constantly struggling with issues for which we have neither the skills, the time, nor the inclination. Yet, we have to make decisions based on advice provided by our advisers. We hire those advisers because we believe they know their field, and we want to have confidence that we can trust their advice. But when we feel a nagging uncertainty, we have to balance our trust in our advisers against our intuitive management sense. As stated earlier, a good lawyer or accountant is not necessarily a savvy businessperson. The lawyer's recommendation to you only reflects his or her legal education and personal bias. Rarely, if ever, is there only one solution to a problem. This applies to architects, graphic artists, and any other profession discussed in this book.

In fact, if an adviser were to tell me that there is only one course of action, I would be very suspicious, especially if that course of action is expensive and would enrich the adviser. Professionals will more likely offer several options and state a preference for one of them. So, how do we view the advice and make an intelligent decision?

Sometimes the best solution is the one that we simply cannot afford and so we must consider a lesser alternative. Therefore, it is important either to quantify the choices ourselves or ask the adviser to quantify the choices (preferably you both should engage in this exercise). You can set up a chart with the options on the vertical axis and the following questions on the horizontal axis:

- How much will this approach cost?
- What are our chances for success?
- What will the benefit or yield be if we are successful?
- What is our downside exposure if we aren't successful?
- How much time and energy will my organization and/or I have to invest?

If you take the time to answer all these questions, you may see graphically how realistic the recommended course of action really is. Ask your adviser/professional to provide answers to the chart while you fill in the answers independent of the adviser's response. Then compare the responses. This exercise will provide you with a very effective management tool.

Ultimately a legal decision, an accounting approach, a design consideration should reflect what is the best for your business. An example might be a start-up company in the midst of negotiations with an outside investor. One of the company's patents has been infringed and management is weighing the options for litigation. The outside investor is turned off by prolonged patent litigation and his infusion of capital into the company is imperative for the company's long-term health. Patent counsel is convinced that it can successfully prosecute the litigation, but the case could take five years and cost $200,000 before a successful conclusion. The right business decision is to get the investor on board and not proceed with the litigation even if you are on firm legal ground. Litigation tends to become an all-consuming exercise and frequently distracts the entrepreneur or manager from the principal reason for being in business. Experienced investors know this and therefore do not like to invest in businesses where the principals are preoccupied with litigation.

I have used three basic sources over the years for second opinions:

1. Friends and business associates.
2. Mentors.
3. Other professionals.

Friends and Business Associates

I have recommended to clients and friends for years to establish a board of directors with at least two outside directors. It makes no difference whether you call this group a board of directors, board of advisers, your "personal board," or your kitchen cabinet. I suggest that you compensate them in some way, have formal meetings on a regular basis, and be certain they are fully apprised of developments within your business. This ought to be the group you go to, either individually—if you need advice between regular meetings, or collectively—if your need for a second opinion can wait until they are all assembled. The cost versus benefit of a dedicated group of advisers is almost impossible to measure.

When my father died and I lost my best resource for second opinions and advice, I decided it was time to set up a board of directors consisting of three outside directors. Only one of the directors was actively engaged in our industry. The two other outside directors were involved in totally unrelated businesses. Problems were brought to these directors at our quarterly board meetings and throughout the year. If I had retained consultants of comparable knowledge and skill, it would have cost me 10 times what it cost me to pay these outside directors their annual retainer and per diem meeting fees and expenses.

Mentors

If you aren't ready to manage quarterly board meetings, the second best solution is to seek out "mentors." A mentor is someone with many years of business experience who is willing to meet with you informally and listen to your problems and offer advice based on his or her years of experience. You may find a mentor who will provide advice on a no-charge basis or you may have to pay the mentor for the time you spend with him or her. A pitfall with both the board scenario and the mentor scenario is that these advisers may not have had experience with the specific problem for which you are seeking a second opinion. The fact that your board or mentors have not personally experienced the specific problem for which you seek a second opinion is generally offset by their wisdom and ability simply to take an objective view of the problem.

Other Professionals

A third alternative is to obtain a second opinion from another professional in the same field as the professional you are evaluating, in much the same way that you might obtain a second medical opinion. There are advantages and disadvantages to this approach. An obvious advantage is that the professional will have germane knowledge and experience. On the other hand, a professional may be reluctant to criticize a colleague. Or, the professional may be unreasonably critical, in the hope of taking over the account. Here again, we as managers must exercise judgment and interpret the reactions of the people giving a second opinion. Engaging an attorney, accountant, or any other professional for a second opinion requires searching for candidates, reviewing their qualifications, and preparing an incident-specific engagement letter. The kind of second opinion you receive may be contingent on the degree of exposure the professional has in the given situation. No one will want to give you a second opinion for $250 if it will expose that person to a $100,000 liability.

A fourth or parallel alternative to those already noted is to study the books I have noted with four stars in the Bibliography. Collectively, these books represent a good reference library. Many of them discuss problems the authors encountered in their businesses and you will gain insight from their observations.

RECAP: MEASURING PERFORMANCE

- Use a daily diary—note the key points of telephone conversations and meetings.
- Maintain a file on each service provider—use the Adviser Review Form. Include copies of relevant pages from your daily diary, performance-related correspondence, and any notes you want to enter about superior or poor performance.
- Get a second opinion—if you have doubts about the advice you are getting or the amount of money you are paying, ask others for advice.

12

TERMINATING A PROFESSIONAL RELATIONSHIP

This book was written to assist you in becoming more professional in your dealings with outside service providers. How you go about terminating employees or outside contractors speaks as much to your professionalism as hiring and managing them.

Although careful selection and management procedures can reduce the risk of termination problems, inevitably—no matter how careful you are—you will still make mistakes and situations will continue to change. You may outgrow a relationship you thought would meet your requirements for an extended period. Your contact may leave the firm you are working with, and you don't like the replacement. You may find an individual or firm better suited to your needs.

Because of my unenviable status of working with many lawyers and other advisers, I know all the wrong ways to terminate a professional relationship. I have paid a heavy price for mismanaging the termination process. I had an accountant who refused to turn over his work papers to the incoming accountant. I had a sales rep instigate litigation for commissions he felt he was entitled. I have had to cope with gaps in service because I didn't plan well enough before a termination.

Very likely, you are reading this chapter, not out of curiosity, but because you are unhappy with a professional adviser and are seeking guidance. I suggest you first review Chapter 1, and then read the chapter pertinent to the profession you wish to terminate, focusing on the selection process. Chapter 9 ("Compensation") and Chapter 11 ("Measuring Performance") may also be helpful. There are three major reasons you may want to terminate a relationship:

1. You feel you are paying too much.
2. You question the individual or firm's competency. This may be a result of a specific incident or a growing sense of dissatisfaction.
3. You have lost confidence in the professional (this relates to the first two reasons).

Other reasons may include:

- New investors require you to make a change.
- Bankers may suggest a change would help your chances in obtaining a loan.
- It may be a condition of going public.
- The adviser has died or become incapacitated.
- The adviser may be unable to provide the additional services you require.
- Sales targets are not being met.

Before terminating a relationship that may have been long term and/or may have an element of friendship, you ought to try to objectively weigh the costs. And undoubtedly there are significant costs. I make this observation because you do not want to get into the habit of thinking you can change lawyers as easily as you change underwear. In Chapter 4, I noted that banks do not like clients who frequently move from bank to bank. If during the search process for an accountant, attorney, or any other professional, candidates learn that you are constantly changing vendors, more than likely they will factor that into the price or the structure of the engagement. Some of the costs associated with a change will include:

- The time you have to invest in searching out and selecting another firm.
- The risk that projects or issues in the works will be bobbled during the transition period.

- The risk that the replacement will require time to be brought up to speed, which you will pay for both monetarily and in lower productivity.
- The impact and upheaval within your organization.
- The damage to your business and your reputation.
- The possibility of having to pay double commissions.

Another element to evaluate is your contribution to the decline of your confidence. I have been guilty of essentially ignoring monthly legal bills (instead of auditing them as they come in), doing a slow burn, and then finally becoming furious when one large bill comes in. Often the conflict develops because you have not carefully negotiated the fees and conditions beforehand and somehow expect the bills to be reasonable or the service immediate. Sometimes you need to vent your frustrations and seek out an adviser's friendly ear; then you get upset when you get a bill for a one-hour telephone conversation that you initiated. In another scenario, you may have shifted directions midway through negotiations causing an expense that was not anticipated or budgeted.

Harold Novick, in *Selling Through Independent Reps*, recommends meeting with the rep and discussing problems in a partnership mode. He also suggests probing to determine the cause of the problem, which may be linked to temporary personal problems such as the loss of a loved one, a divorce, and so on. It could be embarrassing and uncomfortable for you to come down hard on someone for not performing, only to learn the individual has gone through a personal tragedy. Leon Wolf, one of Novick's coauthors, discusses potential problems evolving from "termination for cause" in the chapter on legal trends. Sales reps and real estate agents work essentially on commissions generated from actual sales which may be the by-product of many months of work. Therefore, I reiterate the importance of maintaining a strong paper trail and to have written contracts. Contracts should have clear unambiguous language regarding termination. If you are thinking about terminating a sales rep, invest in Novick's book.

If a disputed billing is in connection with a major project or litigation, you must consider how a change in personnel may affect the outcome. How will a judge or opposing counsel view change of counsel midway through litigation? What will be the cost of changing architects midstream in a construction project? You also need to ascertain whether the transition can be made smoothly and gradually or will alienate the incumbent and cause problems in the transition.

Finally, be careful not to change for the sake of change; be certain the new adviser can make a real difference either in the cost or the outcome. You ought to identify the replacement (if there is to be a replacement) prior to termination. Your new professional should be aware at the outset that he or she is being hired to replace someone and should be aware of the reasons. The replacement can be of great assistance in arranging for a smooth transition by preparing you and even by being an intermediary at some stage.

HAVE A TERMINATION PLAN

If, after considering all the issues, you still feel you want to make a change, then you need to proceed with caution.

Develop a termination plan (see Exhibit 12–1). A termination plan can be a one-page document outlining all the relevant information. It should include a time line that encompasses the planned termination and the date you want the replacement on board.

Review the contract or engagement letter to determine conditions for termination and to verify any financial exposure. Also, look for the anniversary date; it is always best to simply not renew an expiring contract rather than terminate an active one.

CREATE A PAPER TRAIL

In Chapter 11, I outlined the methodology of record keeping and the importance of maintaining a paper trail. *Nowhere is the significance of a good paper trail as important as it is in terminating a relationship.* In much the same way as you would document an employee's failings in their personnel file in anticipation of having to terminate, you ought to be documenting the professional's failings in his or her file.

Early in my business career I learned an important lesson from a payroll service. I had serious problems with unemployment compensation. The rates charged by the unemployment compensation bureau vary based on your experience factor. The more claims and the longer those claims draw against your accountant, the higher your rate becomes. Once your rate is increased, it takes a long time to get it reduced. We had no formal mechanism in place for warning employees when they violated company policy or engaged in behavior that was grounds for dismissal. Often we would terminate an employee for justifiable cause but because we did not have a paper trail for the employee's misdeeds, we would lose at unemployment compensation hearings. The payroll service offered a service that involved setting up policies and procedures to document employee performance. Within six months of the implementation of the system, we began to win unemployment compensation hearings. Within a year we began to see our unemployment rate decline.

Exhibit 12–1   Sample Termination Plan

Adviser name: _____   Current date: _____

Date engagement initiated: _____   Planned termination date: _____

Anniversary date of contract or engagement: _____

Planned date of notification: _____   Date replacement starts: _____

Contract: _____   Letter of engagement: _____

Initialed proposal: _____   Verbal: _____

Reason for termination: _____

_____

_____

Contract provision for termination (if any): _____

_____

_____

Documentation of failure to perform (attach letters, memos, daily log entries,
assign alpha numeric to list below): _____

_____

_____

_____

		Date
_____	Replacement provided list of needed documents.	_____
_____	Replacement engaged.	_____
_____	All needed documents collected.	_____
_____	Reviewed legal exposure with counsel.	_____
_____	Notification sent.	_____
_____	Acknowledgment received.	_____

Always maintain a daily log with notations of conversations where you have complained about service or bills. If you haven't kept an active file with an "adviser review form" or copies of correspondence reflecting your dissatisfaction, you should start such a file in anticipation of terminating the professional. Billing errors and other mistakes should be photocopied with handwritten notes placed on them. In short, you should be building the evidence that the person has not performed to the standard you expect or to an agreed standard.

Why should you go through this effort? You may find yourself in litigation over an outstanding unpaid bill in dispute or a contract violation. Someone may even claim to have been an employee and not an independent contractor. If you prepare for the worse and the termination goes smoothly, the most you will have wasted is some time. If the termination develops problems, however, you will need all the documentation you can accumulate. You should probably take a look at Fishman's *Hiring Independent Contractors* to appreciate the potential problems.

Paper trail also refers to the documents related to the project in which the professional is engaged. If you have done a good job in maintaining copies of all correspondence, drawings, specifications, and work papers, you will be more comfortable in making a change and you will be less likely to be held hostage by a disgruntled professional (see my war story on changing accountants in Chapter 3). Before terminating a professional, develop a list of documents the replacement will require to continue the project and carefully gather any missing data.

"The case files belong to the client, not the attorney. Accordingly, when the relationship has terminated, you have the right to obtain the files in your case. In most cases, the attorney keeps the files because the client fails to demand them. In most states, the attorney cannot withhold your files even if you owe the attorney money."[1] Cliff Robertson may be on strong legal grounds with that advice, but consider this scenario. Your attorney agrees to provide a complete set of the files but wants to be paid for making copies as he won't turn over the originals. The cost of copying is several hundred or even several thousand dollars, which he wants up front. So you may end up ransoming files because you didn't keep a complete file.

I now come to a sort of Catch-22 juncture. If any professionals I have terminated over the years read this section, they will probably chuckle at the inconsistency of my advice vis-à-vis my actions. I suggest, before activating the termination plan, that you confront the professional or firm with which you are unhappy, detail all the reasons you are dissatisfied, state that you have already spoken with a potential replacement, and give the incumbent the opportunity to react and respond to your concerns. If the issue is primarily a billing dispute, you may find the incumbent willing to not only revise the bills submitted to date but also make a substantial concession in the ongoing process. If the issue revolves around service, the incumbent may offer some alternatives that satisfy your concerns.

If the engagement was initiated with a contract or an engagement letter that no longer meets your needs, this is the opportunity to ask that a new or revised contract or engagement letter be prepared. If the engagement began without some sort of written agreement, this is also the time to correct that error. Earlier in this book, I noted that everything can be negotiated. My advice here is that everything can be renegotiated, assuming that you would prefer not to move your account to another firm.

The problem with this advice is that if this confrontation does not resolve amicably, you have tipped your hand and a vindictive professional can become an obstruction to a smooth transition. There is another problem with this advice: It is human nature, especially entrepreneurial human nature, to be unwilling to compromise a decision once you have made up your mind and perhaps even identified someone you think can do a better job.

If you haven't selected a replacement first and are dissatisfied with the results of your discussion with the professional, you will be at severe risk until you do find the replacement.

Whether or not you expressed your dissatisfaction to the incumbent, let's assume you want to proceed with the termination. I recommend the "don't burn your bridges" approach to termination. That is to say, even if the individual is an incompetent, you don't have to tell him or her that to his or her face. Certainly not before you have completed the full transfer of the project, file, or case.

As in my war story about changing accountants in Chapter 3, you ought to be prepared, when you are going to make a change, to have sufficient funds available to "ransom" any records or files that you have been unable to duplicate beforehand. Even if you dispute the balance due, you may have to pay it in full and fight afterward for a partial reimbursement. This situation can occur even when you have maintained a good paper trail and have copies of every document, if the professional is holding certain kinds of originals, such as patents, certificates of incorporation, stock books, and corporate minutes books.

A letter of termination should be carefully crafted. No purpose will be served by challenging the individual's professionalism or integrity when your first and foremost concern ought to be as smooth a transition as possible. At the same time, the letter should not be complimentary if you anticipate a potential dispute going forward. If the letter is confirming a meeting or telephone conversation, it should not be necessary to rehash the earlier conversation (see Exhibit 12–2).

Exhibit 12–2 Sample Termination Letters

Wrong

Dear Jerk:

You have ripped me off long enough! You have not only overcharged me for the past two years, but you are also an incompetent SOB who has cost me a lot of money with bad advice.

Your last bill was the last straw, I have no intention of paying you any part of the bill.

I'll be sending my bookkeeper around to pick up our files, you better have them ready.

Sincerely,

Joe Sucker

Better

Dear John:

You are well aware our company has grown substantially over the past two years. I have felt that your workload has precluded your devoting sufficient time to our account. The bank has advised us that they would like us to have a firm with greater depth handle our affairs. I had hoped you would grow with us. After careful consideration, I have decided to move our account to another provider.

Under the terms of your engagement, either side is obligated to provide ninety-day notice. Therefore, three months from the above date, we will consider the engagement over.

I would be grateful for your cooperation in the smooth transfer of all our files and records to our new service provider. I would also ask you not to initiate any new projects and to try to finish up the projects on which you are currently working. I would like to settle up any outstanding balances prior to the final date.

Cordially,

Some engagements, such as a sales representative, may require ongoing compensation even after the agreement is terminated. You should review carefully the formal agreements you have with sales reps, freelancers, and all other independent contractors, before you prepare the termination letter to be certain you don't violate contractual obligations.

You may wish to terminate an arrangement with an attorney that includes a contingency payment. Your new counsel will have to advise you on handling this potentially difficult situation.

The termination letter should state in clear language you are terminating the contract/engagement, and so on. If there is a contract clause providing for termination, it should be referred to in the letter. If there are documents you want turned over to you or their replacement, they should be itemized either in the body of the letter or as an addendum to the letter. The letter should clearly state the effective date and any other conditions.

Deliver the letter by hand to the professional. It is bad form to send a fax or mail a termination letter, however badly the professional performed or angry you may be. A professional manager should never terminate an employee or an outside service provider through a third party or any other method besides in person. The exception to this rule of professional etiquette would be that you would have to incur a significant travel expense or expenditure of time to terminate the professional in person.

RECAP: TERMINATING A PROFESSIONAL RELATIONSHIP

- Document reasons for termination—maintain a paper trail reflecting your concerns, voiced or not.
- Collect copies of all relevant files—include correspondence, records, forms, and so on.
- Search for a replacement—try to be sure there is someone better than the person you have and prepare for the transition.
- Word termination letters carefully—termination letters should not be destructive or confrontational; however, they should also not be complimentary.

Appendix I

INTERVIEW QUESTIONS

The Interview Questions in Appendix I will provide you with a starting point if you have not previously hired consultants, professionals, or freelancers. These questions should not be construed as representing the universe of information necessary to make an intelligent evaluation. You may wish to ask more or fewer questions, phrase them differently, or place them in a different order. Answers may provoke questions not here and you should follow through on any answers that raise more questions. The general questions should work fairly well for all professions. Thereafter, I have provided specific pages of questions for specific professions in the related chapters or subchapters.

From *How to Get Results from Interviewing*, here are 20 practical suggestions to improve interviewing:

1. Do your homework.
2. Never go beyond your depth.
3. Avoid overgeneralization.
4. Stay clear of prejudice.
5. Be receptive.
6. Avoid tricks or ruses.
7. Never overquestion.
8. Do not worry about conversational gaps.

9. Keep it private.
10. Never ask multiple questions.
11. Keep the initiative.
12. Select the proper approach.
13. Keep your opinions to yourself.
14. Shun the role of the amateur psychologist.
15. Keep an eye on objectives.
16. Maintain a steady pace.
17. Do not be misled by physical appearance.
18. Do not shy away from hard questions.
19. Seek advice.
20. Evaluate carefully.

INTERVIEW QUESTIONS

Career

1. How did you decide to pursue a career in this field/specialty?
2. What are the requirements educationally and otherwise for this field?
3. How many years have you practiced?
4. When did you last attend a continuing education course?
5. What was the subject covered?
6. What do you like least about the field?
7. What do you like most about your job?
8. Have your ever worked with a business such as ours? Describe.
9. What are your professional affiliations?
10. Think back to the last client you lost and explain why that client discontinued your services.

Personal

11. Tell me about your family.
12. What do you do for relaxation?
13. What was the last book you read?
14. What annoys you most about your clients?
15. What would you like to be doing 20 years from now?

16. In which organizations are you active in the community?
17. How do you think friends would describe you?
18. How do you think your clients would describe you?
19. Do you play any sports? What? How often?

My Business

20. Please tell me what you know about my business/industry.
21. Have you ever had a client in a similar business? Describe.
22. What do you think you can contribute that someone else couldn't?
23. What would you do first if I decide to retain your services?
24. How do you think I should measure your performance?
25. Based on what you know about us, how important will we be to your firm?

Your Business

26. If you aren't available, who else in your firm can I rely on, if I need an answer?
27. Have you ever terminated a relationship with a client? Please explain.
28. Please discuss how you would satisfy my concerns regarding accessibility.
29. Does your firm have an established policy for returning phone calls?
30. How long has your secretary/assistant worked for you?
31. What is his or her authority to make decisions in your absence?
32. Is he or she my advocate or your protector?
33. (hourly billing professionals) What are your billing increments?
34. Please explain your billing practices, regarding fax, phone, postage, and so on.

Appendix II

RESOURCE GUIDE

ACCOUNTANTS

American Institute of Certified Public Accountants (AICPA)
1211 Avenue of the Americas
New York, NY 10035-8775
Tel: 800-272-3476, Fax: 212-575-3836

Note: Private Companies Practices Section will provide a member list of 6,500 member firms and a copy of the most recent peer review of candidates.

National Society of Public Accountants (NSPA)
1010 North Fairfax Street
Alexandria, VA 22314-1574
Tel: 800-966-6679, Fax: 703-549-2984

Note: The NSPA provides a referral service to members in your geographic area. It also publishes several brochures (e.g., *How Accountants Set Fees*). The NSPA requires its members to subscribe to a Code of Ethics.

ADVERTISING AGENCIES

American Advertising Federation
1101 Vermont Avenue, Suite 500
Washington, DC 20005
Tel: 202-682-2500

American Association of Advertising Agencies (AAAA)
666 Third Avenue
New York, NY 10017-4056
Tel: 212-682-2500, Fax: 212-682-8391

Note: Publishes directory covering wide range of useful literature, especially *Client's Guide to Conducting an Agency Search.*

ARCHITECTS

American Institute of Architects (AIA)
1735 New York Avenue, NW
Washington, DC 20006-5292
Tel: 800-242-9930

Note: Publishes an excellent mail order catalog, monograph *You and Your Architect*, many local chapters.

ATTORNEYS

American Bar Association
541 North Fairbanks Court
Chicago, IL 60611-3314
Tel: 312-988-5725, Fax: 312-988-5032
E-mail or WWW: abapubed@attmail.com

Note: The Bar's Public Education Division publishes *The American Lawyer—When and How to Use One, Finding the Right Lawyer,* and a lawyer referral services directory.

Practicing Law Institute
810 Seventh Avenue
New York, NY 10019
Tel: 212-765-5700, Fax: 800-321-0093

Patent

National Council of Intellectual Property Law Association
PO Box 2974
Greensboro, NC 27402

Note: May be contacted to determine if there is a local or state association in your area.

Office of Enrollment and Discipline
U.S. Department of Commerce
Washington, DC 20231

Note: Will advise you whether any of the candidates you are considering have complaints registered against them.

Litigation

Association of Trial Lawyers of America
1050 31st Street, NW
Washington, DC 20007
Tel: 202-965-3500, Fax: 202-625-7312

Real Estate

American College of Real Estate Lawyers
733 15th Street, NW
Washington, DC 20005-5710
Tel: 202-393-1344, Fax: 202-783-3780

Estate Planning

American College of Estate Planning Counsel
3415 South Sepulveda Boulevard
Los Angeles, CA 90034
Tel: 310-398-1888, Fax: 310-572-7280

National Association of Estate Planning Councils
PO Box 801226
Dallas, TX 75380-1226
Tel: 214-788-1561, Fax: 214-788-1561

Bankruptcy

American College of Bankruptcy
510 C Street, NE
Washington, DC 20002-5810
Tel: 202-546-6725

BANKERS

American Bankers Association
1120 Connecticut Avenue, NW
Washington, DC 20036
Tel: 202-663-5000, Fax: 202-296-9258

American League of Financial Institutions
900 19th Street, NW
Washington, DC 20006
Tel: 202-628-5624

The Association of Lending and Credit Risk Professionals
1650 Market Street
Philadelphia, PA 19103
Tel: 215-851-9100, Fax: 215-851-9206

Note: Under the name of Robert Morris Associates, publishes the *Statement Studies,* an analysis of industries by SIC code, used by loan officers to compare your business against standard using various ratios.

Independent Bankers Association of America
One Thomas Circle NW
Washington, DC 20005
Tel: 202-659-8111

National Council of Savings Institutions
900 19th Street, NW
Washington, DC 20006
Tel: 202-857-3100

BCS & Associates
PO Box 5108
Scottsdale, AZ 85261-5108
Tel: 800-644-8384

Note: Consultants in managing bank relationships.

COLLECTIONS

American Collectors Association
4040 West 70th Street
Minneapolis, MN 55435
Tel: 612-926-6547, Fax: 612-926-1624

Note: Publishes free brochures *Selecting a Professional Collection Service, A Collection Guide for Creditors.*

International Credit Association (ICA)
243 North Lindbergh Boulevard
St. Louis, MO 63141-1757
Tel: 314-991-3030

Note: Publishes a bimonthly magazine and a monthly newsletter. Also publishes credit management books and will supply a list of members in your area.

CONSULTANTS

General

American Consultants League
1290 North Palm Avenue, Suite 112
Sarasota, FL 34236
Tel: 941-952-9290, Fax: 941-370-6024

Note: Annual directory of members available for $39.00 and a "how to" book for $96.00. Will provide a list of members in geographic area and specialty.

Professional and Technical Consultants Association
PO Box 4142
Mountain View, CA 94040
Tel: 800-747-2822

Note: Publishes directory and an annual survey of rates.

Personnel

Association of Executive Search Consultants
230 Park Avenue, Suite 1549
New York, NY 10169-0005
Tel: 212-949-9556, Fax: 212-949-9560

National Association of Personnel Services
3133 Mt. Vernon Avenue
Alexandria, VA 22305
Tel: 703-684-0180, Fax: 703-684-0071

Note: Awards the Certified Personnel Consultant (CPC) designation.

Management

Institute of Management Consultants
521 Fifth Avenue, 35th Floor
New York, NY 10175
Tel: 212-697-8262, Fax: 212-949-6571

Note: Awards the Certified Management Consultant (CMC) certification.

National Bureau of Professional Management Consultants
3577 Fourth Avenue
San Diego, CA 92103
Tel: 619-297-2207, Fax: 619-692-0351

Note: Awards the Certified Professional Management Consultant (CPMC) designation. Will provide referrals by geographic area and specialty.

Security

International Association of Professional Security Consultants
13819-G Walsingham Road, Suite 350
Largo, FL 34644
Tel: 813-596-6696, Fax: 813-596-6696

Computers

Independent Computer Consultants Association
11131 South Towne Square, Suite F
St. Louis, MO 63123
Tel: 314-892-1675, Fax: 314-487-1345
WWW: http://www.icca.org

Note: Offers referral service. Requires members to subscribe to Code of Ethics.

Information Systems Consultants Association
PO Box 467190
Atlanta, GA 30346
Tel: 404-458-3080

National Association of Computer Consultant Businesses
1250 Connecticut Avenue, NW, Suite 700
Washington, DC 20036
Tel: 202-637-6483, Fax: 202-637-9195

Franchising

Franchise Consultants International Association
5147 South Angela Road
Memphis, TN 38117
Tel: 901-761-3084

Cost Engineering

American Association of Cost Engineers
209 Prairie Avenue
Morgantown, WV 26507-1557
Tel: 800-858-2078, Fax: 304-291-5728

Note: Offers certification program, membership directory and publications catalog. Also publishes magazine—*Cost Engineering.*

Engineering

American Consulting Engineers Council
1015 15th Street, NW, Suite 802
Washington, DC 20005
Tel: 202-347-7474, Fax: 202-898-0068

Database

The Expert Marketplace
Tel: 800-983-9737, Fax: 301-251-4190
WWW: http://expert-market.com/em

Note: Bills itself as the marketplace for consultants, performs matching services between consultants and potential clients.

Material Handling

Association of Professional Material Handling Consultants
8720 Red Oak Boulevard
Charlotte, NC 28217
Tel: 704-558-4749

Business

Institute of Certified Business Counselors
PO Box 70326
Eugene, OR 97401
Tel: 541-345-8064

GRAPHICS AND DESIGN

American Institute of Graphics Arts (AIGA)
164 Fifth Avenue
New York, NY 10010
Tel: 212-807-1990

Note: Publishes a membership and resource directory.

Design Management Institute
107 South Street, Suite 502
Boston, MA 02111-2811
Tel: 617-338-6380, Fax: 617-338-6570
WWW: http://www.designmgt.org

Note: Publishes catalog of articles and books.

Graphics Arts Technical Foundation (GATF)
4615 Forbes Avenue
Pittsburgh, PA 15213-3796
Tel: 800-910-4283, Fax: 412-621-3049
WWW: http://www.gatf.lm.com

Note: Publishes product catalog primarily for professionals but with some interesting titles for beginners.

Industrial Designers Society of America (IDSA)
1142 Walker Road
Great Falls, VA 22066
Tel: 703-759-0100, Fax: 703-759-7679
E-mail: idsanhq@aol.com

Note: Publishes annual membership directory.

Institute of Packaging Professionals (IoPP)
481 Carlisle Drive
Herndon, VA 22070
Tel: 800-432-4085
WWW: http://www.packinfo-world.org

Note: Publishes Who's Who & What's What directory of members.
Good mail-order bookstore.

Printing Industries of America (PIA)
100 Daingerfield Road
Alexandria, VA 22314
Tel: 800-742-2666, Fax: 703-548-3227

Note: Publishes excellent mail-order resource catalog.

INSURANCE

American Association of Insurance Services
1035 South York Road
Bensenville, IL 60106
Tel: 708-595-3225

American Insurance Association
1130 Connecticut Avenue, NW, Suite 1000
Washington, DC 20036
Tel: 202-828-7100

Council of Insurance Agents and Brokers
316 Pennsylvania Avenue, SE, Suite 400
Washington, DC 20003-1146
Tel: 202-547-6616, Fax: 202-546-0597

Note: 300 members, generally the larger brokers and agents in the
United States. Will provide a directory of members with breakdown of
specialty areas served.

Insurance Information Institute
110 William Street
New York, NY 10038
Tel: 800-331-9146

Note: Publishes a variety of brochures discussing purchase of insurance.

National Insurance Association
PO Box 158544
Chicago, IL 60615
Tel: 313-924-3308

Professional Insurance Agents
400 North Washington Street
Alexandria, VA 22314
Tel: 703-836-9340, Fax: 703-836-1279

Note: 18,000 independent agents; will provide a list of members in your area.

Society of Risk Management Consultants
58 Diablo View Drive
Orinda, CA 94563-1507
Tel: 510-254-9472

Note: Will provide a list of members.

OUTSOURCING

The Outsourcing Institute (OI)
45 Rockefeller Plaza, Suite 2000
New York, NY 10111
Tel: 800-421-6767
WWW: http://www.outsourcing.com

Note: Publishes annual *Buyer's Guide*, year-end *Trends & Issues Survey*, an on-line bibliography and a referral help desk.

PUBLIC RELATIONS

Public Relations Society of America
33 Irving Place
New York, NY 10003-2376
Tel: 212-460-1462, Fax: 212-995-0757

Note: Publishes *Bibliography for PR Professionals*, and *Counselors Academy Directory*.

REAL ESTATE

American Industrial Real Estate Association
345 South Figueroa, Suite M-1
Los Angeles, CA 90071
Tel: 213-687-8777, Fax: 213-687-8616

National Association of Master Appraisers (NAMA)
303 West Cypress Street, PO Box 12617
San Antonio, TX 78212
Tel: 800-229-6262

Note: Publishes annual Registry of Real Estate. Affiliated with National Society of Environmental Consultants and the Real Estate Law Institute.

National Association of Realtors
430 North Michigan Avenue
Chicago, IL 60611-4087
Tel: 312-329-8200

Society of Industrial and Office Realtors (SIOR)
700 11th Street, NW, Suite 510
Washington, DC 20001-4511
Tel: 202-737-1150
WWW: http://www.sior.com

Note: Offers a variety of literature at nominal cost and will supply either its membership directory or a list of members in your geographic area.

SALES REPRESENTATIVES

Manufacturers' Agents National Association (MANA)
23016 Mill Creek Road
Laguna Hills, CA 92654
Tel: 714-859-4040

Note: Publishes "Directory of Manufacturers' Agents," a list of its membership.

Manufacturers' Representatives Educational Research Foundation
     (MRERF)
PO Box 247
Geneva, IL 60134
Tel: 708-208-1466, Fax: 708-208-1475

Note: An umbrella organization for some 70 sales representative associations. Will guide you through process of hiring representatives including directing you to appropriate representative associations. Publishes some very useful material.

Appendix III

SAMPLE PATENT APPLICATION

United States Patent [19]

Bisk et al.

[11] E   **Patent Number: Re. 32,269**

[45] **Reissued   Date of Patent: Oct. 28, 1986**

[54] **PLASTIC CLIP**

[75] Inventors: **Leonard Bisk,** Elkins Park; **Gunther Rogahn,** Lansdale, both of Pa.

[73] Assignee: **Independent Products Company, Inc.,** West Point, Pa.

[21] Appl. No.: **587,343**

[22] Filed: **Mar. 8, 1984**

Related U.S. Patent Documents

Reissue of:
[64] Patent No.: **4,335,838**
    Issued: **Jun. 22, 1982**
    Appl. No.: **137,930**
    Filed: **Apr. 7, 1980**

[51] Int. Cl.⁴ A47J 51/095; A47J 51/14; D06F 55/02
[52] U.S. Cl. **223/91;** 24/501; 24/511; 24/562; 24/564; 223/93; 223/96
[58] Field of Search .... 24/137 A, 346, 489, 24/499, 501, 507, 508, 511, 530, 536, 562, 564; 223/91, 93, 96, 85, DIG. 4; 211/115; 248/341; D6/253, 254

[56]   **References Cited**

U.S. PATENT DOCUMENTS

1,151,556	8/1915	Barney	24/564 X
1,684,721	9/1928	Wood	24/501
2,496,109	1/1950	Terry	24/530
2,583,784	1/1952	Maccaferri	223/91
2,666,240	1/1954	Maccaferri	24/501
2,723,786	11/1955	Martin	223/91
3,227,334	1/1966	Samuelsson .	
3,239,902	3/1966	Cohen	223/91 X
3,456,262	7/1969	Coon	24/501
3,963,154	6/1976	Schwartz et al. .	
4,009,807	3/1977	Coon	223/96
4,074,838	2/1978	Blasnik et al. .	

FOREIGN PATENT DOCUMENTS

1159796	2/1958	France	24/511
1210426	9/1959	France	223/96
348684	8/1937	Italy	24/564
7306492	11/1974	Netherlands	24/562
243567	1/1947	Switzerland	223/91
278907	2/1952	Switzerland	24/508
352309	4/1961	Switzerland	24/501
302326	1/1928	United Kingdom .	
477118	12/1937	United Kingdom .	
576423	4/1946	United Kingdom .	
593125	10/1947	United Kingdom .	
624783	6/1949	United Kingdom .	
697866	9/1953	United Kingdom .	
714990	9/1954	United Kingdom .	
715188	9/1954	United Kingdom	223/91
731906	6/1955	United Kingdom .	
916481	1/1963	United Kingdom .	
925386	5/1963	United Kingdom .	
1360965	7/1974	United Kingdom .	

Primary Examiner—Robert R. Mackey
Attorney, Agent, or Firm—Caesar, Rivise, Bernstein & Cohen

[57]   **ABSTRACT**

A molded plastic hanger and a clip for use therewith or with other members. The hanger includes a body portion having a diverging pair of arms including slots therein and a crossbar for mounting garment holding clips. A plastic swivel hook is connected to the body portion at a stem. The stem includes a shaft having an annular locking recess in its periphery which is adapted to be received within a mating socket of the hook to connect the hook and body portion to each other while enabling them to be swiveled readily with respect to each other. The clip is arranged for securement to the crossbar of the hanger or to any other rod-like element and is formed of a three piece construction comprising a pair of plastic jaws and a resilient U-shaped member, also formed of plastic, but having a higher tensile strength and resiliency than the plastic of the jaws.

8 Claims, 5 Drawing Figures

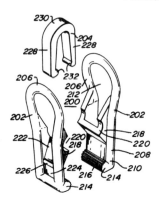

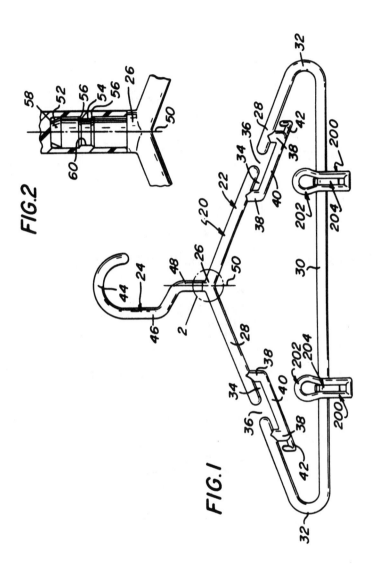

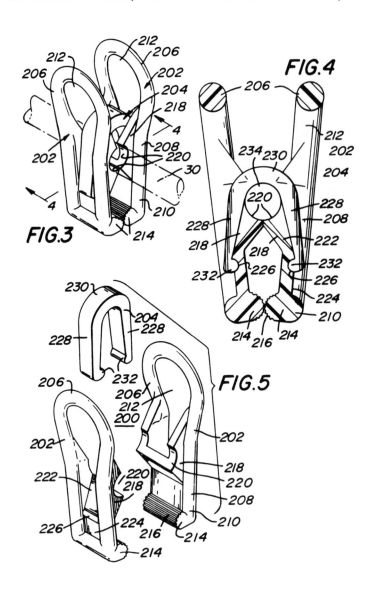

FIG.3

FIG.4

FIG.5

Re. 32,269

1

PLASTIC CLIP

Matter enclosed in heavy brackets [ ] appears in the original patent but forms no part of this reissue specification; matter printed in italics indicates the additions made by reissue.

This invention relates generally to garment hangers and particularly to molded plastic hangers and clips for use thereon, as well as for other uses.

Commercially available hangers are frequently fabricated of plastic material since such hangers can be made relatively inexpensively as compared to wooden hangers, yet are substantially more durable than wire hangers.

Conventional commercially available plastic hangers commonly comprise a plastic body portion and a metal hook. The hook may be pivotally secured to the body to enable the body to swivel with respect to the hook. Examples of hanger structures including a plastic body and a metal suspending hook are found in the U.S. Pat. Nos. 3,406,883 (Crane), 3,282,481 (Maxwell), and 3,407,979 (Patch). All-plastic garment hangers are also commercially available and many have been disclosed in the patent literature. For example, the following United States patents disclose hangers entirely formed of a plastic material: 3,067,917 (Reller, et al.), 3,116,860 (Urich), 3,209,966 (Wach), 3,463,369 (Moskowitz), 3,570,729 (Zuckerman), 3,897,893 (Leinmenes), 3,963,154 (Schwartz, et al), 3,973,705 (Erthein), 4,040,546 (Liebscher), and 4,074,838 (Blasnik, et al). Among the aforementioned patents, the patents to Schwartz, et al, Liebscher and Blasnik, et al, each disclose all-plastic hangers having swivel hooks.

Conventional garment hangers also frequently include pinch-type jaw clips arranged to be located at various positions along a cross-bar at trousers or skirts on the hanger. Examples of such hangers are found in U.S. Pat. Nos. 2,378,578 (Oskow), 2,496,531 (Gray), 2,546,717 (Beetlestone, et al), 2,617,568 (Pechtel), and 3,950,829 (Cohen).

While the aforeidentified plastic hangers do achieve various design goals, such hangers nevertheless suffer from one or more drawbacks, such as complexity of construction, difficulty of assembly, limited utility, limited durability and ruggedness.

Accordingly, it is a general object of the instant invention to provide an entirely plastic hanger and an entirely plastic clip, each of which can be used independently of one another and which overcomes the disadvantages of the prior art.

It is a further object of the instant invention to provide an entirely plastic hanger having a freely swivelable suspender hook.

It is still a further object of this invention to provide an entirely plastic hanger which is low in cost and can be readily assembled.

It is still a further object of this invention to provide an entirely plastic hanger having the capability of holding various types of garments.

It is still a further object of the instant invention to provide an entirely plastic hanger having wide utility and constructed to have an aesthetically pleasing, modern, tubular appearance.

It is still a further object of the instant invention to provide an entirely plastic clip which can be used with said hanger, with conventional hangers or on any rod-

2

like element and which overcomes the disadvantages of the prior art.

It is still a further object of the instant invention to provide an entirely plastic clip which is low in cost and can be readily assembled.

These and other objects of the instant invention are achieved by providing an all-plastic hanger with a swivel hook and all-plastic clips with both the hanger and the clips being usable independently of the other. The hanger includes an integral body portion and hook means connected thereto for supporting the body portion. The body portion includes a neck portion, a pair of arms diverging outwardly therefrom and a cross-bar portion interconnecting the outer ends of the arms.

The body portion and the hook means are each substantially cylindrical in cross-section along their entire length. The hook means includes an arcuate upper portion and a connecting portion. The connecting portion includes a cylindrical socket having a longitudinal axis. The neck portion includes a cylindrical shaft disposed and locked within said socket for swiveling about the longitudinal axis. The socket includes a peripheral collar projecting radially inward and about the longitudinal axis and the shaft includes a mating annular recess for receipt of the collar to lock the shaft within the socket and enable the body portion and hook means to be swiveled with respect to each other.

The clip is arranged for ready assembly and releasable securement to the cross-bar of the hanger or to any other rod-like element having a longitudinal axis. The clip comprises a pair of jaws formed of a first plastic material and resilient bias means formed of a second plastic material. The second material has a higher tensile strength than the first material. Each of the jaws is a generally planar member comprising an enlarged first end portion defining a finger grasping opening, an intermediate portion, and a second end portion including a projection extending normally to the plane of the jaw member. The intermediate portion includes an arcuate recess for receipt of a portion of the periphery of the cross-bar or other rod-like element. The bias means is a generally U-shaped member having a pair of outwardly flared legs, each of which is arranged to engage a respective one of the jaws to hold the jaws on the cross-bar or rod-like element so that the clips can be readily slid therealong and pivoted thereabout.

Other objects and many of the attendant advantages of the instant invention will be readily appreciated as the same becomes better understood by reference to the following detailed description when considered in connection with the accompanying drawing wherein:

FIG. 1 is a plan view of an all-plastic hanger constructed in accordance with one aspect of the instant invention and including an all-plastic clip constructed in accordance with another aspect of the instant invention and mounted on the hanger;

FIG. 2 is an enlarged view, partially in section, showing a portion of the hanger within the area 2 shown in FIG. 1;

FIG. 3 is a perspective view of the clip of the instant invention shown mounted on a rod-like element, such as a portion of the hanger shown in FIG. 1;

FIG. 4 is an enlarged sectional view taken along line 4—4 of FIG. 3; and

FIG. 5 is an exploded perspective view of the clip.

Referring now in greater detail to the various figures of the drawing wherein like reference characters refer to like parts, there is shown at **20** a hanger constructed

Re. 32,269

3

in accordance with one aspect of the instant invention and a clip **200** constructed in accordance with another aspect of the instant invention.

It must be pointed out at this juncture that while the clip **200** is shown mounted on the hanger **20** in FIG. 1, either the hanger **20** or the clip **200** can be used independently of one another. To that end, the hanger **20** may be used without any clip thereon, may be used with suitably constructed prior art clips, or may be used with the clip **200**. The clip **200** may be used with the hanger **20** of this invention, with prior art garment hangers, or with any structural body having a rod-like element or portion on which it is desired to position a clip for longitudinal movement therealong and swiveling movement thereabout. The clip may even be used on a flexible member having a cylindrical surface portion, e.g., a clothesline.

As can be seen in FIG. 1 the hanger **20** basically comprises a body portion **22** and hook means **24** connected thereto for supporting or suspending the body portion from a support (not shown). The hook **24**, as will be described in detail later, is connected to the body portion so that they can be swiveled freely through an angle of 360° with respect to each other.

In accordance with the preferred aspect of the instant invention, the entire hanger **20** is substantially cylindrical in cross-section (see FIG. 3) to provide an aesthetically pleasing, modern, tubular appearance which is now highly desired by the consuming public.

The body portion **22** basically comprises an upstanding neck or stem portion **26**, a pair of arms **28**, and a cross-bar **30**. The arms **28** are connected together at the stem **26** and diverge downward and outward therefrom. Each arm **28** is joined to a respective end of the cross-bar **30** at a rounded shoulder **32**.

As is conventional, the diverging arms **28** serve as a means for supporting a jacket or other similarly constructed garment on the hanger. In order to support dresses or other garments having straps, each arm **28** includes a slot **34** disposed parallel to the arm itself and having a narrow mouth **36**. Each slot is formed by a pair of downward extensions **38** and a cross-piece **40**. A small hook **42** projects outward from the extension **38** which is immediately adjacent the shoulder **32**. The hook **42** serves as a convenient means for holding the straps of delicate garments. The cross-sectional area of the body portion **20** of the hanger is cylindrical throughout its entire length except for the portion forming the hook **42**, which portion is, while also cylindrical, is of substantially smaller cross-sectional area and diameter.

The body portion **22** is molded as an integral unit of a low cost plastic which is strong, lightweight, and durable, such as polypropylene.

As can be seen in FIG. 1, the suspender hook **24** includes an arcuate upper portion **44**, an intermediate portion **46** and a connecting portion **48**. The connecting portion **48** is arranged to connect the hook **24** to the body **22** to enable the body to be supported by the hook, yet be swiveled freely about the longitudinal axis **50** of the stem **26**.

Turning to FIG. 2, it can be seen that the connecting portion **48** includes a socket **52** located therein. The socket **52** is in the form of a cylindrical bore which is coaxial with the axis **50** and includes a peripheral collar **54** projecting radially inward toward the axis **50**. The collar **54** merges with the remaining portion of the socket via a pair of tapered surfaces **56**. The stem portion **26** of the body of the hanger includes a smaller

4

diameter shaft **58** extending coaxially with the axis **50**. The shaft **58** includes an annular recess **60** about its periphery and which mates with the collar **54**. The outside diameter of the shaft **58** is just slightly smaller than the inside diameter of the socket so that the shaft **58** can be snap-fit within the socket and with the peripheral collar **54** being located within the annular recess **60**. Like the body portion **20**, the hook **24** is also formed as an integral unit of a plastic, and is preferably the same plastic as that of the body portion. The use of a somewhat resilient plastic, such as polypropylene, enables the shaft to be readily inserted and snap-fit within the socket, thus facilitating the assembly of the hanger.

When the shaft **58** is snap-fit within the socket **52**, the hook and body can be freely swiveled manually with respect to each other through the full 360° about axis **50**, yet there is sufficient frictional engagement to prevent accidental swiveling.

Referring now to FIGS. 3–5, there is shown the details of the clip **200**. As can be seen, the clip **200** basically comprises a pair of jaws **202** and resilient bias means **204** for connecting the jaws to one another. Each of the jaws is formed of a plastic masterial which is low in cost, lightweight, durable and resilient. The biasing means **204** is also formed of a plastic material but which preferably exhibits a higher tensile strength and resiliency than the material forming the jaws **202**. In accordance with a preferred embodiment of the clip, the jaws **202** are formed of polypropylene, like the hanger **20** described heretofore, while the resilient means **204** comprises polycarbonate, such as sold under the General Electric Company Trademark "LEXAN".

As can be seen in FIGS. 4 and 5, each jaw **202** is formed as a substantially planar loop and includes an enlarged first end portion **206**, an intermediate portion **208** and a narrow second end portion **210**. The jaws **202** are arranged to be disposed side-by-side, with a rod-like element, such as crossbar **30**, forming a fulcrum therebetween, and with the bias means **204** encircling a portion of the opposed jaws and rod-like element to hold the clip together. The opposed end portions **210** form a mouth for the clip which can be opened to receive a garment. The mouth is opened by grasping the clip by its end portions **206** and squeezing those portions toward each other against the bias force of bias means **204**. Upon release of the portions **206**, the bias means **204** pivots the jaws back together to effect the holding of a garment tightly between the opposed jaw ends **210**.

The precise details of the clip **200** and the manner of assembly and disassembly thereof, will now be described. To that end, as can be seen in FIG. 5, the enlarged end portion **206** of each jaw is of generally ring-like construction and includes a central opening **212**. The central opening is suitably dimensioned to enable a user's fingers to be comfortably received therein, but not extend therethrough, so that the jaws can be grasped comfortably to facilitate the opening of the clip. The second end portion **210** of each jaw is generally linear and includes a semi-cylindrical free end projection **214** projecting inward normally therefrom. The opposed free end projections **214** each include a plurality of ridges **216** extending across the full width thereof and are adapted to be the portions of the clip which actually engage the garment to securely hold the garment therebetween under the bias force provided by the bias means **204**. The ridges increase frictional engagement between the clip and the garment.

Re. 32,269

5

The intermediate portion 208 of each jaw includes a wedge portion 218 projecting inward, i.e., in the same direction as the projection 214. The wedge portion 218 includes an arcuate recess 220 which is suitably configured to receive a portion of the periphery of the cross-bar 30 or any other element having a circular surface.

The outside of the intermediate portion of each jaw includes an inclined or ramp surface portion 222 extending downwardly from the edge of the arcuate recess 220 to a planar surface 224 of the end 210. A locking slot or recess 26 is located on the outside of the jaw on the planar surface portion 224. Each locking recesses 226 is adapted to receive a respective end of the bias means 204 to secure the two jaws and the bias means to each other on the element 30.

The resilient bias means 204 is of generally U-shape having a pair of outwardly flaring legs 228 and an arcuate mid-portion 230. Each of the legs termiantes at its free end in an enlarged semi-circular projection 232 which is adpted to be received within a respective one of the slots 226 in the jaws 202.

The assembly of the clip 200 is as follows: The pair of jaws 202 are located opposite to each other on the cross-bar 30 of the hanger 20, or on any other suitably configured rod-like element, with the portion of the cross bar positioned within the opening formed by the respective arcuate recesses 220 in the opposed jaws. The U-shaped bias means 204 is then slipped about the cross-bar 30 so that the projections 232 engage the inclined surfaces 222 of the jaws. By pushing on the arcuate portion 230 of the resilient means 204 toward the jaw ends 210, the bias means slides toward those ends, with the portions 232 of the bias means riding up the inclined surfaces 222 until such portions reach the slots 226 in the planar portion 224. When this occurs, the projections 232 snap into the slots 226, thereby locking the bias means 204 in place and forming a central, circular shaped opening 234 (FIG. 4) in which the crossbar 30 is journalled. Once the clip components are secured, as just described, there is sufficient frictional engagement between the arcuate surfaces 220 and the periphery of the cross-bar 30 to insure that the clip can be readily slid therealong, when desired, but is resistant to accidental sliding. Moreover, the clip can be pivoted through an arc of 360° about the longitudinal axis of the cross-bar 30, since the cross-bar is journalled within opening 234 of the clip.

As can be seen in FIG. 5, the combined angular extent of the two arcuate recesses 220 is substantially less than 360° to enable the clip's mouth to be opened sufficiently wide to accommodate a wide variety of garments. The acruate mid-portion 230 of the clip prevents the jaws from falling off of the crossbar when the clip is fully closed.

If it is desired to remove the clip 200 from the cross-bar 30, all that is required is to grasp the legs 228 of the resilient means 204 to extract the projections 232 from the recesses 226, whereupon the clip can be retracted by pulling its mid-portion 230 away from the mouth of the clip. Such action is facilitated by the inclined surfaces 222 which serve as downwardly extending ramps for the bias member 204 as it is retracted.

As will be appreciated from the foregoing, the hanger 20 and the clip 200 of the instant invention each are simple in construction, can be made at low cost, can be readily assembled and disassembled, and provide the aesthetically pleasing tubular appearance so highly desired in the market place at present.

6

Without further elaboration the foregoing will so fully illustrate our invention that others may, by applying current or future knowledge, readily adapt the same for use under various conditions of service.

We claim:

1. A clip arranged for ready assembly and releasable securement on a rod-like element of a first predetermined diameter and having a longitudinal axis, said clip comprising a pair of jaws formed of a first plastic material and resilient bias means formed of polycarbonate and having higher tensile strength and resiliency than said first material, each of said jaws being a generally planar member and comprising an elongated first end portion defining a finger grasping opening, an intermediate portion, and a second end portion including a projection extending at an angle to the plane of said jaw member, said intermediate portion including an arcuate recess therein for close receipt of a portion of the periphery of said rod-like element when said clip is assembled thereon, said bias means being a generally U-shaped member having a pair of outwardly flared legs each terminating in a free end and an arcuate intermediate portion defining a recess having a first predetermined diameter, the free ends of said bias means being spaced apart by a distance greater than the diameter of said recess to enable said bias means to be readily secured to said jaws, with each of said legs overlying and engaging a respective one of said jaws adjacent said intermediate portion and with the recess in said arcuate portion coacting with the recess in each of said jaws to form a substantially circular opening closely receiving a portion of said rod-like member therein to complete the assembly of said clip by holding said jaws on said rod-like member and whereupon said clip can be readily slid therealong and pivoted thereabout with said rod-like element acting as a fulcrum.

2. The clip of claim 1 wherein said intermediate portion includes an inclined surface terminating in a locking recess and wherein each leg of said bias means includes an enlarged free end which is arranged to slide along said surface and into said recess to facilitate the assembly of said clip.

3. The clip of claim 1 wherein each of said jaws is in the form of a planar loop.

4. The clip of claim 1 wherein said first plastic material is polypropylene.

5. The clip of claim 4 wherein said rod-lik element comprises a portion of a garment hanger.

6. The clip of claim 5 wherein said rod-like element is formed of polypropylene.

7. *A clip arranged for ready assembly on a rod-like element of a first predetermined diameter, said clip comprising a pair of jaws formed of a first plastic material and resilient bias means formed of a second plastic material having a higher tensile strength and greater resiliency than said first plastic material, each of said jaws including a generally planar member comprising a first end portion, an intermediate portion, and a second end portion including a projection extending at an angle to the plane of said planar member, said intermediate portion having an outer inclined surface, and said first end portions being movable relative to each other by a user for moving said second end portions relative to each other from a normally closed position to an opened position, said resilient bias means, in an unbiased state thereof, being a generally U-shaped member having a pair of outwardly flared legs each terminating in a free end and an arcuate intermediate portion defining a recess having a first predetermined diameter, the*

Re. 32,269

7

free ends of said bias means being spaced apart by a distance greater than the diameter of said recess, said spaced-apart distance permitting the free ends of the bias means in said unbiased state to engage the inclined outer surfaces of the intermediate portions of the jaws to enable said bias 5 means to be readily manually secured in a biased state to said jaws by sliding said legs along said inclined surfaces into said biased state, each of said legs overlying and engaging a respective one of said jaws adjacent said intermediate portion for holding said jaws together and biasing 10 said second end portions into said normally closed position, said intermediate portion of each of the jaws also including an arcuate recess therein for closely receiving a portion of the periphery of said rod-like element when said resilient bias means is assembled with said jaws, the recess defined 15

8

by the arcuate intermediate portion of said bias means coacting with the recesses in the intermediate portions of the jaws to form an arcuate opening closely receiving a portion of said rod-like element therein, said first end portions and said second end portions of said jaws being movable relative to each other on an outer peripheral surface of said rod-like element.

8. The clip of claim 7 characterized in that said inclined surface of each jaw terminates in a locking recess and wherein each leg of said bias means includes an enlarged free end which is arranged to slide along said surface and into said locking recess to facilitate the assembly of said clip.

*   *   *   *   *

20

25

30

35

40

45

50

55

60

65

Appendix IV

SAMPLE SALES REPRESENTATIVE EVALUATION FORMS

Representative Recruiting and Start-Up Status Log

Basic Geographical Rep Area/Territory:	Rep Candidates - Co. Name, City, State/Province		
Actions	**Dates**	**Dates**	**Dates**
Letter #1 - Sent			
Letter #2 - 2nd Request - Sent			
Letter #1 - Response Received			
Letter #2 - Response Received			
Letter #3 or #4 - Sent			
Acknowledgement/Holding Letters #5 or #6 - Sent			
First Telephone Contact			
Reference Checks Completed			
Letter #7 (Visit Set/Confirmed)			
Personal Visits/Final Evaluations			
Thank You/Holding Letter #8 (Possible Finalist) - Sent			
Letter #9 ("Cool" Qualified Reps; Possible Future Contact) - Sent			
Letter #10 (Drop all Further Considerations) - Sent			
Letter #11 (Sign Up, Congratulations and Starter-Kits) - Sent			
Letter #12 (Thank You Letter to References) - Sent			
Initial Training Session(s) Scheduled -			
Initial Training Sessions(s) Completed -			
Second Training Session(s) Scheduled -			
Second Training Session(s) Completed -			

Note: Taken from *Thriving With Reps,* by Jerry Frank and Jack McNutt, MRERF, used with permission. Copyright © 1992 IMA Incorporated and McNutt & Co.

Representative Data Sheet

1. Firm name: _____

2. Complete address (home office): _____
   _____

   Telephone _____ FAX _____ TELEX _____

3. Please list all branch offices and the date each was opened:
   _____   _____
   _____   _____
   _____   _____

4. Please give a brief description of your facilities (offices, warehouse, instrument service department, mailing equipment, etc.) _____
   _____
   _____
   _____

5. Please provide a brief description of your computer capabilities: _____
   _____
   _____
   _____

6. Names of owners or principal stockholders and their percentage of the firm:
   _____   _____
   _____   _____
   _____   _____

7. Exact territory covered (send map if available): _____
   _____
   _____
   _____

8. Date established: _____ Proprietorship ☐   Partnership ☐   Corporation ☐
   If a corporation, date and state of incorporation: Date _____   State _____

9. Number of full time employees:

Principals	_____	Telemarketers	_____	Applications Engineers _____
Outside salespeople	_____	Office, Clerical	_____	Warehouse _____
Inside salespeople	_____	Shop/Lab	_____	Other _____

   (please specify)

   Total No. of employees _____

10. Please list your trade / professional association affiliations (ERA, IEEE, etc.): _____
    _____
    _____
    _____

Note: Taken from *Thriving With Reps,* by Jerry Frank and Jack McNutt, MRERF, used with permission. Copyright © 1992 IMA Incorporated and McNutt & Co.

(continued)

Representative Data Sheet   *(continued)*

11. Please complete the following information on your CUSTOMER BASE:

Do You Serve?	YES	NO	Approx. No. Customers* This Group	% Of Your Sales To This Group
a. Electrical/Electronic Mfgrs.	☐	☐	_____	_____
b. Non-Electronics Industrial Firms	☐	☐	_____	_____
c. R&D Labs, Educational Inst.	☐	☐	_____	_____
d. Military & Other Govt. Agencies	☐	☐	_____	_____
e. Industrial Distributors	☐	☐	_____	_____
f. End Users	☐	☐	_____	_____
g. Other: _____ (please specify)	☐	☐	_____	_____

> *Consider each separate division or major facility where independent buying decisions are made as a separate customer.

12. Describe (on additional page) your SALES PROMOTION activities on behalf of your own firm, and the manufacturers you represent (direct mail, local trade shows, ads, etc.): if possible, send sample promotion items.

13. Describe (on additional page) any SPECIAL FACILITIES AND CAPABILITIES at your disposal such as office and laboratory equipment, application engineering talents, and experience directly related to our products.

14. Please send resumes or attach a list showing the following items for EACH MEMBER OF YOUR SALES FORCE: (a) name, (b) advanced education, (c) degrees, (d) field of study, (e) years and kind of business experience, (f) date of joining your firm.

15. Please send us a list giving the following information for EACH PRINCIPAL YOU REPRESENT: (a) company name, (b) complete mailing address, (c) name, title and telephone number of your key contact at the factory, (d) products you handle, (e) date you became their representative and (f) where available, short form and/or condensed catalogs covering the products of each principal.

16. Please indicate your approximate gross sales volume in thousands (+000) for the last five years:

   19 ___ $ _____   19 ___ $ _____   19 ___ $ _____   19 ___ $ _____   19 ___ $ _____

17. Please provide names and addresses of three bank and credit references (not principals):

   a. _____
   b. _____
   c. _____

18. Comments: _____
   _____
   _____
   _____

   Prepared by: _____   Date: _____

Evaluation of a Prospective Representative

Name _____ **Date** _____

Address _____ **Zip** _____

Phone _____

Person Interviewed _____ **Position** _____

REPRESENTATIVE COMPANY INFORMATION

1. History/Background

    a. Are you a corporation, a partnership, or a sole proprietorship? _____

    b. How long have you been in business? _____

    c. Will you furnish a brief company history, resume or brochure? _____

2. Company Growth and Future Plans

    a. Describe your growth history _____

    b. Do you operate on a sales plan and budget? _____

    c. What are your growth plans (where do you
       want to be five, ten years from now)? _____

3. Territory Covered and Market Served

    a. Describe the territory you cover _____

    b. Can you supply a map (county) describing your territory? _____

    c. Will you accept deviations from this? _____

    d. What do you consider to be your
       primary and secondary markets? _____

4. Office Facilities

    a. How many offices do you have (resident salesmen) and what are their locations? _____

    _____

    b. Do you have TWX, Telex or WATS facilities? Other? _____

    c. Are you into electronic data processing
       (NEMRA computer program, etc.)? _____

5. Warehousing

    a. Do you maintain a warehouse? _____

    b. How big is it? _____

    c. How many lines do you presently warehouse? _____

    d. Do you presently stock items in a line for resale (buy-sell)? _____

Note: Taken from *Guidelines*, by National Electrical Manufacturers Representative Association, used with permission.

Evaluation of a Prospective Representative *(continued)*

6. Personnel

a. Total number of employees (including principals) _____

b. How many outside salespeople? _____ How many inside? _____ How many warehouse? _____

c. Can you provide resumes on your salespeople? _____

7. Management

a. Who is actively engaged in the management of your company? _____

_____

b. Can you provide resumes on their backgrounds? _____

c. How active is the management in sales? _____

8. Current Manufacturer Lines Represented

a. Can you furnish us with a list of your manufacturer principals? _____

b. Do you feel their lines are compatible with ours? _____

c. Do any of our product lines conflict with your current manufacturer lines? _____

9. NEMRA Membership

a. Is your firm a member in good standing of NEMRA? _____

b. Is it active in the local and national programs of NEMRA? _____

c. What other professional organizations does your firm belong to? _____

MARKETING SERVICES

1. Sales Forecasting

a. Do you make sales forecasts? How often? _____

b. Are they initiated by you or by the manufacturers? _____

2. Market Surveys

a. Do you provide market surveys for your manufacturers? _____

b. What compensation do you think is fair for conducting these surveys? _____

3. Sales Performance

a. How do you monitor your sales performance? _____

b. Will you advise the manufacturer of performance, if requested? _____

c. Do you keep your manufacturers posted with sales activity
or booking reports (not "call reports" as such)? _____

SALES PROMOTION

1. Direct Mail

a. Do you conduct direct mail programs? _____

b. How many people are on your mailing list? _____

c. Do you have your own company mailer? _____

d. Are there any circumstances under which you would expect your principals to
participate in the production/distribution costs of these mailings? _____

2. Local Shows

a. Do you participate in local trade shows (all-industry sponsored)? _____

b. Do you conduct any counter day promotions and the like? _____

c. Do you conduct any extraordinary promotions in your trading area? _____

d. Do you expect the manufacturer to support these
with equipment, personnel or financial support? _____

Evaluation of a Prospective Representative *(continued)*

3. Catalogs

    a. Do you distribute your own catalog binder? _____

    b. What other means do you use for sales promotion? _____

VISITS BY FACTORY PERSONNEL

1. Policy

    a. What is your policy regarding visits into
       your territory by factory personnel? _____

COMPENSATION

1. Salespeople

    a. How do you compensate your salespeople? _____

    b. Do you have incentive programs? _____ Profit sharing? _____ A pension plan? _____

    c. Do you pay salespeople's expenses? _____

    d. Do you have an insurance program for your employees? _____

    e. What other benefits does your company provide? _____

    f. Do you have any employment contracts with your employees? _____

SALES TRAINING

1. Manufacturer-sponsored Seminars

    a. Will you send your people to factory seminars/training programs? _____

    b. Will you send your people to regional seminars/training programs? _____

    c. What expenses do you expect the manufacturer to pay? _____

2. Representative-sponsored Seminars

    a. Do you conduct your own seminars? _____

    b. Do you have your own sales training seminars in-house? _____

    c. Do you subscribe to any training consultant
       or improvement programs for your people? _____

    d. Do you permit employees to further their education at company expense? _____

    e. What types of training do you provide to
       keep abreast of new areas of technology? _____

ACCOUNT COVERAGE

1. Identification

    a. What type of customers do you concentrate on? _____

    b. Who are your major accounts? _____

    c. How do you cover these key accounts? _____

    d. How are your salespeople assigned—by account, geographical area or lines? _____

BUSINESS PERPETUATION

1. The Next Generation

    a. Have you determined the order of succession in your company
       should you be away from the business for any extended period? _____

    b. Do you have a buy/sell agreement with
       your management personnel and/or employees? _____

REFERENCES

    a. Do you have any objection to our contacting any of your principals/customers? _____

Representative Survey Report (Telephone Reference Check)

Representative: _____

Company Name: _____

Address: _____

Principals: _____

_____

_____

Reference: _____
(manufacturer providing information)

Company Name: _____

Address: _____

Telephone: _____

Individual: _____

Title: _____

1. When did this representative begin to handle your line? _____

2. On a scale of 1 to 5 (one being low and five high) please rate (√) the following attributes of the representative company:

Representative Attribute	Low 1	2	3	4	High 5	Comments
a. Sales volume in territory	☐	☐	☐	☐	☐	
b. Sales coverage	☐	☐	☐	☐	☐	
c. Frequency of calls	☐	☐	☐	☐	☐	
d. Customer penetration	☐	☐	☐	☐	☐	
e. Customer rapport	☐	☐	☐	☐	☐	
f. Sales planning	☐	☐	☐	☐	☐	
g. Sales training	☐	☐	☐	☐	☐	
h. Product knowledge	☐	☐	☐	☐	☐	
i. Application knowledge	☐	☐	☐	☐	☐	
j. Custom design capability	☐	☐	☐	☐	☐	
k. Knowledge of customer needs	☐	☐	☐	☐	☐	
l. Inquiry follow up	☐	☐	☐	☐	☐	
m. Sales promotion	☐	☐	☐	☐	☐	
n. Sales management	☐	☐	☐	☐	☐	
o. Company organization	☐	☐	☐	☐	☐	
p. Financial condition	☐	☐	☐	☐	☐	
q. Office facilities	☐	☐	☐	☐	☐	
r. Service facilities	☐	☐	☐	☐	☐	
s. Warehouse facilities	☐	☐	☐	☐	☐	
t. Business ethics	☐	☐	☐	☐	☐	
u. Initiative	☐	☐	☐	☐	☐	
v. Enthusiasm	☐	☐	☐	☐	☐	
w. Persistence	☐	☐	☐	☐	☐	
x. Commitment to your line	☐	☐	☐	☐	☐	
y. Overall rating	☐	☐	☐	☐	☐	

Note: Taken from *Thriving With Reps,* by Jerry Frank and Jack McNutt, MRERF, used with permission. Copyright © 1992 IMA Incorporated and McNutt & Co.

Representative Survey Report (Telephone Reference Check)   *(continued)*

3. How do you rank them among all of your representatives and why?

_____
_____
_____
_____

4. What are their greatest strengths?

_____
_____
_____
_____

5. What are their most significant weaknesses/shortcomings?

_____
_____
_____
_____

6. If you were starting over, would you rehire them? Why?

_____
_____
_____
_____

7. Is there any other question I should have asked but haven't?

_____
_____
_____
_____

8. Comments:

_____
_____
_____
_____

Prepared by: _____   Date: _____

NOTES

Chapter 1   Beginning the Search

1. Milan Kubr, *How to Select and Use Consultants, A Client's Guide* (Geneva: ILO, 1993).
2. Milan Kubr.
3. Jay Foonberg, *Finding the Right Lawyer* (Chicago: ABA, 1995), 115.
4. Jay Foonberg, 116.
5. Jack Shapiro, Consultant with The Penn Management Group, "Selecting an Advertising Agency," in *Marketing Handbook: Volume 1. Marketing Practices,* ed. Edwin E. and Mark David Bobrow (Homewood, IL: Dow-Jones-Irwin), 568.

Chapter 2   Attorneys

1. Quoted from a 1973 speech, taken from Kenneth Menendez, *Taming the Lawyers* (Santa Monica: Merritt, 1996), 104.
2. Barbara Kate Repa, *The American Lawyer, When and How to Use One* (Chicago: ABA, 1993), 12.
3. Barbara Kate Repa, 16.
4. Cliff Robertson, *The Businessperson's Legal Advisor* (Blue Ridge Summit, PA: TAB Books, 1991), 96.
5. Jay Foonberg, 123.
6. Franklin Foster and Robert Shcok, *Patents, Copyrights and Trademarks* (New York: John Wiley & Sons, 1993), 64.
7. Felix Zandman, *Never the Last Journey* (New York: Schocken, 1995), 257.
8. Jay Foonberg, 157.

9. Sol Stein, *A Feast for Lawyers, Inside Chapter XI: An Expose* (New York: M. Evans, 1989).
10. Suzanne Caplan, *Saving Your Business* (Englewood Cliffs, NJ: Prentice Hall, 1992).

Chapter 3   Accountants

1. *Entrepreneur Magazine Small Business Advisor* (New York: John Wiley & Sons, 1995), 364.
2. *Entrepreneur Magazine Small Business Advisor,* 367.
3. *Entrepreneur Magazine Small Business Advisor,* 367.
4. Cliff Robertson, 100.
5. *Entrepreneur Magazine Small Business Advisor,* 367.

Chapter 4   Banks and Bankers

1. Rick Stephan Hayes, *Business Loans* (New York: John Wiley & Sons), 11.
2. James McGowan, Senior Vice President-Lending, Mid-Atlantic Bank, telephone interview by author, 26 February 1996.
3. B. J. Philips, "Small Banks, Big Expectations," *Philadelphia Inquirer,* 3 June 1996.
4. Robert A. Mamis, "Can Your Bank Do This?" *INC.,* March 1996, 29.
5. Jill Andresky Fraser, "Ways To Keep Costs Low," *INC.,* March 1996, 100.
6. Rick Stephan Hayes, 16.
7. James McGowan, 26 February 1996.
8. James McGowan, 26 February 1996.
9. Robert J. Bifolco, Senior Vice President-Commercial Banking, Progress Federal Savings Bank, interview by author, 5 December 1995.
10. Rick Stephan Hayes, 15.
11. Dennis Suchocki and Andrew Smith, BCS & Associates, interview by author, 7 November 1995.

Chapter 5   Consultants—Business and Technical

1. Bureau of Business Research, *Use of Consultants by Manufacturers* (Richmond, VA: University of Richmond, 1964).
2. The American Consultants League, *Successfully Finding, Negotiating with and Retaining an Expert Consultant* (Sarasota: American Consultants League, 1993), 3.
3. Milan Kubr, *How to Select and Use Consultants, A Client's Guide* (Geneva: ILO, 1993).
4. American Consultants League.
5. Howard Shenson, *How to Select and Manage Consultants* (New York: Lexington Books, 1990).
6. American Consultants League.
7. Howard Shenson.
8. Ray Rauth, National Chairman, Independent Computer Consultants Association, interview by author, December 1995.
9. Ray Rauth.
10. American Consultants League.
11. Herman Holtz, *Choosing and Using a Consultant* (New York: John Wiley & Sons, 1989), 76.
12. American Consultants League.
13. American Consultants League.
14. American Consultants League.
15. Stephen Fishman, *Hiring Independent Contractors* (Berkeley: Nolo Press, 1996), A2.

Chapter 6   Creative Services

1. Dell Dennison, *The Advertising Handbook for Small Business* (Bellingham, WA: Self-Counsel Press, 1994), 84.
2. Jack Shapiro, 569.
3. Jack Shapiro, 569.
4. *Entrepreneur Magazine Small Business Advisor*, 570.
5. Alec Benn, *The 27 Most Common Mistakes in Advertising* (New York: AMACOM, 1978), 4.
6. Alec Benn, 10.
7. Alec Benn, 14.
8. Alec Benn, 18.

9. Dell Dennison, 90.

10. James Barhydt, *The Complete Book of Product Publicity* (New York: AMACOM, 1987), 51.

11. Dell Dennison, 273.

12. James Barhydt, 51.

13. James Barhydt, 52.

14. James Barhydt, 56.

15. Stephen Fishman, A2.

Chapter 7   Insurance Agents, Real Estate Brokers, Collection Agencies, and Outsourcing

1. David I. Scott, *The Guide to Buying Insurance* (Old Saybrook: Globe Pequot), 34.

2. Patricia Borowski, Division Vice President of the Professional Insurance Agents (PIA), interview by author, 7 February 1996.

3. Coletta Kemper, Director of Industry Affairs, Council of Insurance Agents, interview by author, 8 February 1996.

4. Patricia Borowski.

5. *Entrepreneur Magazine Small Business Advisor*, 321.

6. Wade E. Gaddy and Robert E. Hart, *Real Estate Fundamentals*, 4th ed. (Chicago: Dearborn, 1993), 141.

7. Daniel Wilkinson, SIOR, Wilkinson & Snowden, Memphis, TN, letter to Lottie Gatewood, 19 February 1996.

8. SICR Educational Fund, 176.

9. Greg Gunn, SIOR, Wallace Associates, Salt Lake City, UT, letter to Lottie Gatewood, 15 February 1996.

10. Greg Gunn.

11. Greg Gunn.

12. American Collectors Association, *A Collection Guide for Creditors.*

13. Michael Corbett, "The Top Ten Reasons Companies Outsource," *The Outsourcing Institute, 1995 Buyer's Guide*, 29.

14. Louis DeRose, "Outsourcing Users and Providers Ignore Procurement Concepts and Disciplines at Their Peril," *The Outsourcing Institute, 1995 Buyer's Guide*, 32.

15. Frank Casale, Executive Director, The Outsourcing Institute, interview by author, April 1996.

Chapter 8   Sales Representatives and Brokers

1. Ed Bobrow, "Partnering for Profit," *Bureau of Business Practice*, 30 March 1992, 14.
2. Ed Bobrow, "Will Using Independent Sales Agents Meet Your (Clients') Sales Goals?" *MANA Special Report*, 4.
3. Ed Bobrow, 5.
4. Harold J. Novick, *Selling through Independent Sales Reps*, 2nd ed. (New York: AMACOM, 1994), 70.
5. Harold J. Novick, 89.
6. Henry Lavin, "When and How to Use Manufacturers' Representatives," *Handbook of Modern Marketing*, 2nd ed., ed. Victor P. Buell (New York: McGraw-Hill, 1986), 75–5.
7. Jerry Frank and Jack McNutt, *Thriving with Reps* (Geneva IL: MRERF, 1992), 1.1, 2.
8. Henry Lavin, *How to Get—and Keep!—Good Industrial Representatives*, 2nd ed. (Cheshire, CT: Lavin Associates, 1985).
9. Henry Lavin.
10. Henry Lavin.

Chapter 9   Compensation

1. Jay Foonberg, 85.
2. William Gwire, "How the Right Kind of Bill Can Control Your Legal Costs," *Inc.*, February 1995, 116.
3. Cliff Robertson, 97.

Chapter 10   Managing the Unmanageable

1. Neal Whitten, *Managing Software Development Projects*, 2nd ed. (New York: John Wiley & Sons, 1995), 319.
2. Neal Whitten, 319.
3. Sylvia Khatcherian, Esq., "Contracting for Successful Outsourcing," *The Outsourcing Institute, 1995 Buyer's Guide* (New York: Outsourcing Institute, 1995), 37.
4. Suzanne Caplan, 22.

BIBLIOGRAPHY

This Bibliography is organized alphabetically by title rather than by author to enable you to quickly locate books noted in the Reference sections of the chapters. The telephone numbers and prices indicated were correct at the time of publication. I have used the following codes:

* Book out of print but available in libraries.
**** Recommended for your personal library.

The Advertising Handbook for Small Businesses, Bellingham, WA: Dell Dennison, Self-Counsel Press, 1994 ($10.95).

**** *The American Lawyer, When and How to Use One,* Barbara Kate Repa, Chicago: American Bar Association, Public Education Division, 1993 (312-988-5725; $2.50).

Annual Statement Studies, Philadelphia: Robert Morris Associates, 1995 (215-851-9100; $110.00).

**** *Banking,* Theodore A. Platz, Hauppodge, NY: Barron's Business Library, 1991 (800-645-3476).

Banking Smarter: How to Save Money in Your Business Banking Relationship, Dennis M. Suchocki and Andrew M. Smith, Scottsdale, AZ: BCS & Associates, 1995 (602-423-8384).

Beating the Odds, Hattie Bryant, Rocklin, CA: Prima, 1996 (916-632-4400; $16.95).

* *Business Loans,* Rick Stephan Hayes, New York: John Wiley & Sons, 1989.

* *The Business of Optometric Practice,* Chapter 10, "Let Advisors Advise You," Ann Waterman and James Gregg, White Plains, NY: Advisory Enterprises, 1980.

The Businessperson's Legal Advisor, Cliff Robertson, Liberty Hall Press, Blueridge Summit, PA: Tab Books, 1991.

"Choosing a Consultant" (Information Technology Consultants), Jane Bird, *Management Today,* June 1992.

* *Choosing and Using a Consultant, A Manager's Guide to Consulting Services*, Herman Holtz, New York: John Wiley & Sons, 1989.

* *The Complete Book of Product Publicity*, James D. Barhydt, New York: AMACOM, 1987.

Comprehensive Credit Manual, St. Louis, MO: International Credit Association, 1991 (314-991-3030; $175.00).

**** *Conducting an Agency Search*, Allan Gardner, New York: AAAA, 1994 (212-682-8391; $20.00).

The Consultant's Proposal, Fee, and Contract Problemsolver, Ron Tepper, New York: John Wiley & Sons, 1993 (800-225-5945; $22.95).

The Craft of General Management, Joseph L. Bower, Boston: Harvard Business School, 1991 (800-545-7685).

Encyclopedia of Associations, Detroit: Gale Research (313-961-2242).

Entrepreneur Magazine *Small Business Advisor*, New York: John Wiley & Sons, 1995 (800-225-5945).

Eureka! The Entrepreneurial Inventor's Guide to Developing, Protecting, and Profiting from Your Ideas, Robert J. Gold, Englewood Cliffs, NJ: Prentice Hall, 1994.

* *A Feast for Lawyers, Inside Chapter 11, An Expose*, Sol M. Stein, New York: Evans & Co., 1989.

**** *Finding the Right Lawyer*, Jay G. Foonberg, Chicago: ABA Section of Law Practice Management, 1995 (312-988-5760; $19.95).

**** *Getting It Printed*, Mark Beach, Cincinnati: North Light Books, 1993 (800-289-0963; $29.99).

Graphic Arts and Desktop Publishing, Pocket Dictionary, Harvey R. Levenson, Thousand Oaks, CA: Summa Books, 1996 (800-524-3903; $9.95).

Graphic Arts and Desktop Publishing Terminology, Complete Dictionary, Harvey R. Levenson, Thousand Oaks, CA: Summa Books, 1996 (800-524-3903; $26.00).

Growing Your Own Business, Gregory and Patricia Kishel, Perigee Book, New York: Berkeley Publishing, 1994.

The Guide to Buying Insurance, David L. Scott, Old Saybrook, CT: Globe Pequot, 1994 (800-243-0495).

Guide to Wills and Estates, American Bar Association, New York: Times Books, 1995 (312-988-5735; $12.00).

**** *Hiring Independent Contractors*, Stephen Fishman, Esquire, Berkeley, CA: Nolo Press, 1996 (800-992-6656; $29.95).

How Clients Choose, David Maister, David Maister Associates, 1991.

* *How to Get Results from Interviewing*, James Black, New York: McGraw-Hill, 1970.

How to Hire a Home Improvement Contractor without Getting Chiseled, Tom Philbin, New York: St. Martin's Press, 1991.

* *How to Select and Manage Consultants,* Howard L. Shenson, Lexington, MA: Lexington Books, 1990.

**** *How to Select and Use Consultants, A Client's Guide,* Milan Kubr, Geneva: ILO, 1993, (Publications Branch, ILO, CH-1211, Geneva 22, Switzerland).

**** *Industrial Real Estate,* Washington, DC: SIOR Educational Fund (202-737-1150).

**** *Insuring Your Business,* Sean Mooney, New York: Insurance Information Institute, 1992 (800-331-9146; $14.95).

Lawyer Referral Services, Directory, Chicago: ABA, 1995 (312-988-5760; $10.00).

* *The Legal Guide for Starting and Running a Small Business,* Fred S. Steingold, Berkeley, CA: Nolo Press, 1992 (800-992-6656; $24.95).

* *Making the Most of Management Consulting Services,* Jerome Fuchs, New York: AMACOM, 1975.

Managing Software Development Projects, 2nd ed., Neal Whitten, New York: John Wiley & Sons, 1995 (800-225-5945).

* *Marketing Handbook: Volume 1. Marketing Practices,* Edwin E. Bobrow and Mark David Bobrow, Chapter 37, "Selecting an Advertising Agency," by Jack H. Shapiro, Homewood, IL: Dow Jones–Irwin.

Mastering Office Leasing, Washington, DC: SIOR (202-737-1150).

Never the Last Journey, Felix Zandman, New York: Schocken Books, 1996.

Note on Acquiring Bank Credit, Philip Bilden, Boston: Harvard Business School, 1990 (800-545-7685).

O'Dwyer's Directory of Public Relations Firms, Jack O'Dwyer, New York: J. R. O'Dwyer Co., 1996 (212-679-2471; $195).

The Office Building, John Robert White, Washington, DC: SIOR, 1993 (202-737-1150).

Outsourcing Institute, Buyer's Guide, New York: OI, 1995 (800-421-6767; $25.00).

The Practical Guide to Patents, Trademarks, Copyright Designs, Laurence Shaw, Birmingham, England: Bilgrey Samson LTD, 1996 (44-121-456-2269; £19.95).

Raising the Rafters, How to Work with Architects, Contractors . . . , Stephen F. Collier, Woodstock, NY: Overlook Pres, 1993.

Real Estate Fundamentals, 4th ed., Wade E. Gaddy and Robert E. Hart, Chicago, IL: Dearborn, 1993.

* *Real Estate Investing*, Craig Hall, New York: Holt, Rinehart and Winston, 1982.

* *Recruiting, Selecting and Orienting New Employees*, Diane Arthur, New York: AMACOM, 1986.

**** *Saving Your Business, How to Survive Chapter 11 Bankruptcy and Successfully Reorganize Your Company*, Suzanne Caplan, Englewood Cliffs, NJ: Prentice Hall, 1992.

* *The Secrets of Consulting*, Gerald M. Weinberg, New York: Dorset House Publications, 1985.

**** *The Secrets of Successfully Finding, Negotiating with and Retaining an Expert Consultant*, American Consultants League, Sarasota, FL: ACS, 1993 (813-952-9290; $96.00).

**** *Selling through Independent Reps*, 2nd ed., Harold J. Novick, New York: AMACOM, 1994 (800-262-9699; $69.95).

* *The Small Business Legal Advisor*, William Hancock, New York: McGraw Hill, 1982.

Statistical Abstract of the United States, 1994, 114th ed., Washington, DC: U.S. Department of Commerce.

Taking Care of Your Corporation, Vol. 1, Anthony Mancuso, Berkeley, CA: Nolo Press, 1994 (800-992-6656; $26.95).

**** *Taming the Lawyers*, Kenneth Menendez, Santa Monica, CA: Merritt Publishing, 1996 (available through Nolo Press, 800-992-6656; $25.00).

**** *Thriving with Reps*, Jerry Frank and Jack McNutt, Seneva, IL: MRERF, 1992 (708-208-1466; $289.00).

**** *The 27 Most Common Mistakes in Advertising*, Alec Benn, New York: AMACOM, 1978 (800-262-9699).

* *Use of Consultants by Manufacturers*, David Ekey and David Robbins, Richmond, VA: Bureau of Business Research, University of Richmond, 1964.

* *Utilizing Consultants Successfully, A Guide for Management in Business, Government, the Arts and Professions*, Herman Holtz, Westport, CT: Quorum Books, 1985.

**** *You and Your Architect*, American Institute of Architects, Washington, DC: AIA, 1995 (800-242-9930; free).

INDEX

ORDER YOUR FREE ISSUE
NOW!

Entrepreneur
THE SMALL BUSINESS AUTHORITY

And Get FREE Advice To Help Run Your Business

☐YES! Send me my FREE issue of *Entrepreneur*.

Name _____
(please print)

Address: _____

City: _____

State/Zip: _____

54EB8

Mail coupon to: Entrepreneur Magazine, Dept. 54EB8, 2392 Morse Avenue, Irvine, CA 92614

1997 Expo Schedule